States of Grace

SUNY series in Latin American and Iberian Thought and Culture
———————————
Jorge J. E. Gracia and Rosemary Geisdorfer Feal, editors

States of Grace

Utopia in Brazilian Culture

Patrícia I. Vieira

Patricia Vieira is a researcher at the Center for Social Studies of the University of Coimbra, with an FCT Researcher grant from the Portuguese Foundation for Science and Technology (IF/00606/2015). The author gratefully acknowledges the financial support of the Portuguese Foundation for Science and Technology (FCT) under the Strategic Project (UID / SOC / 50012/2013).

Published by State University of New York Press, Albany

For information, contact State University of New York Press, Albany, NY
www.sunypress.edu

Library of Congress Cataloging-in-Publication Data

Names: Vieira, Patricia I., 1977- author.
Title: States of grace : utopia in Brazilian culture / Patrⁱicia I. Vieira.
Description: Albany, NY : State University of New York, 2018. | Series: SUNY series in Latin American and Iberian thought and culture | Includes bibliographical references and index.
Identifiers: LCCN 2017022008 (print) | LCCN 2018009966 (ebook) | ISBN 9781438469256 (e-book) | ISBN 9781438469232 (hardcover : alk. paper) | 9781438469249 (paperback : alk. paper)
Subjects: LCSH: Utopias—Brazil. | Brazil—Description and travel. | Brazil—Economic conditions. | Brazil—Social conditions.
Classification: LCC HX806 (ebook) | LCC HX806 .V25 2018 (print) | DDC 335/.020981—dc23
LC record available at https://lccn.loc.gov/2017022008

For Michael, in the present and in the time to come

Contents

Introduction

A Land of Utopias

A map of the world that does not include Utopia is not worth even glancing at, for it leaves out the one country at which Humanity is always landing. And when Humanity lands there, it looks out, and, seeing a better country, sets sail.

—Oscar Wilde, *The Soul of Man under Socialism*

UTOPIA'S PECULIAR SPATIAL CONFIGURATION is inscribed in the very word coined by Thomas More at the dawn of Modernity, roughly five hundred years ago. The term is ambiguous in that it means "no place" but can also be interpreted as "a good place."[1] For More, utopia is such a good place that there is no space for it in the real world. It is, literally, too good to be true. And the spatial instability inherent in the expression cannot be uncoupled from its temporal ambivalence. Literary utopias such as the island society conjured up by More were perfect communities that, so the fiction goes, existed in some faraway location in the present. Still, the goal of most of these narratives was to criticize the ills of their time—greed, arbitrary exercise of power, corruption, and so on—that emerged in all their abhorrence when compared to the exemplary sociopolitical organization of their literary counterparts. The critical impulse of utopian writings was therefore complemented with a didactic one: such texts were to furnish a blueprint for the improvement of their authors' communities that could aspire to approximate the perfection of utopia in a distant future. Neither fully rooted in a determinate place nor entirely embedded in its time, utopia is always outside and beyond itself, hovering between the real and the imaginary, presence and absence, the present and the future.

In More's book, news of utopia is brought to Europe by a Portuguese sailor, Raphael Hythloday, thus underlining the indelible link between the Old Continent's colonial project, the encounter with disparate landscapes, and the contact with very different peoples, on the one hand, and the ability to envision societies more perfect than the European ones, on the other. The sailor's nationality is an allusion to the Portuguese voyages to Africa, Asia, and, in particular, to America, a continent Christopher Columbus believed to be the location of the Christian paradise on earth when he first reached it. More than any other region, the so-called New World embodied the promise of a better Europe, where a society designed to avoid the faults of Old World monarchies could be built.[2] While the Americas harkened back to the past and reminded explorers and colonizers of the perfection once found in the Garden of Eden, they also pointed in the direction of the future, to a coming community of justice and plenty. Even though he never specifies the geographical coordinates of his imaginary island, More does write that it was located in the "New World," leading readers to believe that he envisioned it somewhere in America, a continent unknown to Europeans until little more than twenty years before the English writer's publication of his renowned book (5).

In one way or another, utopia became ingrained in the imaginary of America and was later included in the mythical makeup of most American nations.[3] Suffice it to think about the United States' self-understanding as a beacon of hope for those reaching its shores, each metropolis a "city upon a hill" that would set an example of tolerance and equality for the rest of the world. This utopian drive is particularly salient in the case of Brazil. Ever since the arrival of the first Portuguese sailors and settlers, the region's lush environment has been compared to the bountiful nature of paradise that obviated the need for human toil, and its pre-Columbian inhabitants have been regarded, at least at first, to be as amicable and innocent as Eve and Adam, as we shall see in chapters 2 through 4. Early Brazil was perceived to be utopia realized and, though it was a far cry from the sophisticated society portrayed by More, we can easily picture Raphael Hythloday favorably comparing the easygoing, money-free existence of its native Indians to the avarice and rapacity of Europeans.

Even when Portuguese colonizers began to realize that the luxuriant tropical forests posed challenges to agriculture and that Brazil's native population was not as amenable to exploitation as they had initially thought, the territory's utopian allure did not fade. To be sure, part of this attraction was considerably removed from the lofty dreams of social, political, and economic justice that tend to drive utopian thought. The fantasy of easy enrichment, grounded on the perception of the region as a treasure trove of natural wealth, has been one of the most powerful utopian forces leading settlers to establish themselves in Brazil. From the prosperity brought by large-scale sugarcane plantations, starting in the first decades of colonization, through the Gold Rush of the eighteenth century, to the riches generated by the Amazonian rubber boom in the early twentieth century, the country has been depicted as an El Dorado at various points throughout its history.

But economic considerations alone do not exhaust the utopian aura of the territory. Both Brazilians and outsiders often identify the nation as a stage where not only great economic but also sociopolitical exploits will one day take place. For instance, Austrian author Stefan Zweig titled his 1941 book on the area *Brazil: A Country of the Future* (*Brasilien: Ein Land der Zukunft*). There, he contrasts the internecine war and racism that devastated Europe at the time to the peaceful coexistence of different races and ethnicities in the South American nation. In his rosy depiction of the country's racial politics he sees the prototype for human relations in the rest of the globe. For Zweig, Brazil is a diamond in the rough. Even though the land was already prospering, he believed its current growth to be just the beginning and predicted that "[the country] is certainly destined to become one of the most important factors in

xii   Introduction

the future development of our world" ("[ein Land,] das doch unzweif-
elhaft bestimmt ist, einer der bedeutsamsten Faktoren in der künftigen
Entwicklung unserer Welt zu werden").[4] "I knew that I had glimpsed
the future of our world," writes Zweig about his travels in Brazil, adding
a little farther down in the text that spending time in the nation "gave
him the feeling of living in a process of becoming, in what is to come,
in the future" ("Ich wußte, ich hatte einen Blick in die Zukunft unserer
Welt getan;" "dieses Gefühl zu empfinden, im Werdenden, Kommenden,
Zukünftigen zu leben"). Zweig's view of Brazil as a country of the future,
where events to come in other regions can already be found *in nuce*,
became etched into its identity. The futuristic architecture of the capital city of Brasília, founded in 1960, testifies to the nation's eagerness to
coincide with and embody the time to come. To this day, Brazilian politicians, economists, scholars, and artists speculate about their country's
ability or failure to live up to its potential and to fulfill its promise as a
land of the future.

A delimited geographical area reminiscent of an indefinite paradise and a land whose present situation is persistently overshadowed by
its glorious future, Brazil, like utopia, never fully coincides with itself.
Its diverse, bountiful, territory first functioned as a space onto which
Europeans projected their manifold fantasies of economic prosperity and
sociopolitical advancement. Later, certain more peripheral parts of the
country served the same function for the nation's elite. The Amazon, a
"dazzling stage, *where sooner or later the civilization of the globe will be
concentrated,*" ("deslumbrante palco, *onde mais cedo ou mais tarde se há de
concentrar a civilização do globo,*" Cunha 219–20), is a case in point, as we
shall see in chapter 2. Brazilian intellectuals perceived the Amazon River
basin as an empty space of prodigious wealth lying in wait to be explored
and exploited. In addition, the country's present tends to be regarded
as a mere step on the path toward a future that perpetually escapes its
population's grasp. The view of leisure as the mode of being characteristic of Brazilians and in store for the rest of humankind, discussed in
chapter 4, illustrates this point. Current events are interpreted in light

of a glorious time to come, the nation's eyes firmly turned toward futurity. It is therefore not surprising that utopia is such an integral part of Brazilian culture. If outsiders tended to project utopian aspirations onto the region, Brazilian intellectuals have, in turn, internalized, modified, and reworked these dreams that became part of the lens though which they reflect upon their nation.

This book looks at key moments in the development of utopia in Brazil. While discussions of utopia may focus on three distinct domains, namely utopian thought, utopian literature, that is, fictional accounts of utopian communities, and practical attempts to found better societies (Claeys 11), this study concentrates almost exclusively on the first. I aim to trace the evolution of utopian thought as it has been configured in Brazil, rather than analyzing specific literary portrayals of fictional utopias set on Brazilian soil or concrete attempts to found perfect communities in the area. Still, these spheres are not watertight compartments, and utopian thought necessarily overlaps with literary and concrete utopias. Antônio Vieira's utopian writings discussed in chapter 1, for instance, had their roots both in theology and in actual Messianic groups that sprung up throughout Europe from the Middle Ages onward and, later, in the Americas.[5] Similarly, the legend of the utopian community of the Amazons analyzed in chapter 2 or the utopian societies of leisure examined in chapter 4 would not have emerged without a palpable, material substratum: the remoteness of the Amazon, in the first case; the natural wealth of Brazil and the country's self-perception as an alternative to Northern capitalist economies, in the second. Furthermore, while utopian thinking is often expounded in essay form, as we shall see in chapter 4, writers also frequently resort to literature as a means to convey these ideas. Chapters 2 and 3 analyze literary writings that cannot be defined *sensu stricto* as utopias but that weave utopian elements into the fictional fabric of the texts.

Throughout the discussion of utopias in a Brazilian context undertaken in this book I espouse a broad understanding of utopian thought. I believe that utopia cannot be reduced to a transhistorical ideal, easy to dismiss given that it will never be reached in the finite temporality of human existence. Rather than unattainable goals, utopias formulate an intrahistorical transcendence, based upon the impulse to go beyond history in history, thus inaugurating new possibilities within reality. Utopian transcendence is therefore not a sphere separated from the real but exists within immanence itself, thus destabilizing the spatiotemporal continuum that stretches between potentiality and its concretization.[6] The present study therefore implicitly refutes the position of thinkers such as John Gray, according to whom all utopias necessarily lead to totalitarian political regimes. In his book *Black Mass: Apocalyptic Religion and the Death of Utopia*, Gray argues that utopias work as normative ideals and are frequently used in order to justify violent acts. Unlike Gray, I do not consider all utopias to be transhistorical notions one would blindly submit to. Rather, they can be interpreted as nonnormative breaches in lived time and space that allow us to envision different ways of existing in a community. True utopias are always incomplete and destined to fail as totalitarian projects, as Fredric Jameson points out: "the best Utopias are those that fail most comprehensively" (xiii). In the case of Brazil, utopian thought derives from the desire to jolt society out of a stagnant status quo and to valorize the possibilities inherent in the country, pointing to new ways of being together that are already latent in the everyday. Brazilian utopian thinking shows that the "utopian impulse," which German philosopher Ernst Bloch defines as a central feature of Modernity, is not a purely negative or nihilistic drive but an attempt to inscribe an element of transcendence in concrete existence—a way to broaden the limits of what is and to consider reality anew.

The states of grace mentioned in the title of the book highlight the transience of utopianism. As Clarice Lispector points out in her texts, analyzed in chapter 3, grace cannot be taken for granted. It emerges as a rupture in our routine and opens up new avenues for interpreting and transforming existing circumstances. The utopian thought analyzed in this study envisions societies living in a state of grace that entails a situation of peace, social justice, and economic equality in the texts examined in chapters 1, 2 and 4, and an interspecies community in the writings discussed in chapter 3. The state, understood not only as a fleeting condition but also as a political configuration, is therefore transformed by grace, which allows us to imagine a better sociopolitical arrangement.

While the notion of a state of grace evokes a moment of union with divinity happening in human history that puts us squarely within a theological paradigm, I hold that utopias have inherited and secularized some of these religious undertones. The state of grace achieved through a close connection to the divine—be it in a prelapsarian, innocent existence in the Garden of Eden or in a Millenarian Kingdom of Christ on earth described in apocalyptic, eschatological Christian doctrine—will be reworked and transformed but never quite abandoned in utopianism. This is particularly true in Brazilian utopian thought, which often goes back to an idealized, paradisiac past, at the same time as it draws on the country's Messianic tradition in its vision of a utopian future.

Many Brazilian depictions of a perfect era to come involve the recovery of an earlier Edenic time, perceived as more egalitarian and just, an arrangement that the authors believe could be secularized and modified to respond to present demands. Utopia performs in this case an elliptical movement that reclaims a theologically configured state of grace and projects it into a secular future, adapting the positive aspects of the former to the changed circumstances of the latter. At the same time, Brazilian utopian projects—and many non-Brazilian ones—often result from the secularization of Messianic aspirations. The faith in a period of peace and prosperity inaugurated by the Second Coming of the Messiah, who will govern the earth for a thousand years before the end of times, as described in the Book of Revelation, is, in and of itself, a projection of a renewed, paradisiac state of grace into the future. This belief is transformed in Modernity into the secular, utopian expectation of an improved community to come. Even literary utopias that postulate the present existence of a perfect group somewhere on earth long for the future betterment of their own societies, hoping they will one day approximate fiction. This is not to say that religion is abolished in all utopian thought; to the contrary, many utopian writings accept the existence of God. But while Messianism relies on divine intervention to facilitate the arrival of the Millennium, the fulfillment of utopian longing depends on human ingenuity alone. Deprived of a heavenly guarantor, utopian states of grace are predicated on uncertainty, since it is doubtful whether human beings will live up to their promise. Utopian thinking draws its strength precisely from this volatility that makes it question and reassess its own tenets at every step.

The structure of this book retraces the development of utopian thought in Brazil from its theological, Messianic origins to the secular utopias of the twentieth century. Chapter 1 analyzes the prophetic writings of Jesuit Priest Antônio Vieira (1608–1697), where he depicts a future, Messianic, Christian Kingdom that would encompass both Portugal and Brazil. This earthly empire of Christ—the Fifth Empire, after the Assyrian, the Persian, the Greek, and the Roman empires—would be predicated on equality and justice. I argue that, for Vieira, the distance between the Native Brazilian population he had encountered in America, the exiled Jews who had fled the Iberian Peninsula because of the Inquisition, and the Christians of Europe would progressively fade, as all would come together in the Fifth Empire. He believed that the colonization of Brazil heralded the advent of a new kingdom of perpetual peace, where people would live in a mystical communion with God and all would have equal rights, mediated by their faith in Christ.

Antônio Vieira's Messianic thought exemplifies the theological paradigm that will leave a lasting imprint in later utopias in the country. Brazil witnessed several concrete utopian experiments grounded on religion, the most famous of which was perhaps the community of Canudos, headed by Antônio Conselheiro (1830–1897). This Messianic leader heralded the impending arrival of a harmonious time of plenty, a message that resonated deeply with the impoverished population of the country's drought-ridden Northeastern region. The rise and fall of Canudos, disbanded in 1897 by the Brazilian Republican Army after a long and bloody campaign, was immortalized in journalist Euclides da Cunha's (1866–1909) sociological and literary masterpiece *The Backlands* (*Os Sertões*, 1902). Canudos retains to this day an emblematic status in Brazilian popular culture, literature, and cinema, as the ultimate example of a real-life utopian community.[7] A historical attempt to establish a utopian society, Canudos lies outside the purview of this study.[8] Still, it testifies to the overlap between theological and political elements already at work in Vieira's thought, a connection tying transcendence and immanence, the beyond and the here-and-now, that we will find in a secularized form in the twentieth-century utopian writings discussed in the rest of this book.

The utopian texts examined in chapter 2 recover the communitarian, egalitarian thrust of Vieira's works. The chapter examines the different representations of the mythical Amazon warriors that lent their name to the Amazon River basin from the time the first European explorers arrived in the region onward. In the past, the legend of a fearsome all-women tribe went hand in hand with a dystopian vision of the territory as a "green hell," according to which unsuspecting travelers and colonizers often fell prey to dangers lurking in the shadows of a threatening natural environment. I contend that, with the development of the Amazon region in the wake of the rubber boom in the end of the nineteenth and early twentieth centuries and, especially, with the rise of environmental concerns, the Amazons became part of an idealized image of the rainforest. The chapter analyzes three modes of utopian representation of the Amazons: Gastão Cruls's (1888–1959) portrayal of a communitarian tribe of women in the novel *The Mysterious Amazon* (*A Amazônia Misteriosa*, 1925); Abguar Bastos's (1902–1995) vision of the land of the Amazons, free from the problems of his time, in *The Amazon Nobody Knows About* (*A Amazônia que Ninguém Sabe*, 1929); and the Modernist fantasy of a matriarchy that would obviate the negative consequences of capitalist rule.

Chapter 3 begins by examining the link between nation and nature in Brazilian thought and discusses the centrality of plants and animals in the country's literature, with reference to the writings of Machado de

Assis (1839–1908) and Guimarães Rosa (1908–1967). Drawing on the work of Brazilian anthropologist Eduardo Viveiros de Castro, I argue that literature can function in a way similar to Amerindian shamanism by attempting to represent the worldview of nonhumans, to regard them as subjects and to espouse their perspective. I call this kind of writing *zoophytographia*, or interspecies literature. The chapter then turns to the texts of Clarice Lispector, which offer a utopian vision of a nonhierarchical world, where plants, animals, and human beings share their living space. On my reading, Lispector suggests two main modes of relating to nonhumans: metamorphosis and encounter. The face-to-face encounter with plants and animals in short stories such as "The Imitation of the Rose" ("A Imitação da Rosa") and "The Buffalo" ("O Búfalo"), or in the novel *The Passion According to G.H.* (*A Paixão Segundo G.H.*), results in a profound transformation of anthropocentric categories such as language or reason, which are now extended to our nonhuman others.

Chapter 4 addresses the positive valuation of idleness as a quintessentially Brazilian way of being-in-the-world that distinguishes the country from the overworked nations of Europe and from the United States. I begin by discussing the ideal of a blissful, work-free Golden Age, present both in Greco-Latin and in Jewish traditions, and then consider various critiques of the current ideology of work by political theorists, economists, and anthropologists, who hope that a leisurely society will arise in the wake of mechanization. I subsequently look into the different ways in which the ideal of leisure has been appropriated in Brazilian culture: the myth that indigenous peoples lived in communion with nature in a Golden Age without labor; the popular figure of the "malandro," someone who moves between organized society and the world of crime; and the ritual of Carnival, together with the dream of a permanent carnivalization of society that would obviate the need to work. I contend that authors such as Oswald de Andrade or Antônio Cândido believe that liberation from work and adoption of a leisurely way of life open the possibility of a utopian world where people could devote themselves to meaningful artistic and intellectual endeavors.

The study of utopian thought in Brazil undertaken in this book aims to contribute to a multifaceted appreciation of the country's ontology, of its self-understanding from a social, political, economic, and environmental points of view. But this multidimensional portrait is split from the start, doubled between the way things are and how they could improve, between the present and an imagined future, which, in turn, often goes back to an idealized past. These temporal dislocations destabilize the existing order and give depth to the present, tapping into its uncharted or neglected dimensions and exploring its latent possibilities. Utopianism disrupts what is, contaminating it with the thought of what could be, and allows one to imagine a more just time to come that would function not as a distant ideal but as a nagging conviction, embedded in our everyday, that another world is possible. This belief nudges us out of complacency, and turns the here-and-now into the very place and time of utopia.

The Theologico–Political Utopia of Father Antônio Vieira

Ele via e ouvia inexistências.
(He saw and heard nonexistences.)
—Manoel de Barros, "Pois Pois," *Tratado Geral das Grandezas do Ínfimo*

A Transatlantic Writing of the Future

How to write a "history of the future," an "account taken from the height of God's designs and from the obscurity of His incomprehensible decrees"? ("história do futuro"; "cômputo tirado da altitude dos desígnios de Deus e da obscuridade dos seus incompreensíveis decretos"). In which ways to penetrate, armed only with the "acumen of the human mind," into the depths of time and recount the end of the world ("argúcia da mente humana," Vieira, *Chave*, 31)? What are the sources used and the method followed in such an investigation and, more relevant still, how to justify the audacity of trying to unveil divine arcana? Throughout his prophetic texts, from the incomplete *History of the Future* (*História do Futuro*) to the later, fragmentary work *Key of the Prophets* (*Clavis Prophetarum*), through the *Representation before the Tribunal of the Holy Office* (*Representação perante o Tribunal do Santo Ofício*) and other texts drafted as a response to the accusations of heresy leveled against him,

Jesuit Priest Antônio Vieira (1608–1697) struggles with these questions. His provisional answers allow us a glimpse into an idealized Kingdom of Christ, a realm of peace and prosperity on earth inspired by the preacher's experiences on both sides of the Atlantic that would leave an indelible mark on subsequent utopian thought in Brazil.

Antônio Vieira was an emblematic transatlantic intellectual who bridged the world of seventeenth-century European centers of learning and the continent's remote colonial outposts. Born in Portugal, he moved to Bahia, Brazil, with his family when he was still a child. He studied at the Jesuit school of Salvador and soon decided to take vows. As a student, he had close contact with the Brazilian indigenous population and learned Tupi so as to better communicate with the Indians and teach them the Christian doctrine. When news of Portuguese independence from Spain in 1640 reached Salvador, Vieira was one of the priests chosen to travel to Lisbon to represent the colony and pay homage to the new king, John IV. This was the beginning of a long-lasting friendship between Vieira and the king, which took the priest to several European countries—France, the Netherlands, Italy, Spain—where he worked as a royal emissary. Key to Vieira's Messianic thought were his contacts with the Jewish community of Amsterdam during this period and his theological debates on Millenarianism with rabbis such as Menasseh ben Israel, to which we will return later.

In 1653 Vieira was sent back to Brazil as the head of the Jesuit missionary efforts in Maranhão and Pará, probably in an effort to distance him from the court and to diminish his influence over the king. In Maranhão he went on a number of missions into the jungle to reach the indigenous population that lived inland and to "make a large number of Christians from our doctrine" ("fazer grande número de cristãos da nossa doutrina," *Cartas* I, 344). Vieira's confrontation with the landowners from Maranhão over the issue of indigenous slavery is well known: while the settlers wanted to use the Indians as slaves to work in their plantations, Vieira wished to keep Native Brazilians in villages headed by Jesuit priests and by an indigenous chief; they would be able to work for the landowners but they would be paid a salary. This conflict prompted Vieira to write the famous "Sermon of Saint Anthony to the Fish" ("Sermão de Santo António aos Peixes," 1654), where he accused the inhabitants of Maranhão of behaving worse than fish, which eat each other out of need but never with hateful intent. With the death of his supporter John IV, Vieira lost ground in the fight against the settlers, was arrested and sent from Pará back to Lisbon in 1661. In a sermon from the same year, given in Lisbon, Vieira wondered: "But what will happen to the poor and miserable Indians who are the spoils, the booty, of this whole War?" ("Mas que será dos pobres e miseráveis índios que são a presa, e os depojos, de toda esta Guerra?," quoted in Castro 61).[1]

After spending nearly six years in prison, accused of heresy by the Inquisition because of his Messianic writings, Vieira left Lisbon for Rome in 1669. There he became a renowned preacher and the confessor of Queen Christina of Sweden, roughly twenty-five years after she had discussed philosophy with René Descartes. Vieira's reputation in Rome's learned circuits led the pope to absolve him from all sentences pronounced against him by the Inquisition. He returned to Portugal for a few years and left again for Bahia in 1681, where he died sixteen years later.

What I would like to highlight from this brief account of Vieira's life is his constant displacement: on the one hand, he grew up and lived in colonial Brazil—in the city of Salvador, in Bahia, and, especially, in Maranhão, where his work as a missionary took him to the depths of the Amazon rainforest; on the other hand, he spent a large part of his life at the Portuguese court of the Restoration period and had close contact with the intellectual elite of seventeenth-century Europe, including learned men (and women) living in Paris, Amsterdam, and Rome. Vieira's conception of a utopian future, particularly his idea that history ineluctably progresses toward a Kingdom of Christ that would encompass all peoples, united under the Catholic faith, is a result of the preacher's position spanning these very disparate realities.

For Vieira, the Portuguese overseas voyages and his work as a missionary in Brazil were proof that a Messianic age was drawing ever nearer.

If the advent of this utopian realm presupposed the Christianization of all human beings, the Portuguese evangelization of Africa, Asia, and, above all, Brazil was a first step in the universal conversion to Catholicism. The Portuguese maritime journeys and the Jesuit missionary efforts overseas were therefore inscribed in a divine plan: "Why could the Portuguese break the impenetrable cloisters of the Ocean and conquer in three other parts of the world, so many, so new and such powerful nations, having such a small kingdom, if not because this was written [in the Sacred Books]?" ("Porque puderam romper os Portugueses os claustros impenetráveis do Oceano, e conquistaram nas outras três partes do mundo, sendo um Reino tão pequeno, tantas, tão novas e tão poderosas nações, senão porque estava escrito?," *História* I, 109). Vieira goes even farther and, in the *History of the Future*, argues that the Old Testament prophets Isaiah and Obadiah had already predicted the Portuguese evangelization of Brazil and Maranhão, which were, at the time, two separate administrative entities (I, 233ff). According to Vieira, the spread of Christianity throughout the world, to which he contributed, was proof that the prophesied Kingdom of Christ was about to arrive.

And yet, Vieira's firsthand contact with colonization and evangelization made him realize that missionary endeavors alone could not reach the goal of universal conversion of all peoples to Christianity and herald a Messianic age. When he considers in the *Representation before the Tribunal of the Holy Office* the means through which conversion would take place, the musings of the theologian are complemented by the preacher's in-depth knowledge of Brazil: "[T]hose who began penetrating the very vast and hidden lands of the gentiles [understand] that the conversion of those gentiles ... will never be achieved through human and natural means," he writes, because of the "totally impenetrable and inaccessible places where many nations live ... closed off with dense woods, rivers, lakes, mountains that one cannot conquer or go through and especially the inclement air and climate ... and the incomprehensible diversity of languages that distinguishes them" ("aqueles que têm começado a penetrar as vastíssimas e ocultíssimas terras das gentilidades [compreendem] que a conversão das ditas gentilidades... se não poderá jamais conseguir pelos meios humanos e naturais... assi pelos lugares totalmente impenetráveis e inacessíveis em que muitas das ditas nações vivem... fechados com brenhas, rios, lagos, montanhas, que de nenhum modo se podem vencer nem romper e sobretudo com a inclemência dos ares e climas... e diversidade incompreensível das línguas com que se distinguem," *Representação* II, 209). Vieira's experience as a missionary influences his utopian views and leads him to acknowledge pragmatically that the goal of evangelizing all peoples could only be reached with the aid of the Holy Spirit.

Vieira is indebted both to his familiarity with the Americas and to his awareness of European intellectual debates for his formulation of the future Messianic age. He often underlines that, by virtue of literally being part of two worlds—the Old and the New—his understanding of theological questions necessarily differs from that of past authors. In a passage from *Key of the Prophets*, he asks: "What could Chrysostom, Augustine and Damascene tell us about the Brazilian barbarians and the rest of the Americans?" ("Que podiam Crisóstomo, Agostinho e Damasceno... indicar a respeito dos bárbaros Brasilenses e dos restantes Americanos?," 106). Unaware of the New World, past theologians necessarily lacked crucial insights into the Christianization of the whole globe that was to herald the Messianic age. Vieira's version of a utopian Kingdom of Christ, like the very concept of utopia, was made possible by the opening up of European thought to the realities of other continents. In an example of cultural relativism, Vieira responds to those theologians writing about Native Americans from Europe: "What should I tell the remaining authors? Just this: that they are in Europe and write in Europe.... Oh, what a difference is there between the appreciations of the wisest sage, philosophizing from afar about distant things, and those of another less wise one, who sees things that are close by, in his presence, the way they are" ("Aos restantes autores... que direi eu? Apenas isto: que estão na Europa e escrevem na Europa.... Oh! quanta diferença há entre as apreciações do mais sapientíssimo, filosofando de longe sobre coisas distantes, e as de outro menos douto que, de perto, na sua presença, vê as coisas como elas são"). He goes on to conclude: "It is inevitable, oh illustrious theologians, that you feel that between your reasoning and mine there is a great abyss, maybe even larger than the ocean that lies between us" ("É inevitável, ó mais ilustres dos teólogos, que sintais que entre os vossos raciocínios e os nossos olhos há um grande abismo e talvez maior que o próprio oceano que se estende entre nós," *Chave*, 107). The preacher's transatlantic positioning allowed him to overcome the limitations of other thinkers from his time and formulate his influential views on a future era of perpetual peace among all peoples.

Vieira's life on the two sides of the Atlantic gave a truly universal dimension to his Messianic writings. He postulates a Kingdom of Christ where the separation between Jews, the native population he had encountered in America, and European Christians would progressively fade, as all would come together under Catholicism. The awareness of his in-betweenness, which resulted from his transatlantic perspective and was most likely responsible for the unorthodoxy of his points of view, drove Vieira on an incessant methodological quest as a way of justifying his contentious beliefs. In his thought, then, the means used to foresee prospective events became as central as the future itself.

How to Predict the Time to Come

Vieira's attempts to legitimize his "history of the future" that surface time and again in his writings cannot be reduced to a mere exercise in rhetoric meant to persuade, in the first instance, Portuguese politicians, then the Inquisition, and, later in his life, the intellectual elite of the seventeenth century of the veracity and inevitability of his doctrines.[2] Even though his obsessive preoccupation with the foundations of his prophetic texts was partly motivated by the controversy they gave rise to, this focus cannot be fully explained by the author's pragmatic intent to defend himself from his detractors. On the one hand, the justification for the pressing need to formulate a "history of the future" and to detail the ways in which such a project is to be articulated derives from the very arguments delineated in the prophetic works. In other words, the author's epistemological considerations grant validity to his conclusions, while his reflections on the ontological status of his "history" demonstrate that the scrutiny of the future is an intrinsic part of the theological-political project of the Catholic Church as he understands it.

On the other hand, the *apologia* of his "history of the future," the explanation of the methods employed in writing it, and the detailed enumeration of the signs that announce the coming of the Messianic age encompass almost the totality of Vieira's prophetic texts, while the actual description of the Kingdom of Christ—a "most happy state" permeated by divine grace—occupies an extremely reduced part of his work ("felicíssimo estado," *Apologia*, 177). This is tantamount to saying that the prophetic works of Vieira are nothing more than a long prologue—epistemological and ontological—to a history of the future that was never written; an extended Prefatory Book (Livro Anteprimeiro) that evolves in response to the shifting political circumstances in Portugal and its colonies and to the development of Vieiran thought as it accompanies these changes. At stake here is neither a flaw in the author's project nor a lacuna that could be filled by extrapolations based on extant texts. The unfinished character of Vieira's prophetic writings formally embodies the incompletion of any attempt at describing a Messianic future, which will inevitably be reduced to prolegomena. If the limited human reason is unable to fully discern the utopian contours of Christ's Empire and if post-Babelic languages fall short of expressing this state of grace, it behooves Vieira to prepare the advent of this divine kingdom with his history of the future, to specify the conditions of its concretion and to offer nothing more than a preview of this era of perpetual peace.

When he announces his intention to write a history of the future, Vieira is conscious of the difficulties in performing this task. Does God really want humans to venture beyond the limits determined by their finite nature and seek the knowledge of what is to come? Furthermore, if so many wise scholars are unable to agree upon the sequence of past events, "how can we presume to find the best account of the future and guarantee that this account can be trusted?" ("como é que nós temos a presunção de encontrar melhor cômputo acerca do futuro e garantimos que ele é digno de confiança?," *Chave*, 18).

Vieira solves the first obstacle by resorting to a variation on a very prevalent trope in Baroque texts, namely, the idea that the world is a stage where a divine comedy is played: "The history of the succession and the events of humankind from the beginning of the world to its end is nothing more than a comedy of God staged in this very theater of this very world" ("A história da sucessão e sucessos do género humano desde o princípio do mundo até o fim dele, não é outra coisa senão uma comédia de Deus representada neste mesmo teatro do mesmo mundo" *Apologia*, 157). However, Vieira ingeniously inverts the implicit fatalism of this worldview by arguing that humans should interpret the play of which they are the protagonists and see it as a mystery to be solved for the delight of God: "God amuses Himself like those who promise a prize to whoever solves a riddle they have devised, so that especially wise men piously and devotedly scrutinize His arcana—something that the Prophets, mentioned and praised by the Prince of the Apostles, would have never done, unless they knew that this was agreeable to God" ("Deus diverte-se à maneira daqueles que prometem um prémio a quem adivinhar um enigma proposto, para que principalmente os sábios se exercitem, pia e louvavelmente, na perscrutação dos seus arcanos, o que nunca teriam feito os Profetas que o Príncipe dos Apóstolos refere e elogia, se não fosse plenamente do seu conhecimento que isso era agradável a Deus," *Chave*, 27).

To recount the future is a form of emancipation with Promethean undertones, given that through their comprehension of coming events humans transcend their condition of puppets in someone else's play and realize that their destiny is to achieve an ever more perfect union with God. Vieiran prophetic writings are inscribed in a hermeneutic process through which humanity gains an increased awareness of its condition, in that it decodes and translates the signs inscribed in the divine comedy.

Vieira thus believes that his texts open the path for the advent of the Kingdom of Christ, seen as the culmination of a process of increasing union between human beings and divinity initiated with the first coming of the Messiah and carried on by the Catholic Church's ongoing interpretation of Christian doctrine.

As to the objection that, given the uncertainty shrouding past events, it would be even more difficult to write a history of the future, Vieira replies by establishing a distinction between the work of the "chroniclers of past times," who determine the "exact moments of the chronology" and "know, define and prove the day, the month or, at least, the year," and his role as an "interpreter of the futures," who treads a "larger and freer path" since he does not "need to know but only to conjecture the future as God knows it" ("cronistas dos tempos passados;" "momentos exactos da cronologia;" "saber, definir e provar o dia, o mês ou, ao menos, o ano;" "intérprete dos futuros;" "uma via mais larga e mais livre;" "[não lhe] é necessário conhecer mas apenas supor o futuro como Deus o conhece," *Chave*, 32). Unlike the chronology of the past, which has to be understood in detail, the history of the future is not rooted in the knowledge of coming events, given that this wisdom belongs to God alone. Humans can only surmise what will happen based on divine revelation. This demotion of history, whereby it becomes mere supposition, does not encumber Vieira's argumentation. In a vertiginous transmutation of values reminiscent of the rhetoric used in his sermons, the author points out the advantages of his interpretation of the future: grounded on reason and divine revelation, the history of events to come is erected upon a more solid terrain than any chronology of the past.

"Whoever wishes to see clearly the falsity of human histories," writes Vieira, "should read the same history written by different writers, and this person will see how the authors clash, how they contradict one another and how they get involved in these events, while it is obvious that the truth could be told just by one of them and it is certain that none of them is telling the truth" ("Quem quiser ver claramente a falsidade das histórias humanas, leia a mesma história por diferentes escritores, e verá como se encontram, se contradizem e se implicam no mesmo sucesso,

sendo infalível que um só pode dizer a verdade e certo que nenhum a diz,"
História I, 137). If past chronologies are clearly erroneous, the "*History
of the Future* is more truthful than all the histories of the past, since the
latter were mostly drawn from a mendacious source, namely human ignorance and malice, and ours was drawn from the flame of prophecy and
expanded by the flame of reason, which are the two sources of human
and divine truth" ("*História do Futuro* mais verdadeira que todas as do
passado, porque elas em grande parte foram tiradas da fonte da mentira,
que é a ignorância e malícia humana, e a nossa tirada do lume da profecia e acrescentada pelo lume da razão, que são as duas fontes da verdade
humana e divina," *História* I, 138). Vieira sets the fallibility of human
memory, the source of the histories of the past, against divine omni-
science, which is revealed to him through prophecy with the guidance
of reason. He unfolds here a postmodern line of argumentation *avant la
lettre*, which highlights the instability of historiographic accounts of the
past, since they are based upon the interpretation of often-contradictory
data. However, the author parts ways with relativism when he identifies
God as a guarantor for his vision of the future and describes himself as
the interpreter of a preestablished reality. Emanating directly from a
divine source, the suppositions of the historians of the future possess a
kind of certainty unattainable for the chronicles of the past, which stem
solely from a limited human understanding. Since the exercise in herme-
neutics Vieira engages in does not amount to knowledge, his portrayal
of events to come will necessarily remain incomplete. Yet, this does not
make his outline of the future any less exact, because it derives from a
reliable, divine source.

Given that Vieira's reflections on the future are substantially different from chronological descriptions of the past, why would the author
choose the word *history* to designate the prophetic writings where
he announced the advent of the Kingdom of Christ on earth? If his
Messianic texts are just incomplete sketches of the time to come and
do not amount to a full knowledge of the future, as Vieira emphasizes,
why does he employ the term *history*, which is etymologically related to

knowing and commonly refers to a minute account of bygone events? Vieira's goal in utilizing this denomination was to emphasize the linear temporality of the future that also entails a chronology, though different from the past one. The author points out that the history of the future inverts the directionality adopted in the narration of the past: "[W]e, on the contrary, by finding a new path in the inverse direction... by going back from the end of the world to the Antichrist, from the Antichrist to the Gospel preached and received everywhere and from the universal conversion of all peoples to our time... will not only go but also arrive. ([N]ós, pelo contrário, encontrando um novo caminho no sentido inverso... retrocedendo desde o fim do mundo ao Anticristo, do Anticristo ao Evangelho pregado e recebido em toda a parte e da conversão universal dos povos até ao nosso tempo... não só iremos senão também chegaremos," *Chave*, 32).

While conventional historians describe events that took place starting with Creation and then move to actuality, Vieira's chronology begins with the end of the world and then proceeds in the direction of the present. An inheritor of medieval Scholasticism, he espouses a theological conception of human history founded upon Church dogma, according to which the future, far from being a repository of possibilities that could either be actualized or forever remain *in potentia*, is defined a priori by God. The divine plan has been in place from time immemorial and, therefore, human endeavors move in the direction of a predetermined *terminus ad quem*. Such worldview necessarily excludes the idea of progress, or rather, the perfectibility of humanity is already part of God's schema for the development of history. The increased perfection of both individuals and sociopolitical groups accompanies the gradual coming together of the kingdom of men and the Kingdom of God up to the point where these merge in the end of time with the advent of the long-awaited Empire of Christ. In this age, there will be a coincidence between the world and the Church, which will thus become truly universal: "But, at the time when finally the plentitude of this light comes to fruition, the magnitude of the Church will correspond to such an extent to the magnitude of the world that there will be reciprocity between the world and the Church and between the Church and the world" ("Mas, no tempo em que final-mente se der a plenitude desta luz, então de tal modo a magnitude da Igreja será igual à do próprio mundo que haverá reciprocidade do mundo com a Igreja e da Igreja com o mundo," *Chave*, 184).[3]

Vieira's "history of the future" can only be understood in the context of a conception of the future that is indistinguishable from the present; or, to put it differently, the future is simply a present that has not yet come to pass. The normative bent of Vieira's thought, which he reveals even more unmistakably in his sermons than in his prophetic works, is rooted in this unshakeable certainty about the contours of the time to come. The author crafted both the sermons and the prophetic texts as instruments to guide the faithful through a path they will necessar-ily have to traverse in order to bring about the advent of the Messianic age and fulfill the destiny of humankind. Vieira's history of the future, then, has both a descriptive and a performative function. It interprets the divine design, elaborates a chronology of future times, and makes it known to all human beings. At the same time, this history determines present events, insofar as, conscious of the imminence of the Kingdom of Christ, all Christians should work to promote its arrival and behave as though it were already in place, that is to say, behave as if the future were, de facto, present.

The second reason why Vieira defines his prophetic writings as a *history* of the future has to do with the traits of the coming Christian Empire that, in his view, will soon encompass the whole of humanity. For the author, this kingdom is not qualitatively different from the pres-ent but, rather, represents its completion. For him, the Messianic age corresponds to the fulfillment of evangelizing efforts undertaken by the Church, including his own activity as a preacher and missionary:[4]

Even though this complete and consummate Empire of Christ is a future empire, it is not for this reason an empire abso-lutely different from the past and the present, but rather the same.... [T]hus the Empire of Christ was small in the beginning, becomes larger as it progresses and in its perfection and augmentation it will be entirely complete and consummate; but even though it will be different in its greatness and extension, in faith and in adoration (which is its substance) it will always be the same Empire of Christ.

Ainda que este Império completo e consumado de Cristo é império futuro, nem por isso é absolutamente império diverso do passado e do presente, senão o mesmo.... [A]ssi o Império de Cristo em seus princípios foi pequeno, em seus progressos é maior e em sua perfeição e aumento há-de ser inteiramente completo e consumado, mas posto que na grandeza e extensão diferente, na fé e adoração (que é sustância) sempre o mesmo Império de Cristo. (*Representação* II, 69)

Similar to what happens in the present, which results from a series of past occurrences, there is continuity between contemporary events and the Messianic future of humanity. Vieira underlines in all of his prophetic texts that the Kingdom of Christ will take place on earth and arise as a more perfect version of the current situation. This Messianic age, also called the Fifth Empire, is the last stage in a sequence of empires that have governed large areas of the world—the Assyrian, the Persian, the Greek, and the Roman empires—and is therefore included in the chronological development of human beings. Vieira's emphasis on the *history* of the future derives from his understanding of the Fifth Empire as an intrahistorical period, imbued with the temporality of human becoming.

The historicity of the Kingdom of Christ, one of the most contentious points in Vieira's doctrine on the future of Catholicism, is crucial for his prophetic vision. The author distances himself on this issue from the canonical orientation of the Church, according to which the Word of God would be completely fulfilled only in the transcendent, spiritual sphere of the Kingdom of Heaven, free from the temptations of the flesh.

Vieiran prophetic thought on this issue echoes the position of many Millenarian groups that highlighted the materiality of a future Christian empire. To the rhetorical question formulated in the Second Section of the *Representation*, namely, "[w]hether the Fifth Empire that we decided would be the one of Christ, is an empire from heaven or from the earth," Vieira replies that it is an "Empire and a Kingdom of the earth or on earth" ("[s]e o Quinto Império, que resolvemos ser de Cristo, é império do céu ou da terra?;" "Império e Reino da terra ou na terra," *Representação* II, 46–47). In the *History of the Future*, the author reiterates the earthly filiation of his Fifth Empire, which "will be in this World" ("há-de ser neste Mundo," II, 50) and adds that it is "both spiritual and temporal" ("juntamente espiritual e temporal," II, 113).[5]

The aporia inherent in the notion of a Kingdom of Christ, "perfect, complete, and consummate" ("perfeito, completo e consumado," *Representação* II, 11), while simultaneously earthly and temporal, is lucidly identified by the author himself: "The kingdoms of the World are all from their own nature corruptible and all ... will end with this very World, which our faith tells us will end. Therefore, if the Kingdom and Empire of Christ and of Christians should be perpetual, incorruptible and eternal, it follows clearly and manifestly that it will not be an empire of the Earth but of Heaven" ("Os reinos deste Mundo todos de sua própria natureza são corruptíveis, e todos, por mais que durem e permaneçam hão-de ter fim com o mesmo Mundo, o qual é de fé que se há-de acabar. Logo, se o Reino e Império de Cristo e dos Cristãos há-de ser perpétuo, incorruptível e eterno, clara e manifestamente se segue que não há-de ser império da Terra, senão do Céu," *História* II, 48). The Kingdom of Christ, necessarily perfect and, as such, immutable, is by nature ahistorical. This is the reason why the Church often places it in the celestial sphere. Vieira is here faced with the difficulty of inserting an extratemporal state into historical becoming, an impasse he will try to overcome by resorting to an intricate theological maneuver: the Kingdom of Christ will first reach its maximum perfection on earth and will subsequently continue this perfection eternally in heaven. "We do not deny, however, and we cannot deny," he writes, that this Kingdom and Empire of Christ and of the Christians will also last with the same Christ and the same Christians after they have been blessed for all eternity in Heaven; but this does not mean that the Kingdom will not possess on Earth the greatness predicted and promised in these texts. Rather, the reason why the Kingdom of Christ will have so much greatness in Heaven is that it will have it first on Earth; in Heaven this greatness will be consummate and most perfect, as it should be in Heaven.

Não negamos, porém, nem podemos negar, que este Reino e Império de Cristo e dos Cristãos, há-de durar também com o mesmo Cristo e os mesmos Cristãos depois de bem-aventurados por toda a eternidade no Céu; mas nem por isso há-de deixar de ter na Terra a grandeza que nestes textos lhe é profetizada e prometida, antes a razão de haver de ter tanta grandeza no Céu, é porque a terá primeiro na Terra, no Céu consumada e perfeitíssima, como se deve ao estado do Céu. (*História* II, 48–49)

The line of argumentation established here is similar to the reasoning developed in the *Apology*, where the author antinomically declares that the Fifth Empire will and will not have an end: "Because the King [*sic*] of Christ in this world will have an end, it will last until the end of the world, and in the other world that will have no end, it [the Kingdom of Christ] will last without an end, as that world will … considering two perpetuities in the Kingdom of Christ (as it will truly come to pass): one in this world and until its end and another in the other world and without end" ("Porque o Rei [*sic*] de Cristo neste mundo há de ter fim, durará até o fim dele, e no outro mundo que não há de ter fim, durará sem fim como ele … considerando no Reino de Cristo duas perpetuidades [como verdadeiramente as há de ter]: uma neste mundo até o fim dele, e outra no outro sem fim," 303). Insofar as the world is finite, the Fifth Empire will end with the world's demise, but it will last forever in the celestial domain.[6] Nevertheless, Vieira does not specify the shape assumed by the temporal Empire of Christ once in Heaven and therefore falls short of offering a fully satisfactory solution for the paradox upon which his prophetic writings are founded.

The vitality of Vieira's prophecies and their lasting impact on Brazilian culture are rooted precisely in the contradiction I have just described: the ahistorical historicity and the eternal temporality of the Kingdom of Christ on earth. The coincidence of temporality and spirituality in the Fifth Empire opens Vieiran prophecies to a social dimension, thus allowing him to go beyond the limitations of a purely theological reflection and create a theological-political utopia predicated on justice, equality among all (Christian) human beings, and perpetual peace.

A Perfect Temporal Empire

Vieira's emphasis on the historicity and temporality of the Fifth Empire leads to a positive understanding of corporeality. Far from being opposed to spirit, in keeping both with the Christian theological dogma and with the Cartesian philosophical model, the body in Vieira complements human spirituality: "That which are [sic] opposed to the body is not always more spiritual.... Those who recognize that Christ has a temporal dominium of the world do not make Christ any less of a Saint and the world any less spiritual because of this" ("Nem sempre é maior espiritualidade o que mais se opõem [sic] ao corpo.... Não fazem menos Santo a Cristo, nem querem fazer menos espiritual o Mundo, os que reconhecem em Cristo o domínio temporal dele," *História* II, 59). Not only is the body not a hindrance to spiritual pursuits, but the temporal Empire of Christ is also compatible with the highest degree of spirituality: "When we call Christ's Empire a temporal Empire, we do not mean to say that His Empire is subject to the changes and instability of time, nor do we mean to say that He receives greatness and majesty from the pomp and the vain splendors of the World's exterior things, which this very

World... rightfully calls temporalities" ("Quando chamamos Império temporal ao de Cristo, não queremos dizer que é o seu Império sujeito às mudanças e inconstâncias do tempo, nem que receba a grandeza e majestade da pompa e aparato vão das cousas exteriores do Mundo, a que o mesmo Mundo... chama, com razão, temporalidades," *História* II, 60).

Vieira underlines that the Kingdom of Christ will be different from all others because it will reject ostentation and futilities. He astutely interprets the Messiah's revelation to Pilatus that "my Kingdom is not of this world" ("Regnum meum non est de hoc mundo") as part of His condemnation of "external splendor and pomp of richness, galas, palaces, horses, carriages, servants and armies" ("aparato e pompa exterior de riquezas, galas, palácios, cavalos, coches, criados, exércitos"), which were the external manifestations of royal power in his time. The preacher points out that Christ does not wish to deny His temporal jurisdiction over the world but only to reject the mundanities usually associated with political power: "One should note here that Christ did not say: *Regnum meum non este de hujus mundi*, but *hoc mundo*, because the Kingdom of Christ was truly from this World and from all the World, the only difference being that it did not have the accidents of vanity and false greatness that shored up the other kingdoms of the World" ("Onde se deve notar que não disse Cristo: *Regnum meum non este de hujus mundi*, senão de *hoc mundo*, porque o Reino de Cristo verdadeiramente era deste Mundo e de todo o Mundo, e só não tinha os acidentes da vaidade e falsa grandeza com que se sustentavam os outros reinos do Mundo," *História* II, 66–67).[7] Vieira evinces his desire to reform the corrupt mores of an imperfect world, a facet that is even more salient in his sermons. The author identifies Christ's renunciation of mundane riches as an example to be followed both by monarchs and by religious men, thus implicitly criticizing the luxurious lifestyle of some members of the clergy: "It was therefore most convenient that in Christ were combined the utmost dominion and the utmost contempt for and abstinence from the things of the World, so that in the same example religious men would learn the mortification of usage and prelates would learn the moderation of dominion" ("Foi logo conveniente íssimo que em Cristo se ajuntasse o sumo domínio e o sumo desprezo e abstinência das cousas do Mundo, para que no mesmo exemplar aprendessem os religiosos a mortificação do uso e os prelados a moderação do domínio," *História* II, 107). Vieira sketches here a utopian form of temporal rule that does not entail the repudiation of corporeality linked to the kingdoms of this world but rather the suppression of any abuse of power, excessive wealth, and luxury. In the footsteps of the Messiah, who abstained from using His temporal, sovereign power and modestly submitted to the authorities when He was alive, the author states that "often the more noble and more generous use of power is not wanting to use it" ("muitas vezes o mais nobre e o mais generoso uso do poder é não querer usar dele," *História* II, 109). The temporal character of the Fifth Empire is thus defined as the enjoyment of a negative freedom, namely, having access to power, riches, and so on, but simultaneously being free from these temptations—a kind of liberty Vieira returns to in his more detailed descriptions of the Kingdom of Christ on earth.[8]

If Vieira vehemently condemns a certain type of temporal empire and exhorts his readers to be humble, he still underlines the corporeal dimension of the Kingdom of Christ, whose sovereignty extends not only to every soul but also to the body of every human being. This union of body and spirit is represented by the two crowns of the Messiah, one made of silver and the other of gold, which would stand for the temporal and the spiritual empires, respectively. Even though the difference in the value of the metals forming the crowns might point to the superiority of spirit, Vieira stresses that these symbolic crowns were "equal and similar in everything and without difference, since the Spiritual Empire of Christ is as universal and perfect as His temporal Empire" ("iguais e em tudo semelhantes, e sem diferença algũa, porque tão universal e tão perfeito é o Império Espiritual de Cristo, como o seu Império temporal," *Representação* II, 219).[9] Christ's nature already prefigured this junction of two kingdoms since, through the hypostatic union, He combined human and divine elements (*História* II, 69).[10] Given that human beings are made of body and spirit, the Kingdom of Christ would be incomplete, and thus less perfect, if it were only immaterial, since "it would not be fair that, as head of men, made of flesh and spirit, [Christ] would have a broken dominion over them; rather He should have a complete dominion, both over things related to the spirit and over things related to the body" ("como cabeça dos homens que são compostos de carne e espírito, não era justo que [Cristo] tivesse sobre eles o domínio partido, senão inteiro, assim sobre as cousas e acções concernentes ao espírito, como as que pertencem ao corpo," *História* II, 104).[11] The temporal character of the Fifth Empire is viewed as a sign of its perfection, since it encompasses the different facets of human life.[12]

Vieira pragmatically observes that the dissemination of the Christian faith has always depended upon the support of existing monarchs: the times when Christianity spread and the Church flourished coincided with periods during which secular power cooperated with ecclesiastic authorities. Based upon this observation, the author concludes that faith needs to take into account the specificities of human nature, which is largely determined by the body: "And if we look for the cause of these effects both amongst Gentiles and amongst Christians, we will find that it depends on human nature and corporeality, which has always been much more influenced by apprehensions entering through the senses, which are those related to temporal power" ("E se buscarmos a causa destes efeitos assi entre os Gentios como Cristãos, acharemos que consiste toda na mesma natureza e corporeidade humana, na qual tiveram sempre muito maior força as apreensões que entram pelos sentidos, quais são as da potência temporal," *Representação* II, 228). The decisions of a king that have immediate consequences for the lives of his subjects are more influential than "the voices, promises, and miracles of twenty Prophets" ("que as vozes, promessas e milagres de vinte Profetas," *Representação* II, 228), which means that the future Christian empire on earth will not only have to take spirit into consideration but, above all, strive to find a harmonious balance between the temporal and the spiritual domains.

The materiality of the Messianic kingdom entails the need for a political structure and a decision about the best way to organize society as a space where the members of the Christian empire will coexist.

According to Vieira, the two crowns of Christ will incarnate in two emperors: the Pope, who has jurisdiction over the spiritual, ecclesiastic domain, and a secular emperor, who will administer temporal issues. Both should exert their authority supplementarily, much in the same way as the sun and the moon alternate in the sky (*Representação* II, 224).[13] Vieira creates with this separation a division of powers that mirrors the Christian trinity. Christ now occupies the place of the Father, who delegates part of His power to the Son and the Holy Ghost, both of whom are transmuted in Vieiran thought into the secular emperor and the Pope, respectively—forming a trinity that will correspond in later Western political systems to the legislative, executive, and judicial powers.

By postulating that the temporal aspects of the Empire of Christ, that is, the organized distribution of the bodies of all the subjects of this kingdom, will be ruled by a secular sovereign, Vieira touches upon three key issues in his vision of the Fifth Empire: the central role of the Portuguese nation in the future Christian realm; the universality of the Messianic age, which would bring together all peoples of the earth, including Gentiles and Jews; and the idea that the Messianic reign will inaugurate an era of perpetual peace guaranteed by a supreme monarch.

If the Kingdom of Christ on earth is to have a temporal emperor, it is necessary to determine the origin of such a sovereign. Vieira does not doubt that the future Christian emperor will be Portuguese: "I find it very probable that the land and the nation of this future Emperor and Empire is the Portuguese land and nation, and the last and more occidental kingdom of the whole world, which is the Kingdom of Portugal" ("[T] enho por muito provável que a terra e nação deste futuro Imperador e Império é a terra e nação portuguesa, e o reino último e mais ocidental de todo o mundo, que é o Reino de Portugal," *Representação* II, 442).[14] The author refers here to the notion that political power follows the movement of the sun from east to west. The geographical location of the four past empires—Assyria, Persia, Greece, and Rome—confirmed this idea and made it clear for Vieira that Portugal, the most occidental country in Europe and with colonies even farther west in Brazil, would be the nation chosen to head the Fifth Empire. Grounding his argumentation on the Portuguese Messianic tradition, Vieira concludes that the future secular emperor will be a descendent of the royal family. In his famous letter "Hopes of Portugal" ("Esperanças de Portugal") addressed to the Portuguese Bishop of Japan, which triggered his trial by the Inquisition, the author interprets the prophetic verses of poet Bandarra to prove that the supreme emperor of the Kingdom of Christ would be Portuguese King John IV. He predicted that the king, who had died recently, would soon be resurrected to lead Portugal as the political kernel of the impending Messianic age.[15]

The identification of King John IV as the secular leader of the coming reign of peace cannot be fully explained as a result of the friendship that united Vieira and the monarch, nor as a mere expression of the author's nationalism, fueled by Portuguese political independence in 1640 after four decades of Castilian domination. Vieira justifies his prediction about the identity of the secular emperor by referring to what he views as the universal calling of Portugal, a nation spread over various continents through its numerous colonies.[16] He highlights that the Portuguese predisposition to embrace other peoples goes back to the mythical foundation of the nation by Moses's grandson Tubal, whose name, according to the etymology unearthed by Vieira, would mean "Mundanus,"—of the entire world. For Vieira, the essence of Portuguese culture resided in its plasticity and adaptability, pinpointed as the sources of the country's exceptionalism. In light of this concept of national identity, which was in itself determined by a strong patriotism, Vieira believed that Portugal was particularly well suited to spearhead the future Fifth Empire that would encompass all nations of the world.[17] The preacher regarded the process of Portuguese colonization and the concomitant evangelization of the colonized regions as a first step in the advent of the Kingdom of Christ, in that the coming empire would extend to all human beings.

Vieira describes the Fifth Empire as a universal kingdom that would include all nations on earth, united by the Christian faith: "[T]here will be a time when all the world will be Christian, all united in one faith, in one baptism, in one adoration and in only one name of the divinity of Christ, and [this world] will constitute and form only one people, namely the Catholic people" ("[H]á-de haver tempo em que todo o mundo seja cristão, unido todo em ũa só fé, em um só bautismo, em ũa só adoração e em um só nome da divindade de Cristo, e constituído e formado de todo ele um só povo, que é o católico," *Representação* II, 113).[18] The preacher reiterates time and again that the Kingdom of Christ will extend to "all roundness of the earth," including the Gentiles and the Jews, which will be converted to the Christian doctrine ("a toda a redondeza da terra," *Representação* II, 71).[19]

In *Key of the Prophets*, Vieira argues against other theologians of his time, such as Father Francisco Suárez, according to whom the so-called Gentiles, that is, those who never heard of God—the category under which Native Brazilians were classified—were guilty of their ignorance about Catholicism and, therefore, incurred a mortal sin and could not be saved. Vieira stressed that, in their simplicity, the indigenous peoples could never have known God through their own means and, therefore, could not be blamed or punished for not being Christian.[20] The coming Messianic Kingdom of Christ would free Indians from their godlessness and welcome them into the fold of Christianity. Once again, Vieira emphasizes the centrality of his experience in the Americas for reaching his conclusions: "This issue cannot be learned though study or discourse [but] through praxis and through experience, as if touched by the hands and observed through the eyes" ("Esta matéria não se aprende estudando e discorrendo, [mas] conhecendo-se pela prática e pela experiência, como que apalpada com as mãos e observada com os olhos," *Chave*, 95).

Similar to the Gentiles, the Jews would also be part of the Messianic Christian kingdom. Vieira's theological discussions with Jews from The Netherlands, particularly with the Madeira-born and Lisbon-educated Menasseh ben Israel, who lived in exile in Amsterdam, persuaded him that there was no incompatibility separating the Christian and the Jewish views on Messianism: "I say that the (material) hope of the Jews can agree with the Catholic faith.... I speak about those with whom I discussed, namely, some Jews from Holland" ("digo que a dita esperança (material) dos Judeus se pode concordar com a fé católica.... Falo daqueles com que disputei, que são alguns Judeus de Holanda," *Representação* II, 317).[21] In a typical twist of interpretation, Vieira argues that the Christian Messiah, the son of God, is of a spiritual nature, whereas the Jewish Messiah is a temporal, political leader. If Jews accept the Christian spiritual Messiah, they can have a political leader for Israel, who would be one of the kings serving under the supreme emperor in the Messianic Kingdom of Christ. It is natural, writes Vieira, that the Jews want to have political control over their land, in the same way as the Portuguese, who had recently fought against the Spanish in order to regain sovereignty over their territory (*Representação* II, 324). Vieira's open sympathy for the Jews, expressed in his frequent comparisons between the Jewish people and the Portuguese—both scattered throughout the world—and his efforts to grant protection to members of the exiled Jewish community so that they could return to Portugal, was one of the reasons for his imprisonment by the Inquisition in 1663.[22]

Having a privileged access to the Gentiles in colonies such as Brazil and enjoying a close relationship to many Jewish communities in Europe, some of which still spoke Portuguese, Vieira believed Portugal was ideally placed to spearhead the future Messianic age. The universalist calling of Portugal as a temporal nation, combined with the universality of the Catholic Church in the spiritual domain, would result in the Empire of Christ on earth, over which the Pope and a Portuguese sovereign would preside. Vieira's conviction that the political leader of the future Messianic age would be Portuguese offered a solution to the serious political and economic problems the country was facing in the mid-sixteen hundreds, from a constant threat to national sovereignty from Castile to the invasion of Brazil by the Dutch. Nevertheless, the need for a temporal emperor in the Fifth Empire went beyond simple patriotism. This monarch was central for Vieira's project bcause he would guarantee perpetual peace, which the author saw as the cornerstone of the Kingdom of Christ on earth.

A Utopia of Perpetual Peace

The union of human beings in the Fifth Empire, made possible by a shared faith that cements their bonds, does not imply the dissolution of all peoples into an undifferentiated whole. When he states that "there will be a time when all the Kings, all the nations, all the languages, all the lands and the whole world will not have a law, a faith, an adoration, a sacrifice other than Christ's" ("há de vir tempo em que todos os Reis, todas as nações, todas as línguas, todas as terras, e todo o mundo inteiro não há de ter outra lei, outra fé, outra adoração, outro sacrifício senão o de Cristo," *Apologia*, 91), Vieira is implicitly recognizing that national, cultural, and linguistic differences will remain in the Messianic age, only subsumed under the larger totality represented by Christian spirituality.

The temporal, intrahistorical facet of Vieira's Messianic project does not allow him to conceive the Fifth Empire as a pan-state where human beings would share the same spirituality devoid of distinctive earthly traits, as will happen in the Kingdom of Heaven. Vieira's emphasis on the Empire of Christ *on earth* is tantamount to a protest against the interpretation of corporeality as a mere accessory, as an appearance that disguises a true spiritual essence. The co-implication of spirituality and temporality in the future Christian empire and the resulting resistance of materiality to the leveling of differences separating various peoples prompts the preacher to distance himself from a conception of the Messianic age as an amalgamation of all nations, subordinated to the power of one monarch. The political expression of a Messianic temporal empire that takes into consideration the multiplicity of world regions will be the continuation of the various kingdoms and principalities already in existence, but now subjected to the higher authority of a secular (Portuguese) emperor.

Anticipating potential criticism leveled against his political proposal of creating a supreme emperor, Vieira reassures the sovereigns of his time: "[T]his scepter that God will send to the world will not take away the Kings from the Kingdoms or the Kingdoms from the Kings, who will remain the heads of the peoples and the lands they ruled, as before" ("[E]ste cetro que Deus há-de mandar ao mundo não há-de tirar os Reis aos Reinos, nem os Reinos aos Reis, os quais hão-de ficar sendo cabeças das gentes e terras que lhes eram sujeitas, como dantes," *Representação* II, 236). The different peoples will still be governed by their respective sovereigns, thus keeping their distinctive traits. The secular emperor will function as a superpower that settles potential disputes between the various nations.[23] He will mediate between princes and thus avoid the constant wars that plague the world, pitting not only Christians and non-Christians but also the different Christian kingdoms against each other.

The main task of the supreme monarch in the Fifth Empire will be to maintain perpetual peace, which is for Vieira the foundation of the coming Kingdom of Christ: "The 1st temporal happiness of this felicitous Kingdom will be that without which nothing else can be called truly happy, and which encompasses all happiness that one can enjoy in this life, namely peace. There will be Universal peace throughout the world and wars and arms will cease amongst all nations" ("A 1.a felicidade temporal deste bem-aventurado Reino será aquela sem a qual nenhuma outra se pode chamar verdadeira felicidade, e a qual em si mesma abraça todas ou quase todas as que se podem gozar nesta vida, que é a paz. Haverá paz Universal em todo o mundo, cessarão as guerras e armas entre todas as nações," *Apologia*, 287).

Vieira differentiates between the peace of the Messianic age and the *pax romana*, characterized by a temporary absence of conflicts while war still looms large as a constant threat on the horizon of political possibilities. Contrary to this state of latent tension that denoted a period of respite between past and future wars, the peace of the Fifth Empire will mean the complete abolition of the concept of war, which will be forgotten by human beings:

[T]he universal peace of Christ... will not only be free from the harm, labors, oppression and ruin that war brings both to those who suffer it and to those who wage it, but it will completely free all men in the world from anxiety, fear, watchfulness, vigilance, caution, suspicion and any other kind of uneasiness or preoccupation regarding war, as there will be no soldiers, captains, arms, no military exercises or military studies, since these will be completely superfluous things and of no use.

[A] paz universal de Cristo ... não só há-de ser livre dos danos, trabalhos, opressões e ruínas que a guerra traz consigo, assi aos que a padecem como aos mesmos que a fazem, mas há-de livrar totalmente a todos os homens do mundo, de temores, receos, prevenções, vigias, cautelas, suspeitas, e qualquer outro género de inquietações ou cuidados da mesma guerra, não havendo soldados, capitães, armas, nem exercício algum ou estudo militar, como cousa totalmente supérflua e de nenhum uso. (*Representação* II, 386)

Vieira compares men of arms to carnivorous beasts, who, in the future empire, will no longer attack one another but will graze "peacefully and in harmony without chasing or eating each other" ("pacífica e concordemente, sem se perseguirem, nem se comerem," *Apologia*, 290, 292). By means of a rhetorical question, the preacher offers a rejoinder to those who might be skeptical about his predictions: "How strange can it be that the world will witness in its last age what it saw in its first?" ("Que muito será que torne o mundo a ver na sua última idade o que viu na primeira?," *Apologia*, 292). Vieira resorts to dialectics in order to conclude that the Kingdom of Christ will bring together in a new synthesis the Adamic paradise and the age of decadence that followed the fall of human beings from their original state of grace. In the Messianic kingdom, human beings will be conscious of what sin, corruption and decay are—they will possess the knowledge of Good and Evil that was out of reach for Eve and Adam—but will still live free from necessity and, more specifically, free from the suffering caused by war.

Negative freedom, which, as we saw above, implied the absence of temptations and a release from the grip of necessity, is precisely what distinguishes the Fifth Empire from the heretical beliefs of the Millenarians. According to Vieira, Millenarianism was reprehensible not because it accounted for human corporeality in the Kingdom of Christ but for allowing the needs of the flesh to determine human behavior, therefore sanctioning sins such as gluttony or lust: "[W]e have the decision of Saint Augustine in / his own terms, who decided that eating should not be abhorrent to the state of the bodies of the blessed; and the only distinction he draws between those and our bodies alive today is that we eat out of necessity and desire, and they can eat out of desire but not out of necessity" ("[T]emos a decisão de Santo Agostinho em / próprios termos, o qual resolve que o comer não tem repugnância alguma com o estado dos corpos bem-aventurados; e a distinção que somente faz entre eles e os nossos em que hoje vivemos, é que nós comemos por necessidade e por vontade, e eles podem comer por vontade, mas não por necessidade," *Apologia*, 275). Like the blessed, who can enjoy bodily pleasures, human beings living in the Messianic Christian empire will have a physical existence but will not be determined by their corporeality.[24] In other words, the body will no longer influence human action, which will be primordially dictated by faith. Activities such as eating or copulating can happen optionally but they will not be regarded as a response to deprivation. The abolition of wars, a centerpiece of the Fifth Empire, should be understood in the context of this general absence of necessity, in that peace is a condition of possibility for the freedom of human beings from corporeal needs. The secular emperor, whose function it is to keep perpetual peace, will fulfill a crucial role in the Kingdom of Christ on earth by promoting harmony among all nations and thus eliminating war.

Vieiran Messianism is a theological precursor for the secular project of perpetual peace later developed in the Enlightenment, which culminated in Immanuel Kant's famous essay "Perpetual Peace: a Philosophical Sketch" (1795). Similar to the kingdom described by Vieira, the era of peace envisioned by Kant would not be established under the auspices of a particular nation that would pacify the regions under its command through the power of its armies, such as the *pax romana* and later the *pax britannica*. Rather, the age of perpetual peace would entail the disappearance of "standing armies" that, according to Kant, "will gradually be abolished altogether" ("Perpetual Peace," 94). As in Vieira's writings,

the notion of perpetual peace devised in the Enlightenment entailed a
federation of united nations. In Kant's text, however, the figure of a secular emperor who mediates between the various peoples is replaced by
the impersonal institution of international law and by the creation of a
league of nations that would arbitrate disputes.

The modern traits of Vieira's Messianism, whence the similarities
between his project and later writings on political philosophy derive, is
rooted in his insistence that the Kingdom of Christ would take place on
earth and therefore would be simultaneously a spiritual and a temporal
reign. In this future empire, the separation between the Jews, the Indians
Vieira had encountered in Brazil, and Christians would progressively
fade, as all would come together under Catholicism. Vieira postulates
a universality based upon a shared Christian faith that prefigures later
universalist projects such as the notion of natural rights, human rights,
and, more recently, global citizenship. He understands that the world
looks radically different when viewed from the Americas, as opposed to
Europe, and it is this ability to shift between different perspectives that
opens up his utopian kingdom to those who were traditionally excluded
from it. By admitting both Jews and Native Brazilians into the fold of
the future reign of Christ, Vieira transforms the very notion of Christian
universality, predicated on the replication of only one model for subjectiv-
ity. His legacy is that of extending the boundaries of Catholic sameness
in such a way that the outcome would be a radically altered version of
Christianity, capacious enough to encompass all peoples.

Far from regarding the Fifth Empire as a desideratum that fades
on the remote horizon of the future and in an uncertain celestial sphere,
Vieira states that he is writing a *history* of the future, a description of
events that will take place in the temporal becoming of the current world
and that therefore needs to take human corporeality into account. His
prophetic writings overflow the narrow boundaries of theology and move
into the political domain, using the notion of perpetual peace, which
entails freedom from physical necessity without abolishing the corporeality that constitutes human beings, to establish a bridge between the
spiritual and the temporal realms. Vieira thus envisions a renewed state

of grace, a time that will be "new and different from all periods in the past" ("novo e diferente de todos os tempos passados," *Apologia* 177), during which human beings will enjoy "all the goods and happiness of heaven and of the earth" ("todos os bens e felicidades do céu e da terra," *Apologia*, 197). The utopia of the Fifth Empire will not take place in another world but in this one and, therefore, it should be operative in the present. Both Vieira's sermons and his Messianic texts are part of the same effort of persuading his contemporaries to bring about the Kingdom of Christ on earth.

Vieira's vision of a just, felicitous, and peaceful realm will resonate throughout Brazil's subsequent utopian thought, as we shall see in the following chapters. Later literary, sociological, and philosophical texts offer various secularized versions of the state of grace postulated by the preacher. In these works, the Messiah, a pivotal figure in Vieiran prophecy, is replaced by the ingenuity of human beings as the spark for an actualized, earthly utopia. The idea of equality will be the cornerstone for communitarian texts that imagine a society grounded upon the principle of sharing. The matriarchal tribe of the Amazons, first depicted in travel writings and later fictionalized in Brazilian literature, incarnates such an idealized community (chapter 2). The inclusive, peaceful Christian kingdom to come depicted by Vieira equally reverberates in literature that portrays the close ties linking humans, animals, and plants. Recent authors highlight the porous boundaries separating humanity from other beings and dream of abolishing the hierarchical understanding of different forms of life, thus creating an interspecies utopia (chapter 3). Vieira's joyous Messianic age, a time when humans will be blessed with life on earth free from necessity, also finds parallels in reflections on leisure. Be it the guilt-free world of the *malandro*, the land of Carnivalesque playfulness, or the place of idleness required for true artistic expression, Brazil has always understood itself as a country of leisure (*ócio*), in stark opposition to the businesslike (*negócio*) attitude of other nations (chapter 4).

2

Amazons in the Amazon
Communitarian Matriarchy
in the Jungle

[T]odos nós desde muito cedo gizamos um Amazonas ideal . . .
([A]ll of us from very early on imagine an idealized Amazon. . .)
— Euclides da Cunha, *Um Paraíso Perdido*

The Realm of the Amazons

The feminization of American territory, envisioned as a vast, natural expanse lying in wait for European *conquistadores* to mold and civilize it, has proven to be an enduring fiction of New World colonization. This conception inherited an age-old understanding of the environment as feminine, the state of nature corresponding to the human condition before the advent of social organization mediated by masculine rationality (Merchant xxiii). In the case of the American continent, land was regarded as womanly, raw, chaotic matter that, following Aristotelian principles, male colonizers were tasked to shape into an enduring, intelligible form.[1] Native American populations tended to be amalgamated with nature as just another feature of the landscape serving as a backdrop for the newcomers' exploits.

It is not surprising that José de Alencar chose an Indian woman, Iracema, to embody the Brazilian land and people at the time of the colonial encounter, in his homonymous novel from 1865.[2] Alencar's

31

narrative became a landmark in Brazilian Romanticism and a foundational text for the country's literature that was to determine the notion of Brazilian national identity for decades to come.[3] Iracema, an anagram for "America," is the virginal guardian of the secrets of her tribe. She falls in love with a Portuguese soldier, Martim, during the early years of colonization, is forced to leave her community, and dies shortly after giving birth to Martim's son, Moacir. The narrative ends with Martim returning years later to Iracema's burial site, accompanied by a priest and other Portuguese soldiers, to found a new town. Even though Moacir symbolizes the fusion of native and European features at the root of Brazilian culture, the novel clearly presents the indigenous contribution and local landscape as vanishing traits, to be sacrificed to the colonizers' civilization.[4]

Feminized nature, depicted in novels such as Alencar's, traditionally took on two competing configurations: that of a virginal woman, who can later become a benevolent, nurturing mother, and that of a wild, uncontrollable being (Merchant 2).[5] The first stands at the origin of pastoral and bucolic literature, in which the environment welcomes humanity and effortlessly provides for its sustenance. In the latter paradigm, nature is a desolate, inhospitable landscape that human beings have to domesticate in order to survive. Both of these views are associated with recognizable patterns of femininity: the passive lover, wife, and mother who respects and obeys her male counterparts; and the wild, unpredictable woman, often depicted as a devil or a witch in Medieval and early modern lore.

European settlers availed themselves of these two archetypes of the environment and of femininity to interpret the foreign landscapes and local customs they encountered in America. The first colonizers often portrayed the continent in edenic hues, as Sérgio Buarque de Holanda meticulously documents in his study *Vision of Paradise* (*Visão do Paraíso*). Such a picture, clearly indebted to the benevolent nature narrative, went hand in hand with an appreciation of the local inhabitants as amiable and naive, an idealization that gave rise to the often-feminized character of the "noble savage," uncorrupted by the vices inherent in European culture. As we saw in the previous chapter, Antônio Vieira's conception of a Kingdom of Christ on earth was beholden to this utopian vision of the Americas as a new Eden, the colonization and evangelization of which would redeem Europe of its degeneracy in the coming Messianic age. As the colonization process progressed and the difficulties of establishing enduring settlements in unfamiliar surroundings became more apparent, however, the paradisiac features attributed to the region increasingly gave way to accounts that highlighted the troubles experienced by those who sought to tame a harsh wilderness and deal with intractable native peoples. These divergent pictures of the American territory as an unspoiled, prelapsarian paradise to be enjoyed, and as a hellish hinterland in need of development, have resurfaced time and again throughout the history of conquest and colonization, and came to form the bedrock of local conceptions of nature long after the independence of American nations.

The Amazon river basin did not escape the stereotypical depiction of America as either edenic or infernal. In fact, the earthly paradise/green hell dichotomy has been a mainstay of writings about the region from the arrival of the first explorers onward. As late as the beginning of the twentieth century, Brazilian writer Alberto Rangel titled his collection of short stories on Amazonia *Green Hell: Scenes and Scenery from the Amazon* (*Inferno Verde: Scenas e Scenários do Amazonas*) but mentioned, in the first short story of the book, that during the rainy season local tidal lakes were "populated by a fauna reminiscent of Paradise" ("populoso de uma fauna de estampa de Paraíso," 40), thus foregrounding the two contradictory aspects of nature in the region.[6]

The remoteness of the Amazon posed particular challenges to European exploration and colonization, problems that generated lasting impressions of the territory. This is perhaps the underlying reason for naming both the river and, synecdochically, the entire region, "Amazon," after the fierce mythological tribe of women warriors who purportedly fought against Ancient Greek soldiers.[7] To be sure, chronicles detailing

the exploits of the first Europeans to arrive in the New World were rife
with news about and even sightings of the Amazons in locations as
diverse as the Islands of the Antilles, present-day Ecuador, the Yucatan
Peninsula, or the South of Chile (Holanda 27–30).[8] The European predisposition to interpret the reality of the new continent through the lens
of preexisting legends created fertile ground for imagining the presence
of the Amazons, as well as of a variety of other mythological creatures,
in different parts of the Americas. One can only speculate why the name
stuck in the case of the "river of the Amazons." The association of the
new land with femininity, combined with the vast and impenetrable
jungle environment, where nature was more like a wild, hostile woman
than a nurturing mother, certainly contributed to cementing the idea
that dangerous female fighters lived deep in the rainforest.

The first encounter with an aggressive tribe of women in the region
was reported in Spanish Dominican Priest Gaspar de Carvajal's text *The
Discovery of the Great River of the Amazons* (*Descubrimiento del gran río
de las Amazonas*). Carvajal accompanied explorer Francisco de Orellana
in his traversal of the length of the Amazon basin from the foothills of
the Andes to the mouth of the river in the Atlantic Ocean in 1541–42.
According to the priest, Orellana's men were attacked by a group of
women, whose bravery in battle was such that they killed many Spanish
soldiers with their powerful arrows and were only defeated after a long
and strenuous battle (213–15). Later in the voyage, Carvajal learned
from an imprisoned Indian that the female warriors were part of a tribe
who lived without men in fairly developed towns with houses made of
stone and wood and connected through walled roads (220–22). The sup-
posed advancement of the Amazons' civilization, when compared to the
fairly simple lifestyle of the other inhabitants from the region, prompted
Carvajal, as well as subsequent chroniclers, to associate them with prodigious wealth. The myth of El Dorado, a city made of gold and located,
according to some accounts, in the depths of the rainforest, often inter-
sected with accounts about the Amazons (Holanda 37–38). This fusion of
the two legends testifies to the perception of the Amazon as a feminized

wilderness harboring incalculable riches that could only be conquered by male explorers ready to overcome countless perils.

After Carvajal's narrative, the Amazons routinely made an appearance in writings about the area. French geographer André Thévet believed that they were direct descendants of their Ancient Greek counterparts living on fortified islands, as he describes in his *The Singularities of Antarctic France* (*Les singularitez de la France antarctique*, 1557) (Holanda 35). Sir Walter Raleigh places the wealthy Amazon kingdom "not far from Guiana" in his *The Discovery of Guiana* (1596), based upon information he gathered among those he met in his American travels. Jesuit priest Cristóbal de Acuña, who, like Raleigh, did not claim to have seen the female warriors, declares himself convinced of their existence in his *New Discovery of the Great River of the Amazons* (*Nuevo descubrimiento del gran río de las Amazonas*, 1641) (121). He reports firsthand testimonies about the women's way of life by various Indians he met in his journey accompanying the Portuguese captain Pedro Teixeira in his return trip from Quito to Belém.[9] Acuña places the territory of the all-female tribe close to a hill he calls Yacamiaba, a designation that would resurface throughout history as the abode of the Amazons (122). In his *Chronicle of the Society of Jesus* (*Crónica da Companhia de Jesus*, 1663), Portuguese priest Simão de Vasconcelos again mentions the group of women, closely following the text of Acuña (Holanda 167–68). Already in the eighteenth century, French explorer Charles de la Condamine is convinced that the Amazons dwell in the interior of Guiana, as he narrates in his *Summarized Account of a Voyage Made in the Interior of South America* (*Relation abrégée d'un voyage fait dans l'intérieur de l'Amérique Méridionale*, 1745). The belief that female warriors inhabit the Amazon lived on until the early nineteenth century, with Drouin de Bercy still arguing for their existence in *Europe and America Compared* (*L'Europe et l'Amérique comparées*, 1818) (Slater 95).

As scientific-driven travel to South America became more frequent, the myth of the Amazons receded into the background. Inspired by the matter-of-fact spirit of the Enlightenment, naturalists such as Alexander von Humboldt, Alfred Russel Wallace, Henry Walter Bates, or Louis Agassiz strove to decipher the hidden mysteries of the rainforest, whether arising from its natural environment or pertaining to the history of its peoples. They created the Amazon as a "field of knowledge," a "scientific construct" to be analyzed through rational, painstaking research (Whitehead 131). In his *In the Land of the Amazons*, originally published in French in 1899, the Amazonian-born Baron of Santa-Anna Nery, a precursor of environmentalism in Brazil, explained away the female-only groups of fighters by pointing out that many indigenous women used to accompany their husbands to battle and even take part in combat, a custom that might have led European explorers to mistake them for the Amazon warriors of the classical period (36). The existence of an all-women tribe was thus easily brushed aside as yet another irrational belief of the prescientific era.

From a very real danger that conspired with other perils—such as strange diseases, wild animals, poisonous plants, and treacherous rapids—to terrorize outsiders, the Amazons became a mere footnote in the long list of misunderstandings about the region. But, as they crossed the hazy border separating reality from myth, fact from fancy, they underwent a subtle transformation. While the Amazons were, at first, part of a dystopian conception of the rainforest as a green hell, their recognition as a mere legend and, hence, no longer a threat, paved the way for their romanticization. In the first half of the twentieth century, feminized Amazonia resurfaced in Brazilian literary and cultural production in two distinct ways that retrace earlier personifications of nature as a woman: as a feminine wilderness to be domesticated by settlers in rubber boom literature; or as the abode of a matriarchal society, often explicitly designated as that of the Amazons, colored in idyllic hues. The disappearance of the perilous all-women group from conceivable reality thus allowed for their rebirth in fiction. As the twentieth century wore on, the "dangerous nature" paradigm gave way to utopianism, and the legendary tribe of the Amazons metamorphosed into an idealized social group, prospering in its environment and devoid of the drawbacks plaguing contemporary Brazilian society.

The Feminized Territory of the Rubber Boom

The so-called rubber boom in the last decades of the nineteenth and the beginning of the twentieth centuries brought unprecedented change to the Amazon river basin. Until then a backwater when compared to the centers of economic and political power located in the south of Brazil, the Amazon jumped into the limelight of national politics as the demand for rubber skyrocketed, bringing extraordinary wealth to the region. "White gold," as the latex from the *Hevea brasiliensis*, or rubber tree, was called, finally seemed to prove the fables of El Dorado true.

The Brazilian state strove toward a better demarcation and patrol of its Amazonian border in areas that had hitherto been neglected but now became attractive thanks to their rubber-producing potential. The conflict over the latex-rich Acre region is a case in point. Nominally part of Bolivia until the late eighteen hundreds, Acre was mostly inhabited by Brazilian rubber tappers. In 1903, it was annexed by Brazil, which, after a few skirmishes, paid Bolivia for the lost territory.[10] The dispute over the Amazonian border between Peru and Brazil also extended into the twentieth century. Brazilian writer Euclides da Cunha toured the region in 1904–05 as head of the Brazilian team in the *Brazilian-Peruvian Joint Commission to Map the High Purus* (*Comissão Mista Brasileiro-Peruana de Reconhecimento do Alto Purus*), tasked with establishing a definitive border between the two countries. Cunha's notes about his travels remain a powerful witness to the approach of early-twentieth-century Brazilian intellectuals to the Amazon.[11]

Cunha was a staunch proponent of technical and economic advancement as a way to bring Amazonia up to speed with the rest of the country. He regarded the plentiful rainforest as a land that had systematically eluded human culture (196).[12] "Thus," he writes, "nature is mighty, but incomplete" ("Destarte a natureza é portentosa, mas incompleta," 117). In another passage, he goes back to edenic rhetoric with a twist: "[The Amazon River] reminded me of an unpublished and contemporary (still incomplete and in the process of being miraculously written) page of *Genesis*" ("[O Amazonas] lembrava (ainda incompleta e escrevendo-se

maravilhosamente) uma página inédita e contemporânea do *Gênese*,"
100). Imbued with turn-of-the-century positivism, Cunha considered
that acts of Creation should not be left to divinity alone, and thought that
human beings had an important role to play in shaping the "incomplete"
natural environment of the Amazon. He advocated for the construction
of railroads throughout the rainforest and for large works of engineer-
ing that would make the territory's many rivers navigable, so as to open
the path for further development.[13] Those who colonize the Amazon,
Cunha concludes, have to "domesticate" it; they "are taming the desert"
("domar"; "estão amansando o deserto," 146). By resorting to zoologi-
cal vocabulary, the writer harks back to a conception of the region as an
enormous living organism, whose power needs to be harnessed by the
forces of civilization.

At the same time as the Brazilian state struggled to establish control over large swathes of Amazonia and to effectively "tame" the region's
hinterlands, thousands of migrants flocked to the territory. Drawn by the
rubber boom, they hailed mostly from the drought-ridden Northeast of
the country and came in pursuit of the dream of rapid and easy enrichment. Rubber boom literature, which focused on the plight of these
workers routinely exploited by powerful rubber lords, inherited Cunha's
views on the need to bring progress to the Amazon. The narratives
often availed themselves of stereotypical images of local nature, portrayed either as a virginal woman who is yet to unveil her riches or as a
ravished female, destroyed by the greed of settlers. In the already mentioned *Green Hell* collection of short stories by Alberto Rangel, as well
as in Carlos de Vasconcelos's novel *The Disinherited* (*Os Deserdados*,
1921) or in Portuguese-born Ferreira de Castro's *The Jungle* (*A Selva*,
1930), for example, personification of the Amazon as a woman is a
common narrative strategy used to symbolize the conflict between the
newcomers and the hostile environment they encountered in the rainforest. The land is depicted as an object of desire to be metaphorically
won over through sometimes violent sexual conquest by male migrants
(Maligo 59, 62–63).[14] Acculturation to the region is represented as a

process of learning how to dominate or, at the very least, cope with, the wilderness of the jungle. In the wake of Cunha's call for developing the Amazon, rubber boom narratives regarded settlers as harbingers of advancement, tasked with bringing progress to the hitherto forgotten, feminized, Amazonia.

Both in Cunha's texts and in later rubber boom fiction the Amazon is seen as a space outside geopolitical coordinates and historical becoming: a "land without history" ("terra sem história," 154–55), in the writer's pointed formulation. In this sense, it epitomizes a *terra nullius*, or no-man's-land, that can be appropriated and shaped according to the vision of the first (Europeans) to lay claim to it. It was this perception of the territory that fueled Cunha's ambitions to integrate it in the march of progress. But the conception of the area as an empty, timeless expanse also allowed for its exoticization and attendant idealization.[15] Writings about the Amazon can broadly be mapped along a continuum that extends from those comprising detailed descriptions of the region and foregrounding local issues to those that use it and its myths as a springboard for reflecting upon Brazilian society as a whole. While many rubber boom texts privilege a documentary style, in which knowledge of regional features was employed as a yardstick to measure authorial competence to discuss the region (Maligo 50–52, 78–79, 81), other narratives moved away from the concrete world of the rainforest and turned it into a fabled location that served as a means to comment upon the institutions of the rest of the country.

Regarded as a land without a past and detached from the constraints of reality, the Amazon often functioned as a screen upon which dreams of alternative social and political models were projected.[16] At various moments throughout history—as the seat of El Dorado, of the Land of Cinnamon, of the city of Manoa—it stood for a quintessential utopian space geared primarily toward the future. As rubber extraction started to decline from the 1920s onward, after the British successfully grew rubber trees in Asia ending the Amazonian monopoly on latex, the utopian bent came to predominate in writings about the region. While some authors were still crafting narratives about the rubber boom (and bust), others were going back to an idealized vision of the Amazon, according to which the area and its inhabitants stood for a better, more pristine version of Brazil, untouched by Western-style culture.

The myth of the Amazons underwent a significant transformation that accompanied the utopian turn in writings about the region. In the past, the legend of a female tribe had been entangled with a dystopian vision of the territory as a "green hell," according to which unsuspecting travelers and colonizers often fell prey to dangers lurking in the shadows of a threatening natural environment. Progressively, this perception of the Amazons changed and they became part of an idyllic image of the rainforest in the new utopian representations of the area. If Amazonia is as much a physical reality as it is a product of the imagination, forged by successive generations of explorers and writers, the legendary Amazons are a creation of fancy to an even greater extent. As such, they lend themselves to widely divergent interpretations, antithetical assessments and fictional reworkings that mirror evolving conceptions of the rainforest environment they have personified from the beginning of European settlement. In the rest of this chapter, we will turn to three modes of utopian representation of the Amazons: Gastão Cruls's depiction of a well-organized, self-sufficient lost tribe of women in *The Mysterious Amazon* (*A Amazônia Misteriosa*, 1925); Abguar Bastos's vision of the promised land of the Amazons, free from the social ills of his time, in *The Amazon no One Knows About* (*A Amazônia que Ninguém Sabe*, 1929), renamed *Land of the Icamiabas* (*Terra de Icamiaba*) in its second edition from 1934; and the Modernist fantasy of a renewed matriarchy as a means to overcome the pitfalls of capitalist, patriarchal rule, in the work of Oswald de Andrade.

Back to the Golden Age: Amazonian Incas

As the rubber boom faltered and Amazonian economic prosperity collapsed, together with the aspiration of importing the technical and economic advancement of Southern Brazilian metropolises to the region, there was a need to reformulate the discourse of progress that had dominated writings about the area in the first two decades of the twentieth century. The underdevelopment and remoteness of the rainforest, decried by intellectuals such as Cunha, acquired positive connotations, as it set the stage for conjuring up a harmonious form of social organization in tune with the environment—the reverse of the scientific excesses, economic imbalances, and political disputes that plague Western civilization.

Gastão Cruls's novel *The Mysterious Amazon*, written at a time when the author had not yet been to the area, exemplifies this idealization of Amazonia.[17] The text's first-person narrator and protagonist is a Brazilian doctor who recounts his adventures during an expedition into the rainforest. He gets lost in the jungle and is rescued by a group of Indians who take him and his companion to a town inhabited only by women. There he meets Doctor Hartmann, a German scientist who had been living in the territory for eight years with his French wife Rosina to conduct secretive experiments. The scientist informs the narrator that they are the guests of the fabled Amazons, descendants of a group of women from the Inca Empire who fled the violence of Spanish conquest.[18] The matriarchal tribe keeps only their female offspring, and no men, apart from occasional outsiders like the narrator, are allowed into the group.[19] In the beginning of the novel, the Brazilian explorer is represented as a detached and impartial observer of the Amazons' customs and of Doctor Hartmann's scientific pursuits. He later becomes emotionally involved with Rosina, thus triggering the narrative's denouement, when the couple tries to escape from the area and the young woman is killed during the attempt.

The environment described by the protagonist reflects his ambivalent relationship toward the rainforest, which goes back to traditional views of the area either as an earthly paradise or as a green hell. On the one hand, he is fascinated by the lushness of the jungle, which surpasses all his expectations. He comments on the "magnificent...gradation of greens" ("magnífica...graduação dos verdes," 11) and adds, farther on, that "[t]he forest displays, at this point, an unmatched grandiosity" ("[a] floresta, neste ponto, é de uma grandiosidade sem igual," 34). The immensity of the landscape dwarfs human measures and thwarts any attempts at cataloging or mapping the region: "It is necessary to know the immensity of the Amazon to be able to evaluate the ridiculous pettiness of geographical charts when we try to use them to reconstruct a path we have already traversed" ("É preciso conhecer o que é a imensidade da Amazônia para poder avaliar a mesquinhez ridícula que assumem as cartas geográficas, quando, diante delas, procuramos refazer algum trecho já percorrido," 20).

On the other hand, the protagonist is sometimes bored by the monotony of nature: "Here, there is not even a gradation of greens. One sole and same somber hue permeates all vegetation" ("Nem mesmo há aqui a gradação dos verdes. Uma única e mesma tinta sombria empasta toda a vegetação," 18). Tedium rapidly turns into apprehension once he gets lost. The environment is now "inhospitable" and the flora turns into a "monster with a green mane that kept us within its grip" ("inóspito"; "monstro de grenha verde que nos retinha entre as suas malhas," 37). While asleep, he has a nightmarish vision of the rainforest coming to life and acquiring mobility, which is juxtaposed to the explorer's sense of powerlessness and entrapment: "As if by magic, all vegetal beings in the forest had lost their cellulose membrane that immobilized them, and were now sensitive beings that moved with ease and wandered freely, slowly dragging their roots, as if these were large tentacles" ("Como que por encanto, todos os vegetais da floresta haviam perdido a membrana de celulose que os imobiliza, e eram agora entes sensificados que se moviam com desembaraço e vagueavam em liberdade, deslocando lentamente o raizame, à maneira de grandes tentáculos," 42). The narrator feels that he is in the clutches of an enormous living being, at once awe-inspiring and threatening.

Cruls's protagonist is aware of the fact that his divergent appraisals of Amazonia are contingent upon his precarious situation as a newcomer to the area. His interpretation of the surroundings is filtered through a vast body of literature that he invokes at every turn. Francisco de Orellana

(106), Hans Staden (55), Carl Linnaeus (47), Alexander von Humboldt (90), Lord Byron (29), Louis Agassiz (18), Richard Spruce (46), Henry Walter Bates (23), and Marshal Rondon (48) are some of the figures he mentions when trying to describe an environment that is utterly foreign to him. This bookish, secondhand knowledge of the territory that results in different opinions on the region, depending on the circumstances, contrast sharply with the immediacy of the Indians' relationship to nature. The narrator comments on the effortlessness with which native Amazonians move in the area: "I was immediately struck by the ease with which those people walked in the woods. Swift and skillful, one would think that the forest was made for them" ("Despertou-me logo interesse a facilidade com que aquela gente andava no mato. Ligeiros e atilados, dir-se-ia que a floresta fora feita para eles," 51). While the narrator's perception of nature was limited to external appearances he often could not decipher, for the Indians "the forest... became a true orchard" ("a mata... transformava-se num verdadeiro pomar," 52), a *locus amoenus* for those who understood its inner workings.

Even though the Amazons are, like the narrator, not originally from the area—according to the text, they descended from the Andes to the Amazon river basin at the beginning of the colonial period—they have, similarly to the native Indian tribes, seamlessly adjusted to their surroundings. When accompanying them in their expeditions, the protagonist reflects: "[I]t was a pleasure to travel with the Amazons. Nature belonged to them and as much on firm land, crossing large forests, as on small rafts... there were no dangers or obstacles for them" ("[D]ava gosto viajar com as Amazonas. A natureza pertencia-lhes e tanto na terra firme, varando as grandes florestas, como sobre as pequenas ubás... não havia perigos e escolhos que se lhes antolhassem," 269). Skillful at fishing and hunting, the Amazons are able to reap full benefits of the abundant local environment.

But the narrator also emphasizes the differences between the women's tribe and other indigenous groups in the region. They live in comfortable houses in well-ordered, miniature cities, with large streets, squares, and gardens (85). Furthermore, they do not depend solely on nature's bounty but have also cultivated extensive fields that yield a variety of crops (88, 98–99). Their warehouses are an emblem of their organizational skills: "[I] did not know what I should admire the most: whether the order in their arrangement, or the diversity and profusion of merchandise stored that testified to the degree of development and industriousness of this people." ("[N]ão soube o que mais admirar: se a ordem que presidia ao seu arranjo, se a diversidade e profusão das mercadorias em depósito, a atestar o grau de adiantamento e operosidade daquele povo," 122).

But what the Brazilian doctor appreciates the most is the proto-communist social organization of the Amazons. Everyone works in activities suitable to their age and ability, and everything is held in common: "goods belong to the community and are equitably divided according to the needs of each person" ("os bens pertencem à comunidade e são irmamente divididos, conforme as necessidades de cada um," 119). It is up to the queen, who is chosen according to her qualities and changes every few years, to distribute produce and other merchandise, depending on necessity (125). In the novel, such a system is traced back to Incan social order. In a hallucinogen-induced vision, the protagonist accompanies Atahualpa, the last Inca emperor, who shows him the capital of his empire, Cusco, whence the Amazons descended. There, as in the all-female tribe, there was no private property and therefore no need for any form of money. The narrator comments on this economic arrangement: "[U]nder the regime of such a wise communism, the nation lived cohesive and prosperous, in the general communion of its goods and beliefs and without ever having known the hatreds and passions that feed on social inequalities and oscillations of fortune" ("[S]ob o regime de tão sábio comunismo, a nação vivia coesa e próspera, na comunhão geral dos seus bens e das suas crenças e sem jamais ter conhecido os ódios e as paixões que se nutrem das desigualdades sociais e das oscilações da fortuna," 164).

The protagonist calls the Inca kingdom "that extraordinary communist empire, which, still today, and for various reasons, could serve as paradigm for the more just aspirations of humanity" ("esse extraordinário império comunista que, ainda hoje, e por vários aspectos, poderia servir de paradigma às mais justas aspirações da humanidade," 163). He paints the portrait of a highly advanced, utopian Incan society in pre-Columbian America, the Amazons being the last remnant of this idealized reign that managed to survive with their communitarian institutions intact precisely because they were never conquered.[20] "Eager for profits, hungry for material gains, and in a permanent delirium of wealth that unleashed their basest instincts," colonizers were diametrically opposed to the communally oriented Incas ("Ávidos de lucros, famintos de proventos materiais, num permanente delírio de riquezas que lhes desaçaimava os instintos mais torpes," 168–69). According to Atahualpa, the greed of Europeans was responsible for the destruction of most of the "blessed continent," together with its native inhabitants, and "countless tribes . . . were completely exterminated . . . throughout Brazil" ("continente abençoado"; "não se contam as tribos . . . que foram totalmente exterminadas . . . por todo o Brasil," 166, 171). The protagonist realizes that the communism practiced both by the Incas and in the tribe of the Amazons was a better form of government than the one prevalent in the society he comes from, which inherited the rapaciousness of the first colonizers. By contrasting the social harmony that reigns among the Amazons to the constant conflicts that plague the Western world, the novel weaves a strong critique of early-twentieth-century values.

The correlation between Western-style civilization and barbarism is nowhere clearer than in the references to World War I, a "breath of madness that stained with blood the most civilized countries" ("sopro de loucura que ensanguentou os países mais civilizados," 29). The narrator calls it "the most horrible of wars" when he describes the conflict to the Frenchwoman Rosina, while they walk among the orderly workshops where the Amazons weave, cook, prepare preserves, and make their pottery ("a mais horrível das guerras," 140). The contrast between a Europe engulfed in war and the peaceful diligence of the laborious Amazons could not be starker.[21] The Amazons, routinely portrayed by past chroniclers as barbaric, ferocious warriors, epitomize in the novel a superior culture that, having embraced communitarianism, is free from the "demented ambitions to rule and dominate" that drove Germany to war ("desvairadas ambições de mando e predomínio," 140).[22] The traditional roles of the civilized and the barbarian, of the developed and the primitive, are inverted in Cruls's narrative, where the utopian kingdom of the Amazons constitutes an example for the rest of the world, peacefully uniting the social cohesion of indigenous tribes with the economic progress of European society.

The Amazons have managed to attain a felicitous equilibrium not only in their sociopolitical structure but also in their relationship to nature. As described above, they have perfected agriculture and reached a high degree of material comfort, while still living in symbiosis with the environment. Conversely, Doctor Hartmann's experiments encapsulate the downside of the Western drive to rule over nature and to mold it to humanity's wildest fantasies. The German tries to keep his scientific pursuits a secret but the protagonist soon finds out about his research goals. He devotes his time to crossbreeding different animals, including humans, in an attempt to prolong life and rejuvenate vital organs, as well as to show the flexibility of what are usually considered to be fixed traits of a given species. For instance, he produced a being that was half-human, half-monkey. Even though he did not ask for permission from the Indian woman who gave birth to the creature, he argues that she stood to gain, since the procedure regenerated her body to such an extent that she became a "mother" when she was sixty years old (230).

While the German doctor is undoubtedly proud of his achievements, the narrator is considerably more skeptical about the experiments. He writes of the scientific creations he is shown: "From then on, in a succession of coops, cages, and pens passed in front of my astonished eyes, in a truly apocalyptic vision, the most curious and unpredictable forms of animals, starting with the unconceivable hybrid of a cigana bird and a lizard, a kind of mythical and disconcerting griffin" (Daí por diante, numa sucessão de gaiolas, jaulas e cercados, passaram aos meus olhos estuporados, numa verdadeira visão apocalíptica, as mais curiosas e imprevistas formas animais, a começar pelo inconcebível híbrido da cigana e do jacruarú, espécie de grifo fabuloso e desconcertante," 231–32). After seeing crossbred creatures involving reptiles, rodents, birds, cetacea, and primates, the protagonist exclaims, "But this is chaos in nature," to which Doctor Hartmann replies: "Not chaos! order... because these crossings will never be produced spontaneously. Order because, in this way, phylogeny is proven through experience" ("Mas isso é o caos na natureza"; "O caos, não! a ordem... porque esses cruzamentos nunca se poderão produzir espontaneamente. A ordem, porque assim nós temos a filogenia comprovada pela experiência," 232).

The German professor, who had moved to the Amazon in order to have easy access to human and nonhuman specimens for his experiments, follows in a long line of fictional creations such as Doctor Faust or Victor Frankenstein, who dream of playing God so as to bend the rules of nature.[23] The parallel with H. G. Wells's scientist from the 1896 novel *The Island of Doctor Moreau* is particularly glaring, and the protagonist himself compares Doctor Hartmann to Doctor Moreau when he first learns of the experiments (209). But while Wells's character transforms nonhuman animals with the explicit goal of making them ape human traits, thus evincing a clear humanist bias, Cruls's researcher is even bolder, experimenting across all species to learn about the dominant characteristics of each. His unscrupulous methods are denounced by his own wife, who accuses him of experimenting on healthy humans, including a merchant who had reached the tribe of the Amazons by chance, just like the narrator.[24] The doctor himself has an inkling that his work will not be well received by the larger scientific community. Using the influence over the Amazons that he had acquired by living for many years among them, he prevents the Brazilian from leaving the tribe, so that the explorer will not misrepresent his research once he reaches the outside world (235–37).

The German nationality of the eccentric scientist, which may be explained with reference to the anti-Teutonic sentiment fueled by World War I, presciently reminds today's readers of the abhorrent Nazi experiments in eugenics that were to take place later in the century. More to the point, however, Doctor Hartmann's efforts evoke Cunha's conception of the Amazon as a land still in construction, with infinite natural resources that human beings are tasked with developing. In his misguided experiments, the doctor is merely taking the mandate to exploit all possibilities of the bountiful Amazonian environment to its logical conclusion. The apocalyptic scenario the narrator encounters in the German's lab is the corollary of the Western drive to dominate nature, impose a form of utilitarian rationality upon it and fashion it according to human whims. The experiments conducted by the scientist reveal, once again, the bestial facet of outsiders, who had already shown their cruelty when they first arrived in the region. Doctor Hartmann's attempts to bend natural laws and to pursue his research no matter what show that Westerners are the real barbarians when compared to the Amazons.

Unlike other authors writing during the rubber boom period, Cruls does not consider progress at all costs to be worthwhile. He decries the more disruptive aspects of modern science and technology in favor of the balanced relationship to their surroundings that the Amazons represent. It is significant that the novel's protagonist was trained as a medical doctor but had abandoned the profession, much like Cruls himself.[25] Unlike Western scientists, the Amazons use technology without trying to overstep natural constraints and have built a highly developed civilization that is in tune with the environment. Allying Indian knowledge of the region with the technological know-how and social organization of the Incas, the Amazons are depicted as an alternative to the simple existence of native Amazonians and the unbridled search for development and desire to shape nature to one's wishes characteristic of modern culture.

The female tribe is described as a people frozen in time, in that they have kept the customs of their Inca ancestors intact and survived in isolation from the rest of country. In *The Mysterious Amazon*, then, the forward-looking, utopian thrust that points toward a better, more socially and environmentally harmonious future, involves a return to the past, to the Amazons' Golden Age of communal organization—a third way between primitivism and modern civilization offered as a social model both for Brazil and for the rest of the Western world.

By setting his jungle utopia in a matriarchal tribe composed only of women, Cruls is implicitly adhering to a series of stereotypes about gender while, at the same time, reconfiguring the usual valuation of these characteristics. War, greed, and corruption are tacitly linked to the patriarchal organization of the West, as is the destruction of nature brought about by modern science, embodied in Doctor Hartmann. The German stands for a quintessential male researcher, oblivious to the consequences and side effects of his experiments. Conversely, cooperation, communal work, and harmony with one's surroundings are perceived as female characteristics. The author suggests that his utopia could only come true if qualities usually regarded as feminine were to be incorporated in modern society, while unrestrained progress and the taming of nature, typically seen as masculine pursuits, would have to be scaled down. Still, *The Mysterious Amazon* is not an explicitly feminist text. The Amazons are defined by what they lack, as "women without husband" ("mulheres sem marido," 64); the main characters are male; and the narrative does not openly advocate for women's empowerment in society at large. But the juxtaposition of two social forms of organization, each with traits associated to a specific gender, highlights the advantages of matriarchal over patriarchal structures and implicitly favors femininity. Cruls resorts to the myth of the Amazons to describe an advanced community free from the violence, selfishness, environmental destruction, and other drawbacks of the contemporary world. As we shall see, the idea that the path to social reform in Brazil would entail a return to the land of the Amazons will reappear in Abguar Bastos's writings, while a renewed matriarchy is central to Oswald de Andrade's reflections on Messianism and utopia.

Utopia in the Land of the Icamiabas

More than in Cruls's text, the Amazons appear as a vanishing signifier in Abguar Bastos's *Land of the Icamiabas*. The novel recounts a series of episodes in the life of its protagonist, Bepe, who is forced to abandon the studies he was pursuing in the city of Belém because of his father's debts, and to move to the small town of Badajoz, in the Amazon rain-forest, where he lives off the land. When he is about to be expropriated from his estate because of a legal technicality, Bepe puts together a make-shift militia and tries to resist the authorities. Faced with the imminent prospect of defeat, as reinforcements from the Brazilian army arrive to fight against the rebellious group, Bepe decides to lead his men to the fabled land of the Amazons, where he hopes to build a better society, a utopian republic free from avarice and from exploitative practices.[26] The Amazons that give the book its title—"Icamiabas" is just another name for Amazons[27]—do not make an appearance in the narrative. Based upon the legend of an all-women tribe, Bastos reduces his Icamiabas to a symbol of a thriving, wealthy community. The fact that Bepe wants to found his utopian city in the land of the Amazons singles him and his men out as inheritors to the promise of prosperity, social cohesion, and communitarian values that the legendary tribe of women stood for.

Land of the Icamiabas shares with *The Mysterious Amazon* a suspi-cion toward modern society that comes through in the contrast between decadent city dwellers and the existence of those who work the land in the rainforest. Urban landscapes bring forth degeneracy, hypocrisy, and deceit, epitomized in the fate of Bepe's two friends, Rejinaldo and Jeremias, both of whom succumb to their amorous disillusionments. The first, a lyrical poet, only loves incorporeal, sickly women who have a ten-dency to die of tuberculosis (27–28). The second, a Romantic writer, falls for a married woman who is assassinated by her lover once he learns of her relationship with the poet (35).

But the moral corruption of the modern city goes beyond dubious love relationships. The novel's third-person narrator condemns the cos-mopolitanism of city life, where foreigners usurp the riches of the land from Native Brazilians. The author of a nationalist manifesto titled "Flami-n'Açu," or "the great flame," Bastos was a rabid detractor of foreigners, and used his novel as a platform to denounce what he con-sidered to be the negative consequences of mass immigration to the country.[28] The text includes a series of rants against those who "abuse the hospitality" of Brazilians ("abuso de hospitalidade," 106). In a telling passage, the narrator exhorts his region to use its "columns of Amazons" to "hurl its blow" in a fight against deleterious foreign domination, so as to "create a Brazilianness of feeling" ("colunas de amazonas"; "arremata o teu golpe"; "faz a brazilidade do sentimento," 95).

While Amazonian cities are perceived as permeable to foreign mores, the rainforest appears in the novel as a last bastion of Brazilian traditional values. The protagonist's retreat into nature, after his short passage through Belém, thus acquires particular significance. For, "Bepe has only one family: his Fatherland. He has only one religion: his Nature" ("Bepe só tem uma família: a sua Pátria. Só tem uma religião: a sua Natureza," 22). The jungle "teaches him, slowly, the terrifying secrets of genesis" ("ensina, lentamente, os segredos terríveis da génese," 39). In the novel, then, Brazilian culture, embodied in the figure of Bepe, derives directly from a close kinship between the people and the environment. Fatherland and nature are presented as two sides of the same coin and the narrator, oblivious to the country's history of immigration, is mistrustful of extraneous customs that corrupt the link between Brazilians and their land.

Bepe's troubles begin when foreign influences start to extend beyond city limits and spread into the jungle. He loses his land to an immigrant, who is supported by local political leaders, thus revealing the corruption of government officials. This is the point in the narrative when the protagonist and his followers leave in search of the land of the Icamiabas. Bepe, the "genius of the place," is glorified as a liberator who will guide the group to a bountiful, new region, akin to the Biblical promised land ("génio do lugar," 8). It is telling that Bepe chooses the territory of the Amazons as the location where he wishes to establish a new society. Unable to find justice within the reality of contemporary Brazil, he pursues his dream of founding a civilization free from dishonesty and true to genuine Brazilian values in the midst of the rainforest. The Amazons appear in the novel as symbols both of a place uncontaminated by extraneous influences and of authentic Brazilianness, unlike their depiction in

Cruls's narrative as descendants of the Incas and, therefore, foreign to the Amazon River basin. In aspiring to occupy a space that once belonged to the mythical female warriors, Bepe hopes to honor, at the same time, their connection to the land and their pugnacious spirit, which drove them to battle against invaders trying to encroach upon their territory, in the same way as foreigners were, according to the story's narrator, invading the cities and even the countryside in Brazil.

In a curious twist, though, the novel depicts Bepe and his men as new *conquistadores*, ready to take over the land that once belonged to the Amazons like the explorers of old. They are guided by a man called "Columbú," a clear reference to Columbus, the only one who "knows where the mysterious land is located—the land that guards the treasures of the men who came from the sea. He knows of its hills of gold, its singing forests, its warrior ants" ("sabe onde fica a terra misteriosa—a que guarda os tesouros dos homens que vinham do mar. Sabe das suas colinas de ouro, das suas florestas que cantam, das suas formigas guerreiras," 155). Bepe, in his turn, "starts to envy the halo of the discoverers and glimpses in historical traces, the crosses, flags, marks, hieroglyphs. . . . He dreams of the sailors who, in the bow of sailboats, crossed the abysses of the oceans" ("começa a invejar a auréola dos descobridores e entrevê, nos rastros históricos, as cruzes, as bandeiras, os marcos, os hieróglifos . . . . Sonha com os marinheiros que, na prôa das caravelas, transpuseram os abismos oceânicos," 175). In Bastos's text, the legendary Amazons and the first explorers of Amazonia are brought together in a synthesis to represent the origins of Brazilian culture, in a move similar to the union of Iracema and the Portuguese soldier Martim in Alencar's novel mentioned above. The feminine and masculine elements come together, erasing the historical friction between the American land and its native peoples, on the one hand, and the colonizers, on the other. In the narrative, Bepe and his followers are portrayed as the true descendants of this unproblematized merger. Threatened by foreigners, they retreat to the land of the Icamiabas, retracing the footsteps of their European ancestors in search of the source of authentic Brazilianness emanating from the rich wellsprings of Amazonia.

In spite of its confused identity politics that amalgamates the colonized and the colonizers and refuses to acknowledge the contributions of new immigrants to the country, Bastos's novel links the Amazons to a utopia that stands in contrast to the rest of Brazilian society. Bepe "dreams of a miraculous Republic," where people will be required "not to wipe their feet but to wipe their spirit" before entering ("sonha com uma República miraculosa"; "não limpem os pés, limpem o espírito," 156). This utopian land, halfway between the city of god and the city of men, is "close to heaven" and combines religious and secular elements ("perto do céu," 156). It will have no courts and public offices, since "God is everything" and human institutions are necessarily imperfect ("Deus é tudo," 156). The narrator points out that "the city will astonish travelers less for its luxury than for its laws" ("a cidade espantará os viajantes menos pelo seu luxo do que pelas suas leis," 156). In this novel city, laws do not need to be coercively enforced, since the moral fiber of its inhabitants, tempered by their Christian belief, will ensure that justice prevails.

Similar to Cruls's narrative, Bastos's text emphasizes the communitarian nature of his imagined, utopian territory. "We have killed envy. We have killed avarice. We have killed egoism," proclaims Bepe ("Matámos a inveja. Matámos a avareza. Matámos o egoismo," 160). In the absence of greed and selfishness, money becomes unnecessary and goods are given to whoever needs them: "There is no money, in exchange for performing a task. There is simply practical compensation.... Because everything is possible when the community is not excluded" ("Não há dinheiro, a troco de funções. Há simplesmente compensações práticas.... Porque tudo é possível quando não se exclui a comunidade," 157). In another passage, the protagonist announces: "Here we do not sell to anyone. We give, with the right to a reciprocal gift" ("Aqui não se vende para ninguém. Dá-se, com direito a uma oferta recíproca," 156). The narrator describes the creation of a new society in a language that echoes the communist revolutions of the beginning of the past century: "The Amazon is being rejuvenated by the warrior song of the oppressed" ("A Amazônia está rejuvenescendo no canto de guerra dos desamparados," 182). The inheritors to the land of the Icamiabas are the Brazilian masses of the dispossessed, who will establish a communal polity based upon the sharing of Amazonian nature's plentiful gifts among all.

The book engages in a thought-experiment, imagining how the new utopian community will be remembered long after it disappears: "Here lies the subterranean conscience of a naked and simple Brazil, which, if one day found again, will be larger, and larger will also be, in that moment, the glory of all of its children" ("Aqui repousa a consciência subterrânea de um Brasil nu e simples, que, se um dia, de novo, for encontrado, estará maior e maior será, nesse instante, a glória de todos os seus filhos," 160). The group, whose memory will outlive the existence of its individual members, stands as a repository of Brazilian virtues, unadulterated by extraneous powers. When, "[o]ne day, these parts change their panorama and all is of a hallucinatory splendor," says Bepe in a speech to the multitude of his followers, "no one will talk about the obscure pioneers who undertook the gigantic work of exploration" ("Um dia, quando estas paragens mudarem de panorama e tudo for um alucinado explendor… ninguém falará nos obscuros pioneiros que fizeram a obra gigantesca da exploração," 174). And he ends with an exhortation to the crowd: "[L]et us create, ourselves, our own history" ("[F]açamos nós mesmos, a nossa história," 174).

The utopian community is a model for a future Brazil that will rise from the ashes of the decadent, contemporary society. Its communitarian ideals will shine forth even after its concrete existence has fallen into oblivion, very much like the legendary tribe of the Amazons. Bastos, like Cruls before him, sees the future as a return to the past, to the mythical land of the Icamiabas that will be the birthplace of the new country of the oppressed. But while Cruls unequivocally denounced European colonizers, who brought untold destruction to the native civilizations of the Americas, and considered the dismantling of the Western approach to social relations and to nature as the only way forward, Bastos adopts a more conservative, reactionary, and, at times, outright racist approach. In his novel, the new society will result from a combination of native elements and the fortitude of early explorers, enervated in the present by foreign influences. The Amazons are absent from his text and function as a mere token of authentic Brazilianness. Still, both authors regarded Amazonia, one of the most underdeveloped regions of the country, as a symbol of hope for a more prosperous and just time to come. The Amazon, together with its mythical Amazons, becomes the land of the future within the greater land of the future that is Brazil. This peculiar temporal loop, whereby the distant past heralds a novel form of civiliza-tion, is also key to the Modernist utopia of a renewed matriarchy.

Matriarchy to Come

The aspiration of the Brazilian Modernist movement to transform the cultural and aesthetic landscape of the country involved both an eman-cipation from a mindless imitation of imported artistic models and, in the case of its most progressive group, an embrace of the nation's diverse, cosmopolitan heritage.[29] Many of the intellectuals, writers, artists, and musicians who came together in the 1922 Week of Modern Art in São Paulo and who subsequently formed the core of the Modernist group sought to return to the indigenous origins of Brazil's culture, while mit-igating this primitivist thrust with an openness to the world outside. Much as in Cruls and in Bastos's novels, the feminized Amazonian land and the myth of the Amazons played a central role in Modernist literary texts, functioning as a counterpoint and offering an alternative to the negative aspects of contemporary Brazilian society.

A case in point is the depiction of the Icamiabas in Mário de Andrade's famous novel *Macunaíma* (1928). The narrative's protagonist, Macunaíma, hails from the Amazon and travels to the city of São Paulo, thus undoing a series of stereotypes common in fiction about the area: instead of portraying an outside explorer penetrating into the rainforest and unraveling its secrets, Andrade's text focuses on a native Amazonian moving to the south of the country (Maligo 100). The city, and not the jungle, becomes an exotic landscape that the reader observes through

Macunaíma's eyes as he navigates its seemingly absurd intricacies. This shift in perspective is nowhere clearer than in the main character's letter to the Icamiabas, where he attempts to explain the bizarre customs of urban life to the Amazons. He does so using an archaic form of the Portuguese language, parodying the stultified version of imported European culture that the Modernists aimed to undermine in their literary praxis.

In spite of its creative engagement with Amazonian myths, however, *Macunaíma* still appears to adopt a traditional view of Amazonia as a land to be dominated by males. Pedro Maligo points out that Macunaíma's attitude toward women is reduced to a desire for sexual gratification, and the Amazons are no exception (104–105). When Ci, described as the "Mother of the Forest" ("Mãe do Mato") and queen of the Amazons, resists the protagonist's sexual advances, he asks for assistance from his two brothers, who hold her down while he consummates the rape. After overpowering Ci and securing control over the environment through sexual conquest, Macunaíma adopts the title of "Emperor of the Virgin Forest" ("Imperador do Mato-Virgem"), thus dethroning the queen from her position as unchallenged ruler of the Amazon (25–26). A sympathetic reading of this and other episodes of female debasement in the text would interpret them, in the ironic, farcical spirit that permeates the novel, not as condoning abuse but, rather, as criticizing it. Macunaíma's use of force to gain ascendency over the queen of the Amazons, known for their sexual independence, would be a satirical representation of the status quo, in which both women and Amazonian land are systematically oppressed. This reading is bolstered by the fact that, in the end of the text, Vei, the female personification of the sun, takes revenge on Macunaíma because he snubbed her daughters, thus precipitating his demise. The last word belongs to a female deity and the main character is ultimately punished for his reckless sexual exploits. Be this as it may, the Amazons in *Macunaíma* function primarily as the other to industrialized, urban Brazil, as in Cruls's and Bastos's novels, but are here devoid of the utopian undertones attributed to the mythical tribe in those narratives.

Mário de Andrade's friend and fellow Modernist writer Oswald de Andrade is more explicit in his positive valuation of the Amazons. When he alludes to Brazil in his 1928 iconoclastic "Anthropophagous Manifesto" ("Manifesto Antropófago")[30] as the "matriarchy of Pindorama"—"Pindorama," or "the land of the palm trees," is a word derived from the Tupi-Guarani language and was the designation used by the native peoples of Brazil to refer to their land—he is foreshadowing the reflections on matriarchy that he was to develop in later, more theoretical texts. Andrade's strategy, both in the "Manifesto" and in his subsequent writings on matriarchy, was to undo the negative preconceptions about his country and, especially, about Native Brazilians, by reclaiming unfavorable labels and giving them a positive spin. Similar to Cruls, he focuses on oppositions such as the one between primitivism and culture, barbarism and civilization. However, while Cruls strove to show that those usually branded as savage, primitive, and barbaric, such as the mythical Amazons, are the true bearers of civilization, Andrade followed a different path. He insisted on the primacy and superiority of primitivism over the mindset of so-called developed nations, perhaps influenced by psychoanalytic theories that looked for the key to understanding human behavior in unconscious psychic energy (Brookshaw 155). The highly problematic association of native peoples to unconscious, irrational conduct notwithstanding, Andrade's originality lies in seeing primitivism as the matrix not only of Brazilian culture, but of civilization as such, progress meaning, for him, a return to the primitive, matriarchal roots of humanity.

The praise of anthropophagy in the "Manifesto" as the basic *modus operandi* of Brazilian arts and culture that digest and assimilate all foreign influences, literally incorporating them into the larger body of the nation, is part of Andrade's reappropriation of elements deemed primitive, in order to attribute to them a broader significance. Likewise, he extols the matriarchal rule associated to Native Brazilian society as superior to the patriarchy that characterizes the modern worldview. He sees the myth of the Amazons as encapsulating the spirit of a matriarchy prevalent throughout the Brazilian territory at the time when the first Europeans arrived on its shores: "Evidently, the word Matriarchy entails the notion of the mother's predominance. It was Matriarchy the fabulous power attributed to the Amazons in Columbian Brazil" ("Evidentemente, a palavra Matriarcado traz consigo a ideia de predomínio materno. Seria Matriarcado o fabuloso poderio atribuído às Amazonas, no Brasil colombiano," "Variações," 201). For Andrade, the Amazons condense features of the numerous tribes of Native Brazilians and their legend remains as a trace of a historical reality erased by colonization. The all-female group's enormous power derives precisely from their matriarchal structure, which Andrade sees as the archetype of a future civilization, built upon nonhierarchical, communal foundations.

In his 1950 text "The Crisis of Messianic Philosophy" ("A Crise da Filosofia Messiânica"), Andrade pits matriarchal against patriarchal societies and teases out the implications of these two forms of organization: "Matriarchy and Patriarchy. The first is the world of primitive man. The latter of civilized man. The first produced an anthropophagic culture, the latter a Messianic culture" ("Matriarcado e Patriarcado. Aquele é o mundo do homem primitivo. Este o do civilizado. Aquele produziu uma cultura antropofágica, este uma cultura Messiânica," "Filosofia Messiânica," 78). Anthropophagy is the process of assimilation of difference into a given community, and was practiced in primitive, matriarchal groups. In contrast, patriarchy relies upon domination and enslavement as a way to subjugate and ultimately eliminate difference. Messianism and the very belief in one God appeared as a result of patriarchal oppression: a promise of rewards in the future that compensated for the abject conditions endured by the vast majority of people in the present ("Filosofia Messiânica," 81).

For Andrade, as for Cruls and for Bastos, matriarchies such as the tribe of the Amazons were communal societies, grounded upon the principle of sharing: "Matriarchy was founded upon a triple foundation: maternal lineage, common possession of the soil, and a classless state, that is to say, the absence of a state" ("O Matriarcado assentava sobre uma tríplice base: o filho de direito materno, a propriedade comum ao solo, o estado sem classes, ou seja, a ausência de estado," "Filosofia Messiânica," 80). Patriarchies, in turn, emerge when one social class takes hold of power and rules over the rest of the population. Matriarchy is a horizontal, and patriarchy a vertical, hierarchical social formation or, to put it differently, matriarchies have close affinities to communism and anarchism, while patriarchy undergirds exploitative, capitalist rule ("Marcha," 189).[31]

In "The March of Utopias" ("A Marcha das Utopias"), first published in 1953, Andrade highlights the connection between New World matriarchy and the socialist and communist utopias that proliferated in Europe from the sixteenth century onward. This "utopian cycle," which began with Thomas More, passed through Karl Marx, and continued all the way to twentieth-century communism, is a return to the matriarchal collectivism of old, of which Europeans were reminded through their contact with American Indians ("Marcha," 147). Yet, for Andrade, most utopias are tainted with an indelible paradox: they preach a return to communitarianism and an abolition of exploitation, all the while imposing a strict discipline and work ethic that is incompatible with a classless, matriarchal way of life. As he pointedly put it: "Militant Marxism was engaged in an economy of Having (Patriarchy), escaping the historical injunctions of the economy of Being (Matriarchy)" ("O marxismo militante engajou-se na economia do Haver (Patriarcado) escapando às injunções históricas da economia do Ser (Matriarcado)," "Filosofia Messiânica," 118). The reason for the emphasis of most utopias and of Marxist communism on a strict regimen of labor is that society needs to have attained a certain degree of technological development in order for human beings to be freed from their drab enslavement to menial tasks that would then be performed by machinery. As we shall see in chapter 4, Andrade believed that humanity had already reached a stage of technical advancement that would allow for the dawn of a new matriarchal age, predicated upon communal organization and boundless leisure. It was only a matter of society catching up with techno-scientific evolution.

Drawing upon Hegelian and Marxist thought, Andrade was of the opinion that historical progress proceeded dialectically. The first period of humankind's history had been matriarchal—"it is clearly established that Matriarchy preceded Patriarchy throughout the world" ("fica claramente estabelecido que o Matriarcado precede ao Patriarcado em toda a terra," "Variações," 203)—, followed by a time of patriarchal rule that culminated in Europe's colonization of vast areas of the globe. The final age of humanity will amount to a synthesis of the other two: "1st term: thesis—natural man. 2nd term: antithesis—civilized man. 3rd term: synthesis—natural man with technology" ("1.o termo: tese—o homem natural. 2.o termo: antítese—o homem civilizado. 3.o termo: síntese—o homem natural tecnizado," "Filosofia Messiânica," 79). In contrast to Cruls, who was weary of scientific, industrial, and mechanical improvements as engines for social change, Andrade regards technology as a springboard for "another Matriarchy that announces itself" ("um outro Matriarcado que se anuncia," "Filosofia Messiânica," 82–83). This novel Golden Age is a return to the communist, classless, and stateless social arrangement of past matriarchies that can now be implemented without giving up the comforts of modern life ("Filosofia Messiânica," 128).

Brazilian culture, which boasts a long matriarchal tradition, would be at the forefront of the matriarchy to come. Andrade regards Brazil as one of the last strongholds of matriarchal principles in a world engulfed by patriarchy: "[W]e Brazilians . . . are a concretized Utopia, for good or for ill, in the face of the mercenary and mechanical utilitarianism of the North" ("[N]ós brasileiros . . . somos a Utopia realizada, bem ou mal, em face do utilitarismo mercenário e mecânico do Norte," "Marcha," 153). Inspired by the utopian ideal of New World matriarchies, the dawn of a renewed matriarchal society is nigh. Brazil, the country of cultural anthropophagy that absorbs all external influences and incorporates them into its everyday routines and aesthetic practices, is the perfect model for a future world where communal habits, sharing, and peaceful coexistence will be the order of the day.

The question remains, however, as to why Andrade saw matriarchies, such as the legendary tribe of the Amazons, as more just, communal, and leisurely than patriarchies. After all, property could conceivable pass from mother to daughter, instead of through a paternal lineage. Furthermore, at least in Cruls's rendition of the Amazons' myth, the women's communist abolition of private property did not preclude a rigid work discipline, a far cry from the laid-back matriarchies of indigenous peoples imaged by the Modernist writer. The key to understanding Andrade's views on the opposition between matriarchal and patriarchal worldviews rests on his considerations on individualism. For him, patriarchy implies a separation between individuals and the society to which they belong. The "father-individual" draws rigid boundaries between himself and his property, on the one hand, and the other members of the group, on the other hand ("pai-indivíduo," "Filosofia Messiânica," 125). This principle of individuation lies at the origin of private property, which, in turn, spawns social oppression and the accumulation of wealth in the hands of those who manage successfully to exploit other members of the community. "In a society where the figure of the father has been replaced by that of society," writes Andrade, "everything tends to change" ("Numa sociedade onde a figura do pai se tenha substituído pela da sociedade, tudo tende a mudar," "Filosofia Messiânica," 125). Not the individual but the well-being of the social group, as a whole, underlies the formation of matriarchal communities. Andrade presupposes that the feminine principle betokens an openness to exteriority incompatible with individualism. Problematic and essentializing as it may be, Andrade's conception of femininity as harboring difference within allows him to dream of utopian anthropophagous matriarchies that welcome alterity and, therefore, are more attuned to the outside and to the commons. This is no doubt the reason why these groups are systematically depicted as communist, both in Andrade's theoretical considerations on a matriarchy to come and in Cruls's and Bastos's literary renditions of the legendary Amazons.

From an association with primitivism and barbarism to later utopian portrayals of their communal society, representations of the Amazons have been closely entwined with divergent perceptions of the Amazon River basin. While, in earlier texts, the mythical tribe frequently symbolized the perils inherent in the exploration and colonization of the rainforest, writings from the beginning of the twentieth century onward saw the legendary all-women group and the environment they inhabited as a matrix for a future society predicated on the values of equality, cooperation, and justice. The Amazons have thus metamorphosed from an epitome of savagery to an idealized blueprint for a better civilization to come.

A constant in the widely disparate depictions of the Amazons has been the female tribe's close connection to the land. The matriarchal society's nonoppositional relation to the outside world and its receptivity to otherness, postulated by Andrade, refers not only to different peoples, customs, and traditions but also to flora and fauna, and is responsible for its harmonious existence in symbiosis with its environment. The group's legendary fierceness in battles against outsiders—a staple of earlier, dystopian views of the Amazons—can thus be understood ecologically. Systematically framed in terms of the need to protect their territory, the women warriors' valor in combat can be interpreted as a way to keep the region from falling into the exploitative grip of colonizers. In later representations, their ferocious behavior vanishes, but their link to the land remains. The utopian, communist society envisioned by Cruls, Bastos, and Andrade seems to portend, therefore, not only an abolition of class privilege and private property but also an ecological allegiance to another type of the commons, namely, the Amazons' shared home, or the Amazon region itself. The next chapter will come back to this environmental awareness in our discussion of zoophytographia, or interspecies writing.

Zoophytographia

Interspecies Literature and the Writings of Clarice Lispector

Não vou ser autobiográfica. Quero ser "bio."

(I will not be autobiographical. I want to be "bio.")

—Clarice Lispector, *Água Viva*

Nation and Nature

European colonizers' perception of Brazil as paradisiac was indebted to the region's bountiful nature, lush forests, and wide variety of plants and animals, many of which were unknown in Europe. From Pêro Vaz de Caminha's Letter to King Manuel (1500), the first written document about this geographical area, describing the arrival of the Portuguese fleet at Porto Seguro, located in what is now the state of Bahia, through the writings of historian Pêro de Magalhães Gândavo in the second half of the sixteenth century, to Jesuit Priest Simão de Vasconcelos's seventeenth-century *Curious and Necessary News of the Things of Brazil* (*Notícias Curiosas e Necessárias das Cousas do Brazil*), to name only a few, the Europeans highlighted the region's abundant flora and fauna, often describing them in detail. Caminha mentions that the trees in the new land "are very many and big and of endless different species" and adds: "I don't doubt that there are many birds in those backlands!" ("arvoredos são mui muitos e grandes, e de infinitas espécies"; "não duvido que por

esse sertão haja muitas aves!"). Gândavo extols the Brazilian vegetables
and fruits, such as manioc, banana, pineapple, and cashew nuts, as well
as animals like the capybara, the tapir, and the armadillo, whose meat is
both tasty and healthful. Vasconcelos, in his turn, devotes a large section
of his book to detailing the virtues of various Brazilian plants (138ff) and
concludes that the region meets all the criteria for being prosperous: good
climate, waters, and vegetation, together with an abundance of fish and
other animals (137). It is telling that the very name of the nation goes
back to a plant, the Brazilwood or, in Portuguese, *pau-brasil*, which was
plentiful in the Northeast of the country and was used both as timber
and to make red dye.

To be sure, the praise lavished upon Brazil's flora and fauna was
tinged with ulterior motives. Explorers and colonizers painted a rosy
picture of the area so as to attract much-needed investment and settlers
(McNee 2–3). Their writings should therefore not be read as simple, dis-
passionate descriptions of what they encountered in the New World but
more as propagandistic pamphlets advertising it to their European audi-
ences. This goal of promoting the region was probably what led Gândavo
to eliminate several negative elements from the final version of his *History
of the Province of the Holy Cross Usually Called Brazil* (*História da
Província de Santa Cruz a que Vulgarmente Chamamos Brasil*), including references to crop-destroying ants and disease-carrying mosquitos
(Dodman). In addition to their propaganda efforts, early descriptions
of Brazil also evince a didactic intent to explain how best to exploit the
natural resources of the land. The texts tend to highlight the medicinal
or nutritional value of plants and animals, hinting at their usefulness to
humans and at their potential commercial value. But beyond pragmatic
concerns, what comes through in these narratives is the authors' sense
of awe when faced with the immensity and variety of the region's flora
and with the diversity of its fauna. Mundane concerns become enmeshed
with aesthetic considerations, as writers cannot help but intersperse their
dry accounts with comments on the majestic beauty of a tree, the fragrance of certain flowers, or the gracefulness of a given animal. Brimming

with wonders, many of which had been hitherto unknown, Brazil was portrayed as a paradisiac land whose munificent nature stood in stark contrast to the tame and tired European environment.

The depiction of Brazilian nature as a cornucopia during colonial times was to shape the country's identity long after this period. The vastness of the land and its environmental richness were some of the arguments adduced to support the region's claim of independence from Portugal in the 1820s (McNee 3). In the postindependence context, nation and environment continued to be inextricably linked. On the one hand, the exuberance and wealth of the Brazilian flora and fauna were used to bolster the young country's political power, as the force of nature was metaphorically transferred to the state. It was common, for instance, to portray the emperor adorned by tropical trees and fruits, so as to reinforce the connection between nation and nature (Pádua, quoted in McNee 3). On the other hand, Brazil's lush landscapes served as a separating marker, distinguishing the region from Europe, in the same way that intellectuals sought to forge a uniquely Brazilian culture, disparate from that of the former colonizers. The paintings of Tarsila do Amaral, for instance, with their stylized representations of local plants and animals, offer powerful images of a natural environment radically different from that of the Old World.

If Brazil's environment has long been at the root of its political and cultural identity, the country's literary production has reflected the national indebtedness to nature. José de Alencar's foundational novel *Iracema* mentions numerous local plants and animals associated with the narrative's heroine, who, in turn, metonymically stands for the Brazilian land, as we have seen in chapter 2.[1] The first two stanzas of "Song of Exile" ("Canção do Exílio," 1843), a poem by Alencar's contemporary Gonçalves Dias, are perhaps the best literary example of the imbrication of nation and nature in the Brazilian context. Living far from his homeland—the Romantic writer studied at the Portuguese University of Coimbra, where he penned the poem—Dias compares the European landscapes to the luxuriant environment of Brazil:

My land has palm trees,
Where the *Sabiá* sings;
The birds who chirp here,
Do not chirp like they do there.

Our sky has more stars,
Our valleys have more flowers,
Our woods have more life,
Our life has more love.

(Minha terra tem palmeiras,
Onde canta o Sabiá;
As aves, que aqui gorjeiam,
Não gorjeiam como lá.

Nosso céu tem mais estrelas,
Nossas várzeas têm mais flores,
Nossos bosques têm mais vida,
Nossa vida mais amores.)

One of the best-known texts of the Brazilian literary canon—the poem has been reworked and reinterpreted by several later writers, including Oswald de Andrade ("Song of Return to the Homeland," "Canto de Regresso à Pátria"), Murilo Mendes ("Song of Exile," "Canção do Exílio"), Carlos Drummond de Andrade ("New Song of Exile," "Nova Canção do Exílio"), and Ferreira Gullar ("New Song of Exile," "Nova Canção do Exílio"), among others—"Song of Exile" is structured around the simple opposition here/there, which, though this is never mentioned explicitly, is usually interpreted as referring to the differences between Portugal and Brazil. Plants and animals abound "there"—note the repetition of "more" in all the lines of the second stanza—and are in general lovelier than their European counterparts ("The birds who chirp here, / Do not chirp like they do there"). From this already ideologically charged statement about the excellence of Brazilian nature the poet deftly moves to assert the advantages of life in his homeland: "Our life has more love." Part of the nationalistic literature created in the aftermath of Brazilian independence from Portugal in 1822, the poem nevertheless goes back to a common trope of writings from the colonial period. It sings the praise of life in Brazil, its superiority tied to the country's lavish and charming nature.

Nationalism and nature continue to be linked in Brazilian literature throughout the twentieth century. Modernist writers have drawn on the environment to reconfigure national letters, which, in their view, were too dependent upon foreign cultural and literary models. Mário de Andrade's *Macunaíma*, discussed in the previous chapter, and Raul Bopp's *Norato Snake* (*Cobra Norato*, 1931), for instance, draw upon Amazonian flora, fauna, and folkloric traditions as a source of inspiration. Both writers turned to the Amazon as an emblematic Brazilian landscape that distinguishes the country from other European and North American nations.[2]

In the narratives of "regionalist" writers such as Graciliano Ramos, José Lins do Rego, and Guimarães Rosa nature likewise plays a crucial role in defining the country's identity, which, in this case, is viewed through the prism of social injustice. Suffice it to think about the drought so eloquently portrayed in Ramos's *Barren Lives* (*Vidas Secas*, 1938) to realize that, far from being reduced to a mere background where events unfold, the environment is the main protagonist of the novel. Unlike the images of lush forests that Brazil usually evokes, the country's arid Northeastern region offers an alternative outlook upon the nation's landscapes. Significantly, the novel is framed by the death of two animals: a pet parrot slaughtered for food in the beginning of the text, when the main character's family is on the road looking for a place where they can settle after the drought has reached their village; and the killing of the dog Baleia, shot down by the father to prevent her continued suffering from a disease most likely caused by malnutrition, toward the end of the narrative, when the family is about to hit the road once again to escape another onset of drought. For Ramos, the Northeast stands as an emblem of the class struggle that has pitted rich landowners against landless peasants throughout the nation. The drought in the region is portrayed both as an environmental problem and as a metaphor for the rest of Brazil, a country where even areas that benefit from a verdant nature have been bled dry of their resources, usurped by a few, who leave the vast majority of the population behind.

While Brazil's environment has left a lasting imprint on the country's literary output, not all Brazilian texts about flora and fauna are linked to a political agenda. Perhaps because the region has historically been understood through the lens of its natural landscapes, plants and animals crop up in the nation's letters in myriad different ways. A salient example is the work of nineteenth-century author Machado de Assis, arguably the most significant Brazilian writer to this day. A supporter of vegetarianism—"God... is vegetarian. For me, the question of earthly paradise can be clearly and simply explained by vegetarianism. God created man for vegetables and vegetables for man.... Eat everything, He told him [man], except the fruit of this tree. Well, this so-called tree was simply meat." ("Deus... é vegetariano. Para mim, a questão do paraíso terrestre explica-se clara e singelamente pelo vegetarismo. Deus criou o homem para os vegetais, e os vegetais para o homem.... Comei de tudo, disse-lhe, menos do fruto desta árvore. Ora, essa chamada árvore era simplesmente carne," Machado, *Semana*)—Machado criticized cruelty against animals in texts such as "Short Story from Alexandria" ("Conto Alexandrino"), which decries the practice of vivisection, or "The Secret Cause" ("A Causa Secreta"), and gave voice to our nonhuman companions in several of his writings.[3]

In "Ideas of the Canary" ("Idéias do Canário"), Machado conjures up a speaking bird whose vision of the world changes according to his current circumstances and increasingly expanding horizons, much in the same way as it happens with humans. A *crónica* from 1892 stages a conversation between two donkeys, who reflect about the recent introduction of electrical trams in Rio de Janeiro and the impact this will have on their lives.[4] While one of them believes the innovation will free donkeys from their servitude of constantly pulling trams, the other is more skeptical. He points out that, throughout history, humanity has always found new ways to exploit and enslave animals, and there is therefore no reason to believe that the plight of nonhumans is about to change. These texts deploy the fine irony characteristic of Machado's prose to question human feelings of superiority vis-à-vis animals, as well as the scientific weltanschauung of his time that underwrote much of our callous behavior toward other living beings in the name of knowledge. The novelist invites his readers to shift their point of view and put themselves in the place of an animal, a change in perspective implicit in many reflections on animal-human relations, from Montaigne's foundational "Apology for Raymond Sebond"—"When I play with my cat, who knows if he is not amusing himself more with me than I am amusing myself with him?" ("Quand je joue avec mon chat, qui sait s'il ne s'amuse pas plus de moi que je le fais de lui?"), asks Montaigne—to pop culture products such as the various installments of the film franchise *Planet of the Apes*.

Still, Machado's texts often remain tied to an anthropocentric perspective, since his animals adopt a manner of speaking, logical reasoning, and even ideals of freedom in no way different from those of humans. The author readily acknowledges this shortcoming and, in a typical, self-reflexive manner, embeds it in the dialogue of the two donkeys. One of the animals blames his friend for thinking like a human—"I see, the donkey on the right retorted melancholically, I see that there is much of a human being in your head" ("Vejo, redarguiu melancolicamente o burro da direita, vejo que há muito de homem nessa cabeça")—an accusation that could be leveled against many of the texts produced about or in the name of animals, let alone plants.

Even though we cannot fully obviate our human bias, as Machado points out, some writers have tried to escape the narrow confines of anthropocentrism to imagine what plant and animal life and language would be like. In the rest of this chapter, I analyze the work of Brazilian authors whose encounter with other living beings has been at the core of their texts. Moving beyond utopias based upon the exploitation of a lush flora and abundant fauna put at the service of the colonial and, later, the nationalist cause, I will focus on writers who have imagined a utopia of *living with* and *learning from* plant and animal modes of being. Their texts and literary language testify to the transformative power of such thought experiments.

Zoophytographia: Literature as Shamanism

Plants and animals feature not only as the subject matter or, in other instances, one of the characters, in Brazilian writings; they are often both the topic of and, at the same time, the inspiration for narratives and poetry heavily influenced by their own languages and existences. These literary productions incorporate flora and fauna in the process of writing to such an extent that they become co-creators of the texts. I define this imbrication of plants and animals in literature as *zoophytographia*, or interspecies writing.[5] The idea that a literary text can be co-written by nonhumans appears, at first brush, to be a fanciful notion, to say the least. After all, human cultural productions can hardly escape an anthropocentric framework determined by our particular way of experiencing the world and by our long history of interaction with and exploitation of vegetal and animal beings. We are able, at most, to ventriloquize the voices of flora and fauna, so as to convey what we think they might say if their worldview were indeed ever translated into verbal language, an imaginary speech that projects our desires and aspirations upon others. At the same time, plants and animals have their own way of expressing themselves, a language that remains, for the most part, inaccessible to humankind.[6] Still, some texts attempt the perilous crossing of the chasm separating our standpoint from that of nonhumans. They strive to approach plant and animal life and to integrate their specific being-in-the-world into literature. Such a literary face-to-face with others yields two different but complementary outcomes: on the one hand, it triggers a probe into the meaning of humanity and of life itself; on the other hand, it pushes written language to the limits of the unutterable, as literature is contaminated by nonverbal forms of expression.

Widening the boundaries of literature, so as to encompass the existence and expression of animals and plants, zoophytographia enriches
human experience, cracking open the edifice of anthropocentrism to let
others in and to allow humanity to peer out. But interspecies writing is
not without its pitfalls. The risk of exerting violence over flora and fauna,
superimposing one's preconceptions onto them and thus preventing them
from speaking at the very moment when one lends them a voice, is very
real. The utopian thrust of zoophytographic writing resides in the belief
that literature can propitiate an encounter with the lives of nonhumans
that does not necessarily entail subsuming them to our own parameters.
An encounter that does not involve conquest but operates through a give
and take, transforming each party in the process and resulting in a novel
literary language. The authors discussed in the remainder of this chapter,
Guimarães Rosa and, more at length, Clarice Lispector, are examples of
such a transformative literary undertaking.

The impulse to create a Brazilian interspecies literature is indebted
to the country's native heritage, which forms a powerful counternar-
rative to the European colonizers' wish to exploit natural resources, to
the appropriation of nature in order to bolster nationalistic claims in
the postindependence period, or even to the use of plants and animals
as merely the topic of anthropocentric tales. Anthropologist Eduardo
Viveiros de Castro has vividly delineated the main differences separating indigenous views on flora and fauna from those prevalent in
Western culture. "[I]f there is a virtually universal Amerindian notion,"
writes Castro, "it is that of an original state of undifferentiation between
humans and animals, described in mythology. Myths are filled with
beings whose form, name and behaviour inextricably mix human and
animal attributes in a common context of intercommunicability, identical
to that which defines the present-day intra-human world" ("Amerindian
Perspectivism," 471). Western thought's point of departure is the unity
of nature that encompasses the bodies of plants, animals, and humans,
all subject to the same mechanistic laws, and a multiplicity of human
cultures, a view that has multiculturalism as one of its latest avatars.
Amerindians, to the contrary, presuppose a spiritual unity of all beings,

coupled with a corporeal diversity, an ontology that Castro defines as "multinatural" ("Exchanging Perspectives," 466).[7]

For Amerindians, humanity is the common condition of both humans and nonhumans, given that all beings possess a similar soul or spirit, a universal given: "For Amazonian peoples, *the original common condition of both humans and animals is not animality but, rather, humanity*. The great separation reveals not so much culture distinguishing itself from nature as nature distancing itself from culture.... *Animals are ex-humans (rather than humans, ex-animals)*" ("Exchanging Perspectives," 465).[8] The main difference between humans and other entities lies in their bodies, whose differentiation happened a posteriori and does not annul the communion of their souls:[9] "[I]t is this inversion of our usual pairing of nature with the universal and culture with the particular that I have been terming 'perspectivism,'" writes Castro. "Amerindian thought proposes ... a representational or phenomenological unity that is purely pronominal or deictic, indifferently applied to a radically objective diversity. One culture, multiple natures—one epistemology, multiple ontologies" ("Exchanging Perspectives," 474).

What are the consequences of Amerindian perspectivism for the literary depiction of plants and animals? For Castro, "To say ... that animals and spirits are people ... is to attribute to nonhumans the capacities of conscious intentionality and social agency that define the position of the subject" ("Exchanging Perspectives," 467). By virtue of having bodies that differ from those of humankind, nonhuman beings have a particular point of view, whereby they are created as subjects.[10] The world, then, is not an objective reality that exists independently from each subject but is co-created by the particular perspective of each being. In other words, the world is not represented differently by various entities; it is the world itself that differs, which is tantamount to saying that there is no world, only worlds.[11] Amerindian thought is in this respect close to the notion of *Umwelt* developed by biologist Jakob von Uexküll, according to whom animals should be understood as completely integrated in and adapted to their environment, which may differ greatly from that of humans.[12]

In tune with perspectivist tenets, zoophytographia entails an attempt to imagine what plant and animal *Umwelten* are like and to render such thought experiments through a literary language inspired by these worldviews, in a utopia of coexistence among human and nonhumans lives.

A second implication of perspectivism resides in the possibility of one being turning into another. Castro underlines that "the passing between species is much more fluid than in the case of our exceptionalist and anthropocentric cosmological vulgate," given that "the individuals of each species are able to 'leap' from one species to another with relative ease" ("Interview"). Shamanism designates "the capacity evinced by some individuals to cross ontological boundaries deliberately and adopt the perspective of nonhuman subjectivities in order to administer the relations between humans and nonhumans" ("Exchanging Perspectives," 468). While shamanic power resides in a person's ability to leave the human realm and benefit from experiencing reality from the perspective of nonhumans, the latter can also enter human consciousness, in an unending exchange or feedback loop. Zoophytographic literature also involves a shamanic process, in that it requires embracing the plant and animal points of view to such an extent that they becomes one's own. Clarice Lispector's texts discussed below are an example of this shamanic literature, or rather, of literature as shamanism: her prose often documents the very process of transformation into nonhumans, both on a thematic and on a linguistic level.

A final offshoot of perspectivism is an inversion of what Western culture regards as knowledge. In the West, to know is to objectify or, as Castro puts it, "[t]he form of the other is *the thing*" ("Exchanging Perspectives," 468). Amerindian perspectivism espouses the opposite ideal: "To know is to personify, to take on the point of view of that which must be known. Shamanic knowledge aims at something that is a someone—another subject" ("Exchanging Perspectives," 468). Objectification signals, for Amerindians, an incomplete or flawed knowledge. "If in the naturalist view a subject is an insufficiently analyzed object," writes Castro, "in the Amerindian animist cosmology the converse holds: an

object is an incompletely interpreted subject. The object must either be
'expanded' to a full-fledged subject—a spirit; an animal in its human,
reflexive form—or else understood as related to a subject" ("Exchanging
Perspectives," 470). Furthermore, knowledge is not limited to humans:
"Being conscious subjects able to communicate with humans, these natural beings are able fully to reciprocate the intentional stance that humans
adopt with respect to them" ("Exchanging Perspectives," 469). That is to
say, plants and animals are able to "personify" humans—to know us—in
the same way as we personify them. Interspecies literature is predicated
on this reciprocity between humans and nonhumans. Zoophytographic
texts lend a voice to nonhuman subjects, radically decentering humanity
by envisioning plants and animals as beings who direct their attention to
the world and to us and who respond intelligently to their surroundings.
The encounter between the human and the animal gaze—or, in Castro's
terms, the moment when two beings recognize each other as subjects and
get to know one another—is frequently thematized in zoophytographic
literature, most notably in Clarice Lispector's writings.

Philippe Descola, a fellow anthropologist and collaborator of Castro,
teases out the implications of perspectivism for the relations between
humans and nonhumans. "Many so-called primitive societies," writes
Descola, "have never imagined that the frontiers of humanity extended
no farther than the human race and have no hesitation in inviting into
their shared social life even the most humble of plants and the most
insignificant of animals" (*Beyond Nature*). For Amerindians, plants and
animals are subjects endowed with a specific point of view and, hence,
not only have a sociality of their own but are also part and parcel of the
social life of human beings. The source of interspecies literature is precisely this shared sociality that brings together humans and nonhumans
in an encounter, resulting in a mutual process of learning. The prose
of Guimarães Rosa, which draws inspiration from life in the Brazilian
backland (*sertão*), where people traditionally lived in close proximity to
and dependence on the natural environment, offers us a glimpse into a
utopian world where humans, plants, and animals are connected through

close ties of affinity. "The greatest animalist of our [Brazilian] literature," in the words of Maria Esther Maciel, Rosa's zoophytographic texts have become a blueprint or, at least, a point of departure for all subsequent Brazilian interspecies writing (75).

The human-animal social interaction comes through at its most vivid in Rosa's "Conversation—with Cowboy Mariano" ("Entremeio—com o Vaqueiro Mariano"), part of *These Stories* (*Estas Histórias*), a collection of short stories published posthumously in 1969. Based on events that took place during a trip the author undertook to the region of Mato Grosso do Sul in 1952, the text is a literary rendition of a dialogue with a cowboy (*vaqueiro*), who describes his lifelong experience with cows and bulls. Not only has the cowboy acquired some of the characteristics of the animals in his ongoing dealings with them—he had a "learnt slow tameness" ("vagarosa mansidão aprendida," 118); he walked while "ruminating" ("ruminando," 127)—but the cattle are also personified. He mentions each bull by name and these often act like human beings, as the one who "died of sadness" ("morreu de tristeza," 117) when he was lassoed and humiliated by a group of men. The cowboy summarizes the interdependence of people and animals in a pointed inversion of usual roles: "Here, it is the cattle that raises people" ("Aqui, o gado é que cria a gente," 118). He acknowledges his community's profound debt toward cattle that goes beyond food and raw materials, in that the bulls' brave and stoic behavior serves as a role model for human action.[13]

Rosa's work offers countless other examples of an alternative understanding of plants and animals, along the lines of the perspectivism Viveiros de Castro attributes to Amerindian thought. In "Conversation of Bulls" ("Conversa de Bois"), included in the short story collection *Sagarana* from 1946, the narrator, a ne'er-do-well from the backlands, tells a tale to prove that "nowadays, now, just now, here, there, over there, and everywhere . . . animals [can] talk and be understood, by you, by me, by everyone" ("hoje-em-dia, agora, agorinha mesmo, aqui, aí, ali, e em toda parte, . . . os bichos [podem] falar e serem entendidos, por você, por mim, por todo o mundo"). He claims to have heard the story from a tayra (irara) who had witnessed it firsthand. The narrative revolves around a group of bulls who slowly pull a heavy wagon along a winding road. Routinely flogged by the man who leads the cart, they rebel and, when he falls asleep on top of the wares they are transporting, they shake the vehicle, the man falls and is crushed by the weight of the wheels.

The story develops slowly, imitating the cadence of the bulls' pace, and consists mostly of a dialogue between the animals. As their exchange progresses, the bulls acquire what, for lack of a better term, we could define as "species consciousness," in analogy to the Marxist notion of class consciousness. They decry those who roam free in the fields and "do not know that they are bulls" ("não sabem que são bois"), an awareness they themselves have gained by working for and being exploited by humans. "Man is an animal without horns that should not exist," says one bull, and another one adds later on: "It is bad to be a wagon-bull. It is bad to live near men.... Bad things are from man" ("O homem é um bicho esmochado, que não devia haver;" "É ruim ser boi-de-carro. É ruim viver perto dos homens.... As coisas ruins são do homem"). The close contact with humans is both the source of the animals' ills and the reason why they have gained the ability to reflect upon their plight and, therefore, to unite and rebel against their yoke: "We can think like man or like bulls.... It's because we have to live near man, we have to work.... Like men.... Why did we have to learn how to think?" ("Podemos pensar como o homem e como os bois.... É porque temos de viver perto do homem, temos de trabalhar.... Como os homens.... Por que é que tivemos de aprender a pensar?"). Living among human beings, the bulls learn to employ a typically human strategy to get rid of their oppressor. They unite and work together to kill the driver of the wagon without others suspecting that that his death was anything but an accident. For the bulls, human thought is therefore both a blessing and a curse: it helps to set them free, all the while leading them to commit a crime, even if the assassination of their master is the only path toward liberty. Tellingly, the initiation rite for human cogitation is murder.

The implicit parallel between the bulls' plight and the fate of the working class is revealing in this context. Used as tools, food, and raw materials by human beings from time immemorial, plants and animals play the role attributed to proletarians vis-à-vis capitalists in Marxist thought. As in the communist revolution, when the oppressed gain the upper hand by becoming conscious of the capitalists' reliance upon the products of their labor, the bulls also free themselves by understanding that the wagon driver ultimately depends upon them. Clarice Lispector will add another layer to this analogy between nonhumans and the working class by giving it a feminist spin, as we shall see below. Women are often exploited in the same way as nonhumans and (male) proletarians, but they can also occupy a position of power. Be this as it may, Rosa's story highlights human indebtedness to animals, at the same time as it underlines that cattle have a worldview of their own. Using a very simple, repetitive language in an effort to verbally depict the thought processes of the bulls, Rosa's story adheres to their standpoint and portrays reality from their angle. Similar to what happens in perspectivism, the text presents cattle as subjects with intentionality and desires of their own that often clash with those of human beings.

If in "Conversation of Bulls" animals acquire some human traits, such as the ability to think like people, due to their close contact with humanity, in the short story "My Uncle the Jaguar" ("Meu Tio o Iauaretê"), included in *These Stories*, it is a human being who slowly turns into an animal. A jaguar hunter spends so much time stalking his prey that he adopts some of their characteristics, including physical features such as long sharp nails and thick fur. He later starts killing other human beings who upset him, feeding their bodies to the jaguars. He acknowledges that "[j]aguars are my people, my relatives" ("Onça é povo meu, meus parentes," 219) and states, toward the end of the story, that "I am a jaguar" ("Eu sou onça," 234). The hunter's fascination with his prey turns into identification, as he slowly begins to embrace the jaguars' way of life, in the same way as Amerindian shamans turn into animals and espouse their points of view. Yet, while the shamans described by Castro enter the world of animals only to return to the fold of humankind enriched by that experience, the protagonist of Rosa's story immerses himself ever deeper into the existence of jaguars, progressively leaving his humanity behind. The short story ends with the growls and snarls of the hunter who, unable to resist the pull of animality, is now utterly transformed, a mutation signaled by the fact that he relinquishes that quintessential human feature, verbal language.

In the zoography of Rosa, the coming together of animals and humankind is not always peaceful; more often than not, it is fraught with violence. Still, his tales point in the direction of a utopia of sorts: a world where the border separating humans from our others is nothing but a porous division that frequently collapses, and a writing so influenced by animality that it becomes difficult to ascertain who or what is actually the subject of enunciation in the stories. Animals inscribe themselves—their mannerisms, their language—in the text to such an extent that they become unwitting co-writers of Rosa's interspecies literature. Their textual inscription takes on two complementary but distinct forms. On the one hand, interspecies writing has an existential dimension, in that the lives of humans are altered by their encounter with plants and animals, even as flora and fauna's being-in-world is also transmuted by their close contact with us. Literature, in this case, sets the stage for and registers the process of this transformation. On the other hand, there is a strong component of linguistic reflection in zoophytographic texts, in that they play with modes of expression of animals and plants and welcome their specific languages in literature. In the wake of Rosa's short stories, subsequent Brazilian zoophytographia will incorporate both of these facets. In the rest of the chapter we will analyze the work of Clarice Lispector, whose writings bring together the existential and the linguistic aspects of interspecies literary texts.

Lispector's Plants and Animals

Clarice Lispector reported in one of the texts she published in *Jornal do Brasil* about a conversation she once had with Guimarães Rosa: "then [he] told me something I will never forget, so happy as I felt at the time:

he said he read my texts, 'not for literature, but for life'" ("então [ele] me disse uma coisa que jamais esquecerei, tão feliz me senti na hora: disse que me lia, 'não para a literatura, mas para a vida,'" *Aprendendo*). Disparate as Rosa's and Lispector's oeuvres certainly are—the first, usually classified by literary critics as a regionalist writer, deeply embedded in the language, traditions, and folklore of his native region of Minas Gerais, focuses mainly on male characters, often cowmen or outlaws; the latter, a Jewish Brazilian woman whose texts frequently lack clear temporal or geographical coordinates, are devoid of any regional linguistic markers, and read like parables or fictionalized philosophical essays, has been heralded as a feminist, her style cited as an example of *écriture féminine*[14]—the two share a concern with the foundations of human life, our relation to transcendence and the pivotal, albeit often seemingly insignificant, moments and events that put our systems of belief to the test, thus profoundly altering them.[15] Rosa was probably alluding in the conversation cited above to the existential dimension of Lispector's texts, to her effort to come to terms with what appears to be the meaninglessness of being. As he incisively noted, hers is not a literature of linguistic flourishes and stylistic embellishments. Rather, her austere prose strives to move beyond the adornments of literary language in an incessant quest to reach the heart of actuality. She writes in order to overcome blabber, to obviate the shallowness of human language so as to get in touch with the unadulterated, nonverbal core of the real. Hers is therefore an "un-literary" literature, which explains why Rosa read her texts "not for literature but for life," a succinct piece of literary criticism that perceptively condenses the essence of her endeavor as a writer.

Lispector considers that life, even in its humblest instantiations, trumps the most elaborate of texts. In "The Man who Appeared" ("O Homem que Apareceu"), part of the collection of short stories *The Via Crucis of the Body* (*A Via Crucis do Corpo*, 1974), she stages the following dialogue: "You swear that literature does not matter? / I swear, I replied with a certainty that derives from an intimate truthfulness. And I added: any cat, any dog, is worth more than literature" ("—Você jura que a literatura não importa? / —Juro, respondi com a segurança que vem de íntima veracidade. E acrescentei: qualquer gato, qualquer cachorro vale mais do que a literatura," *Contos*, 165). Far from a belittlement of animals, this conversation should be read literally as an acknowledgment that texts are only a way to reach out to the world, a window through which we can contemplate actuality. Or, as this chapter will point out, that literature is one of the many forms of expression of living beings, which writers incorporate in their aesthetic praxis.

Like Rosa before her, Lispector attributes to nonhuman beings pride of place in the exploration of reality's enigmas, the ultimate goal of her writings. Cats and dogs are not only worth more than literature but she also finds in them, as well as in other animals and plants, the main source of her reflections on existence. Nonhumans figure prominently in her narratives in a variety of roles: from adornment, in the case of flowers, to companion pets; from silent interlocutors to springboards for a journey into the wellsprings of what is. It is through our relations to our others that we come to understand our co-belonging in the continuum of life. Literature as zoophytographia is therefore just a passageway into pure life living itself—something humans cannot experience but through the mediation of aesthetics—and its perfection would spell out a falling back into the nonverbal modes of expression characteristic of nonhumans. Plants and animals are Lispector's guides in this utopian immersion into primordial life, co-writers of her texts, upon which they etch their modes of being, therefore redefining what it means to be human.

Judging by her comments in autobiographical writings, Lispector had a close connection to nonhumans ever since her childhood. The very name she received in Chechelnik, the Ukrainian city where she was born before her parents immigrated to Brazil, points in the direction of a special relation to plants and animals. She was called Chaya, which means "a living creature" in Hebrew and, throughout her life, friends and associates often compared her to different animals (Moser 33; 55–56).[16] She mentions in the short story "One Hundred Years of Pardon" ("Cem Anos de Perdão"), a first-person narrative with clear autobiographical undertones, how a little girl used to steal the roses she admired from the garden of a wealthy house in Recife. She was surrounded by cats as a child and spent countless hours in the yard playing with chickens, resulting in a close identification with hens—through a knowledge of their "intimate life," ("vida íntima," quoted in Moser 56), as she put it—that gave rise to several short stories, including "The Egg and the Hen" ("O Ovo e a Galinha"), "A Hen" ("Uma Galinha"), and "A Story of so much Love" ("Uma História de tanto Amor"), as well as to the children's tale *The Intimate Life of Laura* (*A Vida Íntima de Laura*, 1974).

Already as an adult, Lispector continued to be attracted to plants and animals, an appeal that seeped into her prose. In two short stories included in *Family Ties* (*Laços de Família*, 1960), "Love" ("Amor") and "The Imitation of the Rose" ("A Imitação da Rosa"), the female protagonists experience an epiphany triggered by flora—more on that below. In a later autobiographical novel, *Água Viva* (1973), a continuous monologue directed to an unidentified "you," the female voice decides to "talk about the pangs of flowers to better feel the order of what is" ("falar da dolência das flores para sentir mais a ordem do que existe," 46). What follows is a long list of flowers featuring a description of the modes of existence of each and of what they evoke in the protagonist (46–49). Flowers are depicted as having a personality of their own, each standing for a particular approach to reality. In these examples, plants profoundly impact human beings. Far from the passivity so often ascribed to it, flora acts upon and transforms the women in the narratives, who are drawn to its vigor, vitality, and seductive beauty.

Other writings testify to Lispector's ongoing concern with humans' relationship to animals. Similar to Machado de Assis, she decried gratuitous cruelty against other living beings. In one of her *crónicas* for *Jornal do Brasil*, about a whale beached in Leblon, a seaside neighborhood of Rio de Janeiro, she condemns those who take advantage of the dying animal: "Some said that the Leblon whale still had not died but that its flesh was cut while it was alive and sold by weight.... How to believe that we would not even wait for death before one being would

eat another?... [W]e are as ferocious as a ferocious animal, just because
we want to eat that mountain of innocence that is a whale, as we eat
the singing innocence of a bird" ("Uns diziam que a baleia do Leblon
ainda não morrera mas que sua carne retalhada em vida era vendida
por quilos.... Como acreditar que não se espera nem a morte para um
ser comer outro ser?.... [S]omos tão ferozes como um animal feroz, só
porque queremos comer daquela montanha de inocência que é uma baleia,
assim como comemos a inocência cantante de um pássaro," *Aprendendo*).
Still, Lispector did not romanticize our connection to animals and, unlike
Machado, was not an apologist for vegetarianism. In another *crónica*,
she writes: "My lack of courage to kill a chicken and, still, to eat it once
dead confounds me, astonishes me, but I accept it" ("Minha falta de coragem de matar uma galinha e no entanto comê-la morta me confunde,
espanta-me, mas aceito," *Aprendendo*).[17] In her fiction, she also struggles
with the paradox that humans eat the flesh of other beings. A little girl
in "A Story of so much Love" is heartbroken when one of her favorite
hens is slaughtered for food. She learns from her mother, however, that
"when we eat animals, the animals become more similar to us, being thus
inside us" ("[q]uando a gente come bichos, os bichos ficam mais parecidos
com a gente, estando assim dentro de nós," *Contos*, 128). When another
hen she liked is killed, its flesh cooked for a meal, the girl eats it knowing that the hen "would be incorporated into her [the girl] and would
become hers more than it was when it was alive" ("se incorporaria nela
e se tornaria mais sua do que em vida," *Contos*, 129). Such an attempt
to justify our carnivorous habits, naive as it may seem, speaks to a desire
to become closer to and internalize animals, a longing that will deserve
further analysis later in this chapter.

Beyond dietary concerns, Lispector was fascinated with various
other animals. She had a lifelong interest in horses that comes through
most clearly in "Dry Point of Horses" ("Seco Estudo de Cavalos"),
where she writes: "The shape of the horse represents what is best in
human beings. I have a horse within me that rarely expresses itself"; and
"[I]f I could have chosen, I would have liked to have been born a horse

("A forma do cavalo representa o que há de melhor no ser humano. Tenho um cavalo dentro de mim que raramente se exprime"; "[S]e pudesse ter escolhido queria ter nascido cavalo," "Seco Estudo de Cavalos," *Contos*, 227). Lóri, the protagonist of *An Apprenticeship or The Book of Pleasures* (*Uma Aprendizagem ou O Livro dos Prazeres*, 1969) also identifies with horses: "There is a being living inside me as if the house was his, and it is. I am talking about a black and sleek horse" ("Existe um ser que mora dentro de mim como se fosse casa dele, e é. Trata-se de um cavalo preto e lustroso," *Aprendizagem*, 23).

But the animal with which Lispector forged a tighter connection was certainly the dog. She reminisces about her pet dog Dilermando, who kept her company when she lived in Naples: "Our relations were so close, his sensibility was linked to mine to such an extent that he sensed and felt my difficulties.... No human being ever gave me the feeling of being so totally loved as I was loved without restrictions by that dog" ("Nossas relações eram tão estreitas, sua sensibilidade estava de tal modo ligada à minha que ele pressentia e sentia minhas dificuldades.... Nenhum ser humano me deu jamais a sensação de ser tão totalmente amada como fui amada sem restrições por esse cão," *Aprendendo*). The traumatic experience of having to leave Dilermando behind when she moved to Bern was what led her to write "The Crime of the Mathematics Professor" ("O Crime do Professor de Matemática") about a man who attempts to expiate the guilt of having abandoned his dog (Moser 165).[18] Later in life, Lispector grew extremely attached to another dog, Ulisses. She wrote about him in several texts and even composed a children's story, *Almost True* (*Quase de Verdade*, 1978) in his voice (Moser 331–32).

Lispector writes that "the relationship between humans and animals is not replaceable by any other. Having pets is a vital experience. And those who have not lived with an animal lack a certain kind of intuition of the living world" ("as relações entre homem e bicho são singulares, não substituíveis por nenhuma outra. Ter bicho é uma experiência vital. E a quem não conviveu com um animal falta um certo tipo de intuição do mundo vivo," *Aprendendo*). She traces the origins of several of her fictional prose pieces directly to her "love of animals," which she describes as "one of the accessible forms of people" ("amor por bichos"; "uma das formas acessíveis de gente," *Não Esquecer*).[19] This idea is reiterated by the narrator of *The Hour of the Star* (*A Hora da Estrela*, 1977), who confesses that he "gets along better with animals than with people" ("eu me dou melhor com os bichos do que com gente"). And, from her first novel onward, the female protagonists of Lispector's narratives, often interpreted as the author's alter egos, are incessantly compared to different animals. Joana, the main character of *Near to the Wild Heart* (*Perto do Coração Selvagem*, 1943), for instance, is likened to a viper, a wildcat, a horse, a dog, and a bird at different moments in the text (Moser 122). For Lispector, animals teach us about our nature and animal-like characters such as Joana lay bare the drives that determine our behavior.

This brief excursus, reading a sample of Lispector's writings on plants and animals through a biographical lens, shows the deep imbrication of nonhuman beings in the writer's life and work. However, such an approach merely broaches the subject. The author's appreciation of flora and fauna goes beyond their usage as stylistic devices that illuminate the distinctive features of human characters in her texts. Nor can the presence of plants and animals in her prose be reduced to a thematic reading, according to which her sympathy for nonhumans would straightforwardly translate into a variety of references to flowers, pets, or other animals in fiction. Significant as Lispector's enthrallment with other living beings certainly is for understanding her literature, the most thought-provoking appearance of nonhumans in her fiction cuts across and even goes against her biographical attachment to certain plants or animals.

For one thing, her prose often blurs the boundaries between fiction and nonfiction, with biographical details merging seamlessly with fantasy. As the protagonist of one of her novels puts it: "I do not want to have the terrible limitation of those who live only on what can make sense. Not me: what I really want is a made up truth" ("Não quero ter a terrível limitação de quem vive apenas do que é passível de fazer sentido.

Eu não: quero é uma verdade inventada," *Água Viva*, 19). Within this
privileging of invention over facts, or rather, the creation of facts through
invention, it becomes problematic to interpret Lispector's writings
biographically. Furthermore, her narratives often produce an alienation
effect (*Verfremdungseffekt*), akin to the one popularized by Bertolt Brecht
in his plays, in that our everyday relationship to nonhumans is de-
familiarized, scrutinized, and questioned. Not only are we prompted
to see other living beings in a new, often startlingly unexpected light,
but also, instead of integrating them into our own predefined plots—
through their aestheticization, in the case of flowers, or domestication
as pets—we are also confronted with their specific, idiosyncratic modes
of being. Lispector's utopian zoophytographia, then, is an approach to
plants and animals against the grain of cultural norms and expectations,
in a phenomenologically inspired attempt to cut through the layers of
sedimented wisdom regarding nonhumans, in order to discover more
about them and about ourselves.

Writing One's Life with Others

Lispector states time and again that she wants to avoid humanizing animals, so as not to impose our constraints upon them. In one of her *crónicas*
she censures a man who has domesticated a coati (quati), treating the
wild animal as if it were a dog and walking it on a leash. She imagines
herself asking the man: "[W]hy are you doing that? What need makes
you conjure up a dog? And why not choose a real dog, then? ... Or did
you not have another way to possess the grace of that animal but through
a leash? But one crushes a rose if one presses it hard!" ("por que é que
você faz isso? que carência é essa que faz você inventar um cachorro?
e por que não um cachorro mesmo, então? ... Ou você não teve outro
modo de possuir a graça desse bicho senão com uma coleira? mas você
esmaga uma rosa se apertá-la com força!" *Não Esquecer*). The animal is
destroyed by its domestication, being reduced to a ridiculous shadow of

its former, wild self: "that animal no longer knew who it was" ("aquele bicho já não sabia mais quem ele era," *Não Esquecer*). Lispector envisions the moment when the coati realizes that it has been denatured, its being corrupted by the whims of the man: "But what if one were to reveal to the coati the mystery of its real nature?... I am well aware, it would have the right, once it found out, to massacre the man with hate for the worst thing one being can do to another—to falsify its essence in order to use it" ("Mas se ao quati fosse de súbito revelado o mistério de sua verdadeira natureza?... Bem sei, ele teria direito, quando soubesse, de massacrar o homem com o ódio pelo que de pior um ser pode fazer a outro ser—adulterar-lhe a essência a fim de usá-lo," *Não Esquecer*). She finds the drive to tamper with and mold animal nature to human needs an abhorrent cruelty. It debases the animal and, at the same time, demeans the humans responsible for such acts.

The episode with the coati exemplifies the opposite of what Lispector hopes to achieve in her writings on plants and animals. Instead of alienating flora and fauna, forced by humans to pose as something they are not, the author hopes to alienate human beings themselves, to defamiliarize our habits and social norms, viewed differently when considered through the prism of non-humans. Wild animals cannot be tamed and turned into pets, and even companion animals such as cats and dogs retain an irreducible foreignness, their most captivating feature, which the author hopes will contaminate humanity. This inversion of commonplace viewpoints comes through clearly in "The Crime of the Mathematics Professor," when the protagonist acknowledges: "I am now quite sure that I was not the one who had a dog. You were the one who had a person" ("Agora estou bem certo de que não fui eu quem teve um cão. Foste tu que tiveste uma pessoa," *Laços*). The illusion of mastery over animals is shattered in the short story, as the main character recognizes that the influence his pet exerted over him was far deeper than whatever impact he had on the behavior of the animal;[20] the professor was the one to be "possessed" by his dog, not vice versa. The man committed the "crime" of abandoning the animal to free himself from the pet's domination—"this crime [abandoning the dog] replaces the larger crime I would not have the courage to commit" ("este crime substitui o crime maior que eu não teria coragem de cometer," *Laços*), most likely the assassination of the animal—only to acknowledge his indebtedness to the dog at the end of the text.

For Lispector, defamiliarization, in the process of which we are touched by the existence of plants and animals and compelled to contemplate our lives anew, can turn into full-fledged metamorphosis, akin to the becoming-animal of shamans described by Viveiros de Castro. "But I do not humanize animals, I think this is offensive—one has to respect their natura—I am the one to be animalized," she writes, only to add: "It is not difficult, it comes easily, one should just not fight against it, just deliver oneself to it" ("Mas eu não humanizo os bichos, acho que é uma ofensa—há de respeitar-lhes a natura—eu é que me animalizo. Não é difícil, vem simplesmente, é só não lutar contra, é só entregar-se," *Aprendendo*). Animalization takes place once we give in to our drives and accept the animal within us. In the novel *Água Viva*, the female protagonist, who could be interpreted as Lispector's alter ego, also comments on the pull of animality: "Not to have been born an animal is one of my secret nostalgias. They sometimes cry out from the distance of many generations and I cannot reply but by being restless. It is the calling" ("Não ter nascido bicho é uma minha secreta nostalgia. Eles às vezes clamam do longe de muitas gerações e eu não posso responder senão ficando inquieta. É o chamado," 43).[21] The main character is nostalgic for a past she has not lived but that lives on in the makeup of each human being, hailing us from the depths of time.

The process of becoming a plant or an animal is a recurring trope in Lispector's fiction. The protagonist of *Água Viva* hears the call of wild animals and, at the same time, also dreams of turning into a plant: "I dive into the quasi-pain of an intense happiness—and leaves and branches are born between my hair as adornment;" "I am a tree that burns with hard pleasure;" "My impulse gets linked to that of the roots of trees" ("Mergulho na quase dor de uma intensa alegria—e para me enfeitar nascem entre os meus cabelos folhas e ramagens;" "Sou uma árvore que arde com duro prazer;" "Meu impulso se liga ao das raízes das árvores," 20; 33; 35).[22] Such vegetal transmutations, evocative of Ovid's *Metamorphoses*, nonetheless have a very different role from the one they play in the Latin poet's writings. While, in Ovid, humans were imprisoned in their vegetal form that was often adopted as a means to escape persecution or meted out as punishment for a transgression, becoming plant or animal in Lispector's narratives is perceived as a kind of liberation from the shackles of human rules and customs.

Becoming nonhuman means getting "in touch with the animal primitive life," and turning into a "diffuse blur of instincts, sweetness and ferociousness" ("contacto com a vida primitiva animálica," *Água Viva*, 40; "mancha difusa de instintos, doçuras e ferocidades," *Aprendendo*). It is a return to humankind's primeval origins, to an era when our existence was ruled by our inclinations. The multiple transformations of humans into nonhumans in Lispector's prose easily lend themselves to a reading inspired in Gilles Deleuze, who, together with Félix Guattari, developed the concepts of "becoming-plant" and "becoming-animal" that denote the freeing up of human flows of desire usually straightjacketed in psychosocial configurations such as the Oedipal triangle. For the two philosophers, becoming-plant or animal is therefore an emancipatory gesture, meant to unchain us from (self-)imposed boundaries, so that we can give free rein to our desires (232–309). It is through this philosophical lens that we should understand the narrator's statement in *An Apprenticeship or The Book of Pleasures* that "she despised the human itself and experienced the silent soul of animal life" ("desprezava o próprio humano e experimentava a silenciosa alma da vida animal," 35): humanity's limitations are a shortcoming to be surmounted by surrendering to the nonhuman substratum within us. But turning one's back on the human and delivering oneself to becoming-plant or animal, in Deleuze and Guattari's terms, is not without its dangers, as we saw in Rosa's short story "My Uncle the Jaguar." One risks dissolution into one's drives, a disarticulation of one's singular existence as one disintegrates into an impersonal whole.

Lispector will skirt the danger of being drawn into the undifferentiated bareness of life by turning to another way of relating to plants and animals: a face-to-face encounter with their mode of existence.

The novelist writes in a *crónica* that "[s]ometimes I get electrified when I see an animal. I am now hearing the ancestral call within me: it seems like I no longer know who is more of a creature, me or the animal. And I get all confused. I seem to get afraid of facing the muffled instincts that I am forced to admit to when I stand before the animal" ("Às vezes eletrizo-me ao ver bicho. Estou agora ouvindo o grito ancestral dentro de mim: parece que não sei quem é mais a criatura, se eu ou o bicho. E me confundo toda. Fico ao que parece com medo de encarar instintos abafados que diante do bicho sou obrigada a assumir," *Aprendendo*). This passage encompasses several topics we have already touched upon: becoming-animal as a form of regression into the past of humanity, to a time when instincts determined our existence, and an inversion of hierarchies, making it unclear who controls whom, who is more creaturely, the animal or the human, as the author puts it. But the relationship to animality does not involve a metamorphosis in this case. Rather, Lispector describes an encounter—signaled by the use of the verbs *to see*, *to face*, and *to stand before*—between animals and humans, in the course of which we are confronted with the reality of our selves.

This encounter with nonhumans is not limited to animals. The short story "Love" describes one such transformative brush with flora. The narrative revolves around a woman who experiences an existential crisis triggered by plants. The story is set in the afternoon, at a time when, according to the narrator, "the trees she had planted laughed at her" ("as árvores que plantara riam dela"). Even though the trees in this quote are metaphorical—they refer to the routine, middle-class life of the woman: her growing children, the meals she prepares, her household—the scorn with which these everyday affairs laugh at her is sparked by real trees. The protagonist goes to Rio de Janeiro's Botanical Garden, where she contemplates the "deep ... decomposition" of "laden trees" in an environment "so rich that it rotted" ("decomposição ... profunda"; "árvores

carregadas"; "tão rico que apodrecia"). She reflects that "[t]he morality
of the Garden was different," at odds with the petty bourgeois concerns
that usually preoccupied her ("A moral do Jardim era outra"). It was a
world that pulsated with the different stages of life, from flowering and
fructification to decomposition and death, all of them equally crucial.
Her encounter with the amoral proliferation of plants jolts her out of
her drab existence as she ponders the "tranquil . . . rawness of the world"
("crueza do mundo . . . tranquila").

In "The Imitation of the Rose" Lispector depicts once again a
face-to-face encounter with plants as a life-changing event. The female
protagonist, who suffers from an unspecified psychological illness, cannot
resist the "extreme beauty" of a bunch of roses ("beleza extrema"). The
perfection of the flowers acquires religious undertones, as they are implicitly compared to Christ through the trope of the *imitatio*. The woman
felt that "whoever imitated Christ would be lost—lost in the light but
dangerously lost" ("quem imitasse Cristo estaria perdido—perdido na
luz, mas perigosamente perdido") and this dissolution of self is what
befalls her when she sits facing the flowers and gives in to their allure.
Delivering herself, almost against her will, to the inhuman undertaking
of imitating the roses, she abandons her conventional, prosaic life and
goes insane at the end of the narrative.

The final short story of *Family Ties*, "The Buffalo" ("O Búfalo"),
portrays another encounter with nonhumans, this time with an animal.
As in most of Lispector's writings, the text revolves around a female protagonist, who goes to a zoo is search of a living being that would echo her
anger. "Where, but where, could she find an animal that would teach her
to have her own hatred?," writes the narrator ("Mas onde, onde encontrar
o animal que lhe ensinasse a ter o seu próprio ódio?). The woman finally
finds her match in a buffalo. Within the scopic regime that governs the
zoo, a place where humans go to observe animals, the buffalo is the one
living being who "faces" the woman ("encarou-a") and returns her gaze:
"There they were, the buffalo and the woman, face-to-face. . . . She looked
at its eyes. And the eyes of the buffalo, the eyes looked at her eyes. Small
and red eyes looked at her. The eyes of the buffalo" ("Lá estavam o búfalo

e a mulher, frente a frente.... Olhou seus olhos. E os olhos do búfalo, os olhos olharam seus olhos.... Olhos pequenos e vermelhos a olhavam. Os olhos do búfalo"). The animal reciprocates the woman's look, his silent "tranquil" ("tranquilo") hatred for the humans who imprisoned it a response to her own state of mind. The deep connection established between the woman and the buffalo, their encounter in the depths of their hatred for others, is what empowers her to go through with her plan. She buries a dagger in her body and commits suicide, drawing her resolve from the calm strength of the animal.

The face-to-face encounters with plants and animals narrated in the short stories we have been analyzing preclude a metamorphosis of the self into the other. Rather, the protagonists dwell in flora and fauna's difference, all attempts to imitate nonhuman existence a priori condemned to failure. The latent tension in these narratives results precisely from the elusiveness of plant and animal life that we can never completely grasp. Such a relationship to nonhumans evokes the encounter with the Other that is the cornerstone of Emmanuel Levinas's philosophy.[23] According to Levinas, the subject is constituted in the moment when the I faces the Other, who hails the I from its unbridgeable difference (*Totality*, 33ff). Unlike what happens in a transformation, where the identification of the I with the Other is such that a transmutation of the one into the other— of a human being into a plant or an animal, in Lispector's terms—occurs, a face-to-face encounter is grounded upon detachment. For Levinas, the Other is unknowable and wholly separate from the I, who can therefore not empathize with the one facing it ("Transcendence," 151). Still, the subject is created by the call of the Other that, paradoxically, not only arrives from the most remote of distances but also originates within the self. Subjectivation takes place when the I recognizes the foreignness of the Other within, a formulation reminiscent of Lispector's ancestral call of animality mentioned above.[24]

Even though the Levinasian Other is always a person, one could broaden this category to include nonhumans.[25] In the work of Lispector, absolute transcendence—the other, the highest, figurations of god—often comes full circle and incarnates in the most concrete, immanent, and often abject being. The latter can be a plant or an animal, the encounter with which engenders a new human subject, all the while questioning the relation between divinity, humanity, and nonhuman beings.

Animal Encounters: *The Passion According to G.H.*

The best-known and most powerful example of a face-to-face encounter with a nonhuman other in Lispector's oeuvre happens in *The Passion According to G.H.* (*A Paixão Segundo G.H.*, 1964).[26] The novel's female main character and first-person narrator, known only as G.H.—an acronym that can stand for "género humano," or "human race," thus turning G.H. into an allegory for the whole of humankind (Williams 253)—finds a cockroach inside a closet in a room that used to be occupied by her former live-in maid, and the text consists in working through the repercussions of this ostensibly mundane event. The encounter is, at first, framed by the "disgust" the protagonist experiences when she sees cockroaches, an "archaic horror" that makes her feel "revolted" whenever she is close to the animals ("nojo"; "arcaico horror"; "repugnara," 37). The woman's repugnance will compel her to focus her attention on the cockroach and probe the source of her distaste for the insect. What ensues is a far-reaching reflection on the roots of life that goes well beyond humanity.

After the initial shock of coming across a cockroach in her home, G.H. realizes that the animal is slowly crawling out of the closet and, overcome by an irrational fear, tries to kill it by slamming a door against it. But the cockroach, although crippled, does not die. As she prepares to administer a final *coup de grâce*, banging the closet door once again against the insect, G.H. encounters it face-to-face: "It was then that I saw the face of the cockroach. It was facing me, at the height of my head and eyes. . . . But then because of a fraction of a second it was too late: I saw. . . . I, in truth—I had really never seen a cockroach. I had only been repulsed by its old and always present existence—but I had never faced it, not even in thought" ("Mas foi então que vi a cara da barata. Ela estava de frente, à altura de minha cabeça e de meus olhos. . . . Mas eis que por um

átimo de segundo ficara tarde demais: eu via.... Eu na verdade—eu nunca
tinha mesmo visto uma barata. Só tivera repugnância pela sua antiga e
sempre presente existência—mas nunca a defrontara, nem mesmo em
pensamento," 43–44).[27] The remainder of the text unfolds the consequences of contemplating the cockroach beyond the culturally mediated
disgust it usually elicits in humans. G.H. faces the animal concretely, in
its corporeality, and in thought, up to a point where the two modes of
relating to it become one and the same, as bodily functions and thought
processes are revealed to be both part of the ongoing becoming of life.[28]

Similar to the buffalo in the short story discussed above, the cockroach reciprocates G.H.'s gaze with her "radiant and dark... eyes. The
eyes of a bride" ("olhos... radiosos e negros. Olhos de noiva," 44). "I don't
know if it saw me, I don't know what a cockroach sees. But it and I were
looking at each other," writes G.H. ("Não sei se ela me via, não sei o que
uma barata vê. Mas ela e eu nos olhávamos," 60). What transpires in this
exchange of gazes upends the protagonist's worldview, exposing a realm
of actuality that she did not suspect existed. It is worth transcribing the
moment when the concrete sight of the animal metaphorically opens
G.H.'s eyes to a hitherto unexplored dimension of life:

But if its [the cockroach's] eyes did not see me, its existence
existed me—in the primary world where I had entered, beings
exist other beings as a way of seeing each other.... The cockroach did not see me directly, it was with me. The cockroach
did not see me with the eyes but with the body. / And I—I saw.
There was no way not to see it. There was no way of denying:
my convictions and my wings were rapidly burnt and had no
more purpose.... And I could not even, like before, resort to
an entire civilization that would help me deny what I saw.

Mas se seus olhos não me viam, a existência dela me existia—
no mundo primário onde eu entrara, os seres existem os outros
como modo de se verem.... A barata não me via diretamente,
ela estava comigo. A barata não me via com os olhos mas com

o corpo. / E eu—eu via. Não havia como não vê-la. Não havia
como negar: minhas convicções e minhas asas se crestavam
rapidamente e não tinham mais finalidade…. E nem podia
mais me socorrer, como antes, de toda uma civilização que me
ajudaria a negar o que eu via. (60)

What G.H. contemplates in her face-to-face with the cockroach is the
animal's mode of existence, which is wholly distinct from her own. Unable
to explain away the foreignness of the insect by resorting to the clichés
spawned by an "entire civilization," the woman is forced to consider life
beyond humankind. She realizes that the way of relating to others in
Western culture, through seeing and objectifying, does not apply in the
case of the cockroach, which interacts with its environment using its
entire body—"The cockroach did not see me with the eyes but with the
body." Once again, Levinasian thought is pertinent here. As the I, in his
philosophy, cannot know the Other in its difference but finds traces of
the Other within, so does G.H. recognize that the insect, which relates
to her through its body, is, at the same time, inside her: "It was with me."
The animal is, then, a paradigmatic example of the uncanny, that is, it
is simultaneously alien and strangely familiar, which explains the revul-
sion mixed with attraction experienced by the protagonist when she first
sees it (Nascimento 25ff). The cockroach's "being with" G.H. does not
amount to a transformation of the human into the animal or vice versa
but to a recognition that, despite the abyss separating the two, they are
able to relate to one another by virtue of the shared life that traverses
them both. This is how we can read Lispector's idiosyncratic formula-
tions: the cockroach's "existence existed me," since "beings exist other
beings as a way of seeing each other." The cockroach "exists" humans
insofar as both are living organisms, the former a much older species
than the relative newcomer *Homo sapiens*, and therefore folded into the
phylogenic development of humanity.[29]

Be it through metamorphosis into a plant or an animal, like the
ones we discussed above, or, as in *The Passion*, through a face-to-face

confrontation between humans and nonhumans, what Lispector conveys in her fiction is an immersion into the wellsprings of life. As G.H. deftly put it, what she saw in the eyes of the cockroach was "life looking at me" directly, without the mediations afforded by culture ("a vida me olhando," 45). The author refers to this primordial life by many different terms throughout her oeuvre. G.H. calls it, among other names, "raw life," "primary world," "the nucleus," "the neutral," "the nothing," and "primordial matter" ("vida crua," "mundo primário," "o núcleo," "o neutron," "o nada," "matéria primordial," 47; 60; 64; 67; 73; 81). In other writings it is defined as "primitive life" ("vida primitiva," *Contos*, 83), "live jelly," ("geleia viva," *Não Esquecer*), "the living neutral of things" ("neutro vivo das coisas," *Aprendizagem*, 100), "plasma," "placenta," and "the invisible nucleus of reality ("plasma," "placenta," "invisível núcleo da realidade," *Água Viva*, 9, 20). All of these expressions point in the direction of a reality that antecedes humanness. "I felt ... that 'my being' came from a source much older than the human and ... much larger than the human," writes G.H., only to add a few pages later: "[F]acing the living cockroach, the worst discovery was that the world is not human, and that we are not human.... [T]he inhuman is the best of us" ("[E]u sentia ... que 'eu ser' vinha de uma fonte muito anterior à humana e ... muito maior que a humana"; "[D]iante da barata viva, a pior descoberta foi a de que o mundo não é humano, e de que não somos humanos.... [O] inumano é o melhor nosso," 45; 55).[30] Primordial life, of which the existence of the cockroach is just one of many instantiations, is about life's yearning for itself, a longing for being that is not yet (or already not) differentiated into a specific individual. What is at stake is a depersonalized *conatus essendi* of life striving for existence, as Spinoza, one of Lispector's favorite philosophers, postulated in his *Ethics* (75).[31] The face-to-face encounter with plants and animals reminds humans that they belong to this becoming of life, which unites all of the living.

For Lispector, the human immersion in primordial life does not amount to an enjoyable oceanic feeling of communion with the whole. The experience of originary existence comes at the cost of our

"sentimentalized life" ("vida sentimentalizada," *Paixão*, 55). In order to
enter the core of reality humans need the "diabolic courage to let go of
feelings" and have to divest themselves of the pieties of morality, a violent
separation from life as we know it ("coragem diabólica de largar os sen-
timentos," *Paixão*, 105). "I was freeing myself of my morality," observes
G.H., "even though this gave me fear" ("Estava me libertando da minha
moralidade—embora isso me desse medo," 68). In *The Passion*, primordial life is therefore frequently qualified as infernal: "And that seemed
like hell, that destruction of archeological human layers upon layers. Hell
because the world no longer had a human meaning for me, and man no
longer had for me a human meaning. And without that humanization,
without the sentimentalization of the world—I get terrified" ("E isso me
parecia o inferno, essa destruição de camadas e camadas arqueológicas
humanas. O inferno, porque o mundo não me tinha mais sentido humano,
e o homem não me tinha mais sentido humano. E sem essa humanização
e sem a sentimentação do mundo—eu me apavoro," 55–56).[32] But if the
depersonalization required to get in touch with unmediated life may
seem like hell, it is also, at the same time, reminiscent of paradise: "My
first hesitant steps in the direction of life, and abandoning my life. The
foot stepped on air and I entered paradise or hell: the nucleus" ("Meus
primeiros passos hesitantes em direção à vida, e abandonando a minha
vida. O pé pisou no ar, e entrei no paraíso ou no inferno: no núcleo,"
64). Life happens in a zone of indistinctness between the categories of
hell and paradise or, rather, when what seemed to be hell from a narrow,
human point of view reverts to a utopian paradise when considered from
the depersonalized, non-perspectival, absolute stance of life itself.

G.H. testifies that "in order to escape the neutral, I had long ago
abandoned being for a persona, for a human mask. When I got human-
ized ... I also lost the forests, and I lost the air, and I lost the embryo
inside me" ("Para escapar do neutro, eu há muito havia abandonado
o ser pela persona, pela máscara humana. Ao me ter humanizado ...
perdera também as florestas, e perdera o ar, e perdera o embrião dentro de
mim," 73). Humanization, then, is a mask we don to help us escape the

harshness of reality. This persona entails a loss that the narrator of *The Passion* attempts to overcome by abandoning her "human organization" and recovering her link to primordial life ("organização humana," 78). This is a painful process fraught with risk—"Had I asked for the most dangerous and forbidden thing?" ("Havia eu pedido a coisa mais perigosa e proibida?" 105). The "passion" in the title of the novel, which evokes the Biblical passion, or suffering, of Christ, denotes the protagonist's anguish in her struggle to reach depersonalized existence.

In the narrative, G.H. only draws the full consequences of her face-to-face encounter with the cockroach once she embraces "[t]he inhuman within the person" ("O inumano dentro da pessoa," 123). She proves that she has achieved this goal in the final pages of the novel when she eats a piece of the white paste oozing from the cockroach's crushed body. Once again, the Christian undertones of the text are clear: much like the Eucharist, which bespeaks a communion with Christ, G.H.'s action signifies a togetherness with life itself, represented by the body of the insect. But, similar to the Catholic ritual, eating part of the animal does not imply a metamorphosis. The woman and the cockroach remain thoroughly distinct, and tasting the latter's body as a religious host is a token of this unbridgeable difference, whereby G.H. literally becomes a host to the body of the Other she ingests, a stranger in her home.

In order to eat a piece of the cockroach's oozing matter the protagonist of *The Passion* has had not only to overcome her feelings of disgust but also to renounce the categories of beauty and the good. "I lost the fear of the ugly," states G.H., who longs for "a life so much larger that it does not even have beauty" ("perdi o medo do feio"; "uma vida tão maior que não tem sequer beleza," 16; 127).[33] "The world has no intention of beauty... there is no aesthetic plan in the world, and not even an aesthetic plan of kindness, and this would have shocked me before," adds G.H. later in the text ("O mundo não tem intenção de beleza... no mundo não existe nenhum plano estético, nem mesmo o plano estético da bondade, e isto antes me chocaria," 125). Beauty is in the eye of the human beholder and does not inhere in reality beyond our subjective

appreciation.[34] By the same token, the good and ethics are human creations that make no sense from the point of view of life itself:[35] "God is
greater than goodness with its beauty" ("O Deus é maior que a bondade
com a sua beleza," 125). What is at stake here is not the deity of any
particular religious tradition but the Spinozan "God, *or* nature"—"Deus
sive natura" (*Ethics*, 114)—in other words, a divinity that is indistinct
from the forms of life that make up Creation: "pre-human divine life," in
G.H.'s words ("vida pré-humana divina," 80). God is not to be found in
a transcendent being but in any plant or animal, even an abject one such
as a cockroach. Human aesthetics and morality therefore do not apply
to a god coextensive with nature and with all living beings.[36]

G.H. reflects that, by touching and eating a chunk of the cockroach,
she has violated the Biblical injunction to keep unclean beings at bay. She
speculates that unclean animals are those that have remained the same,
without ornaments or change ever since Creation (57). "[T]he unclean is
the root" of life, the true fruit of good and evil ("o imundo é a raíz," 57).
Jewish religious law forbids humans to experience this reality and keeps
us in the sphere of entities that only "pretend to be alive," a protected
realm that allows us to "build a possible soul" ("disfarçadamente vivo;"
"construir uma alma possível," 57). By eating the body of the cockroach,
the ultimate unclean matter, G.H. is expelled from a "paradise of adornments," the restricted Eden of Eve and Adam, and thrown into pure life,
a genuine, amoral paradise ("paraíso de adornos," 57). *The Passion* thus
depicts a Christianized and, at the same time, Nietzschean challenge:
to endure the suffering of tearing the veils that mask actuality and to
embrace life beyond good and evil.

Interspecies Literature

G.H.'s encounter with the cockroach in *The Passion* teaches her that what
she had hitherto called "humanness" was a shallow, false form of existence, a "rough humanity that had always been made of rough concepts"

("grossa humanidade que sempre fora feita de conceitos grossos," 105).
She writes that humans are soaked in a fake humanization, which precludes the emergence of true humankind and its humanity (124). In any
case, she suggests, "a person is human, so one does not need to fight for
it: to wish to be human sounds too pretty" ("a pessoa é humana, não é
preciso lutar por isso: querer ser humano me soa bonito demais," 123).
Beyond this easy humanness, G.H. considers, "[t]here must be a good so
different that it will not look like the good," an inhuman goodness akin
to the primordial life she found in the body of the cockroach ("Tinha que
existir uma bondade tão outra que não se pareceria com bondade," 70).

But G.H.'s critique of humanity does not spell out its complete
rejection. She realizes toward the end of the novel that what she is
striving for is not simple dehumanization but a more acute awareness
of what being human actually means: "'not human' is a great reality
and ... this does not mean 'inhumane,' to the contrary" ("'não humano'
é uma grande realidade, e ... isso não significa 'desumano,' pelo contrário,"
134). The trivial humanness of G.H.'s former life makes a mockery of
genuine humanity, which is achieved only when we accept the inhuman
within: "At last, at last my casing was really broken, and I was without
limits. ... What I am not, I am. Everything will be in me. My life does
not have only human meaning, it is much larger ... and I would only
realize my specifically human destiny if I were to deliver myself ... to
what is no longer me, to what is already inhuman" ("Enfim, enfim que-
brara-se realmente o meu invólucro, e sem limite eu era. ... O que não sou
eu, eu sou. Tudo estará em mim. ... Minha vida não tem sentido apenas
humano, é muito maior ... e só realizaria o meu destino especificamente
humano se me entregasse ... ao que já não era eu, ao que já é inumano,"
140). One finds in this passage, again, echoes of Spinoza, according
to whom the difference between the I and its surroundings, as well as
between body and soul, matter and mind, *res extensa* and *res cogitans*,
is one of degree. True, all living beings are different, but they partake of
the same life principle and there is as a result no absolute divide separating the body of a cockroach from human thought. What is more, in

the same way that the kernel of humankind can already be found in an insect, humanity also finds traces of all life forms in itself.[37]

To be human is to become aware of the other(s) within and to consciously accept it (or them). It is a going back to primordial existence, without completely dissolving in its originary amalgamation. Discovering humanity entails peeling the layers of constructs we have created to obfuscate our proximity to plants and animals—"I had gone back until I knew that the deepest life in me is before the human" ("Havia recuado até saber que em mim a vida mais profunda é antes do humano," *Paixão*, 105)—, which amounts, simultaneously, to a leap forward, to a humanness that knows its kinship with the rest of the world: "My kingdom is of this world . . . and my kingdom was not just human. I knew" ("Meu reino é deste mundo . . . e meu reino não era apenas humano. Eu sabia," 99). Genuine humanity is therefore a process of learning to be less and more than human: to be so humble as to approximate a cockroach and to recognize all life within our human existence. "[W]e have the freedom to fulfill our fatal destiny," writes G.H., and "it is up to me to become freely what I fatally am. I own my fatality and, if I decide not to fulfill it, I will remain outside of my specifically living nature. But if I fulfill my neutral and live nucleus, then, within my species, I will be specifically human" ("temos a liberdade de cumprir ou não o nosso destino fatal . . . de mim depende eu vir livremente a ser o que fatalmente sou. Sou dona de minha fatalidade e, se eu decidir não cumpri-la, ficarei fora de minha natureza especificamente viva. Mas se eu cumprir meu núcleo neutro e vivo, então, dentro de minha espécie, estarei sendo especificamente humana," 99). The specifically human mode of existence is freely to embrace the nonhuman others that inhabit our selves.

The intimacy with other living beings and with the processes of life allows humans to experience a utopian state of grace, in which they are reconciled with the world around them. This amounts to a *stasis*—a Greek word that denotes both an uprising or disturbance and a standstill or stability—since it unsettles life-as-usual, bracketing the routine in favor of a calm enjoyment of what is. The protagonist of *Água Viva* vividly describes this condition: "The state of grace I am talking about is used for nothing. It is as if it arrived just so that we would know that we truly exist and that the world exists. In that state, beyond the tranquil felicity that irradiates from people and things, there is a lucidity that I only call light because in grace everything is so light" ("O estado de graça de que falo não é usado para nada. É como se viesse apenas para que se soubesse que realmente se existe e existe o mundo. Nesse estado, além da tranquila felicidade que se irradia de pessoas e coisas, há uma lucidez que só chamo de leve porque na graça tudo é tão leve," 70).

The state of grace is a time outside the regular course of history, a period of inoperativeness akin to the moments of leisure or idleness we will discuss in the following chapter. G.H. associates it with the Jewish Sabbath, a day of rest devoted to the divine that allows one to reflect upon one's conduct during the rest of the week. "I had entered the orgy of Sabbath," she records in the aftermath of her encounter with the cockroach, adding that, in this state, "[o]ne enjoys the thing that things are made of" ("Eu entrara na orgia do sabath"; "[f]rui-se a coisa de que são feitas as coisas," 81). The contact with the real in the state of grace permits one to grasp the world at its clearest, since one is no longer bound by limitations or categorizations: "Beatitude begins the moment when the act of thinking frees itself from the need of form.... True incommensurability is the nothing, which has no barriers and is where one can spread one's thinking-feeling" ("A beatitude começa no momento em que o ato de pensar liberou-se da necessidade de forma.... A verdadeira incomensurabilidade é o nada, que não tem barreiras e é onde uma pessoa pode espraiar seu pensar-sentir," *Água Viva*, 72). The secularized beatitude found in the state of grace is made possible when we take a leaf out of the plants' and animals' book and learn that we must open ourselves to the world.[38] We realize that feeling and thinking are two correlated modes of processing the imprint reality leaves upon us.

Lispector mentions in *An Apprenticeship* that animals enter a state a grace more often than human beings. "Humans have obstacles that do not encumber the life of animals," writes the narrator, "such as reasoning,

logic, understanding.... [A]nimals have the splendor of what is direct and
directs itself directly" ("Os humanos tinham obstáculos que não dificul-
tavam a vida dos animais, como raciocínio, lógica, compreensão.... [O]s
animais tinham esplendidez daquilo que é direto e se dirige direto," 108).
Animals have a more unmediated approach to reality that makes it possible for them to bond with their surroundings. However, nonhumans
are unable to recognize that they are in a state of grace. The awareness
of this condition is a distinctive trait of human beings who are all the
more human the more they realize their possibilities of beatitude (108).

The state of grace envisioned by Lispector should not be confused
with inspiration, "a special grace that happens so often to those who deal
with art" ("uma graça especial que tantas vezes acontece aos que lidam
com arte," *Água Viva*, 70). "[A]fter the freedom of the state of grace the
freedom of imagination also happens," writes the protagonist of *Água
Viva*, but the aesthetic impulse does not originate in grace ("depois da
liberdade do estado de graça também acontece a liberdade da imag-
inação," 73). In fact, for the main character of *An Apprenticeship*, it is
fortunate that human beings do not fall into a state of grace too often,
since it precludes a shared language and, along with it, the arts: "[W]e
might definitively pass to the 'other side' of life, because that other side is
also real but no one would ever understand us: we would lose a common
language" ("[T]alvez passássemos definitivamente para o 'outro lado' da
vida, que esse outro lado também era real mas ninguém nos entenderia
jamais: perderíamos a linguagem em comum," 108–109).

For Lispector, human language always falls short of the state of
grace. G.H. writes in *The Passion* that there is an "abyss between the word
and what it was attempting [to reach]" and, later in the novel, reflects:
"The name is an addition, and it prevents the contact with the thing. The
name of the thing is an interval for the thing" ("abismo entre a palavra e
o que ela tentava [atingir]"; "O nome é um acréscimo, e impede o contato
com a coisa. O nome da coisa é um intervalo para a coisa," 53; 110). The
state of grace, when humans get in touch with primordial life, transpires
in the "silence that makes up life," the "inexpressive," since, in this beatific

condition, "talking to things is mute," that is to say, it happens without the mediation of language ("silêncio com que a vida se faz"; "inexpressivo"; "[f]alar com as coisas é mudo," *The Passion*, 73; 123; 126).[39]

What is, then, the role of writing and of literature in Lispector's existential thought? As the protagonist of *Água Viva* puts it, "Writing, then, is the mode of whoever has the word as a bait: the word fishing for what is not a word. When that non-word—the between-the-lines—takes the bait, something got written." "Once one has fished the between-the-lines, one could throw away the word with relief," she continues, only to add: "But the analogy ends here: by taking the bait, the non-word incorporated it" ("Então escrever é o modo de quem tem a palavra como isca: a palavra pescando o que não é palavra. Quando essa não palavra—a entrelinha—morde a isca, alguma coisa se escreveu. Uma vez que se pescou a entrelinha, poder-se-ia com alívio jogar a palavra fora. Mas aí cessa a analogia: a não palavra, ao morder a isca, incorporou-a," 19). Literature is an attempt to capture the ineffable, knowing full well that one will never be completely successful in this endeavor. A certain word or expression may manage to "bait" the real and articulate it in language but it is unable to replace what is in its immediacy. Words can hope, at most, to be contaminated by life, which engulfs, incorporates, and ultimately renders meaningless the language that strives to encompass it.

Before we write Lispector off as the ultimate anti-Derridean, striving for a mystic merging with a world above and beyond the triviality of language, though, we should pay closer attention to the fine grain of her prose. To be sure, she often expresses the belief that language is doomed to failure. G.H. writes, for instance, that "[i]t is precisely through the failure of the voice that one will hear for the first time one's own muteness and that of others and of things, and accept it as a possible language" ("É exatamente através do malogro da voz que se vai pela primeira vez ouvir a própria mudez e a dos outros e a das coisas, e aceitá-la como a possível linguagem," 137). It is worth reflecting upon the nuances of this statement. On the one hand, entering the state of grace and communing with the world around us demands a breakdown of the voice, understood not simply as vocalized speech but as the whole of human language. But, on the other hand, this collapse of vocalization refers merely to human expression and not to language as such. As G.H. puts it a little farther in the novel, "[t]he unsayable can only be given to me through the failure of *my* language" ("[o] indizível só me poderá ser dado através do fracasso de *minha* linguagem," 138; emphasis added). It is the language of humanity, imbued with our preconceptions, that prevents us from understanding "others and . . . things." We regard them as mute, passive beings at our disposal, because they do not share verbal communication with us. For G.H., then, the challenge is to interpret the muteness of others and to recognize it as a form of language we can also partake of.

In her reflections on language Lispector is addressing a distinction already outlined by Walter Benjamin in his 1916 essay "On Language as Such and on the Language of Man."[40] Benjamin argues that all beings and even things partake of language (72). Similar to the Brazilian writer, he saw verbal communication as only one possible mode of expression amongst the many other mute languages of the world. Still, he believed in the superiority of human language that was able to name things, establish relations between them, and therefore release them from their enforced muteness, a capacity that conferred upon humans the power to rule over the entire Creation (65).[41] As we have seen, Lispector is less sanguine about human language. Contrary to Benjamin, she deems verbalization to be often a hindrance, rather than an asset, preventing humanity from listening to the mute modes of nonhuman expression.

The final sentences of *The Passion* can be of help in shedding light upon Lispector's understanding of literature. The novel ends in an abrupt fashion, with G.H. considering the limitations of human language: "Then how could I say without the word lying for me? how will I be able to say if not timidly, thus: life is to me. Life is to me, and I do not understand what I say. And then I adore. — — — — — —" ("Pois como poderia eu dizer sem que a palavra mentisse por mim? como poderei dizer senão timidamente assim: a vida se me é. A vida se me é, e eu não entendo o que digo. E então adoro. — — — — — —," 141). The protagonist struggles with words that can lie and contrast with life's immanence and immediacy. The primordial life that she comes into contact with when she encounters the cockroach simply happens in/to and through her without words, at the breaking point of *logos*—"I do not understand what I say." The last words of the narrative, "I adore," denote a surrender to life, of which G.H. is in awe, and an abandonment of rational thought and verbal expression, signaled by the dashes.[42]

But Lispector, who wrote a number of novels, short stories, and journalistic texts, is not exactly advocating for an end to verbal language and to literature. "What am I?" she asks in one of her *crónicas* published in *Jornal do Brasil*. "I am a person who tried to put into words an unintelligible world and an impalpable world. Above all a person whose heart beats with an extremely light joy when she manages to say in a sentence something about human or animal life" ("O que sou então? . . . sou uma pessoa que pretendeu pôr em palavras um mundo ininteligível e um mundo impalpável. Sobretudo uma pessoa cujo coração bate de alegria levíssima quando consegue em uma frase dizer alguma coisa sobre a vida humana ou animal," *Aprendendo*). For Lispector, literature is a way to articulate the muteness of the world and to say the unsayable. "Sometimes—sometimes we ourselves express the inexpressive—one does this in art . . . to express the inexpressive is to create," writes G.H. ("Às vezes—às vezes nós mesmos manifestamos o inexpressivo—em arte se faz isso . . . manifestar o inexpressivo é criar," 112). Bordering on the ineffable, *The Passion According to G.H.*, as well as many of the writer's other texts, bears witness to literature's ability to push the boundaries of the unspeakable and to articulate the real in a language humans can understand.

Literature is a paradoxical institution. It is made by and for humans using a verbal language only they can grasp. But, at the same time, its utopian aspiration is to overcome the constraints of its human origins and to express what is beyond humanity. It is not by chance that plants and animals figure so prominently in Lispector's fiction. Faced with the double bind of literary language, she turns to nonhumans as her companions in the process of writing. In order to convey the muteness of the world, to go beyond human language and to articulate language as such, literature needs to include nonhumans and their modes of expression. In other words, it needs to become a zoophytographia. Plants and animals are embedded in Lispector's literary language, transforming it from within. The author's tendency toward impersonal grammatical constructions—"life is to me," "a vida se me é")—, her simple yet often utterly unexpected turns of phrase, her pervasive use of plant and animal metaphors, all reveal her efforts to incorporate the lives of nonhumans into her writing.

The first-person narrator of "The Egg and the Hen" writes that "[m]y mystery, that I am just a means and not an end, has given me the most malicious of freedoms: I am no fool, so I take advantage of it" ("O meu mistério que é eu ser apenas um meio, e não um fim, tem-me dado a mais maliciosa das liberdades: não sou boba e aproveito," 52). Inverting the famous Kantian dictum, Lispector finds that, in interspecies literature, the artist is a medium, akin to the figure of the genius so dear to Romanticist thought. However, she does not believe that her task as a writer is to mediate between god and humans, as the geniuses of old tried to do, and not even to be the medium through which different human voices are expressed. The heteroglossy she aims at is much more radical than the one Bakhtin identified as a key attribute of the novel ("Discourse," 271–73). The writer for her is a means—or a shaman— through which primordial life, flora and fauna articulate themselves in human language. She takes advantage of the freedom artistic creation affords to enunciate a utopian communion with plants and animals, both in life and in writing, that is to say, to craft a zoophytographia.

Toward the end of *The Passion*, G.H, makes a startling discovery, namely, that the state of grace is a permanent condition. "For the state of grace exists permanently: we are always saved. Everyone is in a state of grace.... [N]ow I know: the state of grace in inherent" ("Pois o estado de graça existe permanentemente: nós estamos sempre salvos. Todo o mundo está em estado de graça.... [A]gora eu sei: o estado de graça é inerente," 115). The nonhuman languages that come through in Lispector's texts echo the primordial life inside us and teach humanity that the state of grace, whereby we commune with the world around us, is always within reach. Even though we tend to regard humanity as permanently hovering between the hither side of being and the beyond, between beast and god, between fallenness and the state of grace—a wavering that is, in itself, the source of the artistic impulse in its multiple instantiations—zoophytographic literature reveals that this dichotomy is an obfuscation. Redemption is immanent; it has happened from the beginning of time or, to put it differently, there has never been a Fall, since we have always partaken of life's becoming. In this sense, Lispector merely highlights a quality of all literary texts: literature is always an interspecies undertaking, in that writing necessarily reveals the others within the human. This is how we should understand the epigraph of the present chapter, "I will not be autobiographical. I want to be bio" ("Não vou ser autobiográfica. Quero ser 'bio," 30), from *Água Viva*. "Autobiography" is a tautological word, in that writing, even fiction, always has the I as a point of departure. The utopian challenge of Lispector's literary praxis is to leave the self behind as her sole reference and to embrace the lives of others, to become *bio* or, better still, *zoe*, thus creating a zoophytographia.

4

Idling in the Tropics
Utopias of Leisure

[C]hama-se de Utopia o fenômeno social que faz marchar para
a frente a própria sociedade.
([T]he social phenomenon that makes society itself move forward
is called Utopia.)

                    —Oswald de Andrade, *A Marcha das Utopias*

Leisurely Golden Ages and the Ideology of Work

The fantasy of a past Golden Age of plenty, when human beings reaped
the bountiful produce of the land and enjoyed an easy, leisurely life
devoted to pleasurable pursuits, has long been a staple of the Western
worldview. In Ancient Greece, Hesiod described in his *Works and Days*
a "golden race of mortal men" who lived "like gods" off the abundant
fruit of the earth, "free from toil" and "merry with feasting" (II, 109–20).
Already in the Roman period, Ovid's *Metamorphoses* offered another
glimpse into the imagined primordial Golden Age of humanity, an era
when food "grew without cultivation" and "sometimes rivers of milk
flowed, sometimes streams of nectar, and golden honey trickled from
the green holm oak" (I, 89–112). Similar to Greco-Roman thought, the
Jewish tradition also posited a time without toil in the Book of Genesis,
when Eve and Adam roamed happily in the Garden of Eden, "eating
freely of every tree" (2:16). In all of these instances, the current state of

humanity is perceived as a fallen condition that demands hard work. Hesiod, for instance, is sorry to live in the Iron Age, when "men never rest from labor and sorrow" (II, 170–201). His praise of productive activity can only be understood in the context of a decadent humankind, whose only path to virtue is through exertion (II, 286–92). In Genesis, humans are evicted from paradise after the original sin and condemned to work for a living, eking their meager existence out of a cursed earth covered in "thorns" and "thistles" (3:18).

Given humanity's perceived fallen state, it is not surprising that literary writers and thinkers endeavored to return to the Golden Age. In his famous Eclogue IV, Roman poet Virgil dreamed of a new era of peace when toil would become unnecessary and agriculture redundant, as the land would once again provide enough sustenance for all without cultivation. Such a transposition of the Golden Age of humankind from an immemorial past to a time in the future would have momentous consequences for Western thought. Christianity adopted this temporal shift from a harmonious, bygone age to a peaceful and leisurely time to come in its various Millenarian movements and in Messianic thought, an example of which is the Kingdom of Christ that Antônio Vieira announces in his writings, analyzed in chapter 1. The Millennium stands for a thousand years of prosperity heralded by the coming of the Messiah, which will take place on earth and not in the distant Kingdom of Heaven. A secularized version of Millenarian beliefs, many utopias espouse a similar confidence in the advent of a more egalitarian and often more leisurely human society, mediated this time not by divine intervention but, rather, by human ingenuity, cooperation and more just sociopolitical institutions, an example of which would be the tribe of the Amazons we discussed in chapter 2.

From the Enlightenment period onward, when economic and material progress became entangled with the desire for moral advancement, and the drafting of blueprints for better functioning, socially engineered communities was the order of the day, authors often resorted to Golden Age myths so as to substantiate the possibility of creating a more perfect society. As Vincent Geoghegan shows, Left-leaning intellectuals were particularly adept at making use of conjectures about the past as both models and evidence for the anticipated establishment of a new Eden. Geoghegan is careful to point out that Marxist thinkers did not simplistically advocate a return to the olden days. Rather, they sought to incorporate some of the features of those earlier periods—the absence of private property being the most salient of these—in their projects for a communist society. At stake, therefore, was not regression but a judicious adaptation of old structures to the technical and economic conditions of Modernity, as we have seen in chapter 2 (79). An example of this trend can be found in Engels's *The Origin of the Family, Private Property and the State* (1884), which draws on Lewis H. Morgan's anthropological studies to describe the more egalitarian lifestyle of our ancestors, who only divided labor between the sexes according to the dictates of nature. With increased social differentiation, however, work started to be apportioned based upon a person's position in society, and the number of tasks most people had to perform greatly increased in order to allow for a new class of workless masters to thrive (150). This first watershed between exploiters and exploited was, for Engels, what communism would reverse by reviving the "*higher form of the liberty, equality and fraternity of the ancient gentes*" (Morgan, quoted by Engels, 164).

The vision of past communities sketched by many intellectuals often combined speculations about a Golden Age of humanity with the experience of real encounters with and studies of premodern societies in a continuum that extended from outright fabrication to rigorous anthropological research. Rousseau, for instance, based his idea that the "happiest and most durable" stage in human development took place right before the emergence of private property upon a largely conjectural projection of his social and political views onto prehistory. For Rousseau, humanity was destined to remain at that stage, the "real youth of the world" in which "most savages were found," and it was some "revolution" or "fatal accident" that removed us from this condition, an accident that "for the common good, should never have happened" (119).

Other authors ground their belief in the superiority of past societies upon the findings of anthropology. Marshall Sahlins uses anthropological data to define hunter-gatherer communities as the "original affluent society" (1). Far from leading the dismal life plagued with scarcity that is usually attributed to them, hunter-gatherers had few material needs and these were easily met with the supplies at hand without excessively strenuous work, their well-known prodigality testifying to their wealth and abundance of resources. Following in the line of Rousseau, Kent Flannery and Joyce Marcus have also relied on anthropological studies to correlate the increase in inequality with the development of agriculture, the rise of large empires, forced labor, and private property. These disparate authors share an implicit positive estimation of the more egalitarian existence in prehistoric communities and hint at the fact that contemporary society should strive to follow their example and adopt a simpler, less consumption-focused, more leisurely lifestyle.

As in the literary depictions of a Golden Age and in the theological positing of a Garden of Eden, more recent, anthropologically driven notions about prehistoric societies often convey value judgments on labor. The portrayals of a work-free Golden Age from the Greco-Roman period arose within a social context where many occupations were disparaged. In Ancient Greece, Plato seemed to recognize the need for labor and for a division of tasks among members of different social groups in *The Republic*, but, as he put it in *The Laws*, the citizens of the state should not engage in productive activities.[1] Aristotle was even more adamant in his condemnation of work. He viewed it as demeaning for citizens, whose primary occupation should be with political affairs. Being absorbed in guaranteeing the material conditions of existence was deemed an inferior enterprise that would prevent men—Aristotle was primarily concerned with male freedom—from pursuing a life of virtue beyond the so-called realm of necessity. Nevertheless, for Aristotle, a society without labor was a fanciful notion, only possible in fiction: "[I]f every tool could perform its own work when ordered... like the statues of Daedalus in the story... if thus shuttles wove and quills played harps of themselves, master-craftsmen would have no need of assistants and masters no need of slaves" (*Politics*, 1253b).[2] In the absence of instruments that labor by themselves, work was regarded as an unavoidable evil that should ideally be performed by servants, slaves, and women, leisure being reserved for citizens as a condition of possibility for freedom within the *polis*.

Aristotle's denigration of work and the understanding of leisure as a prerequisite for freedom and a virtuous life derived from his conception of humans as ontologically contemplative and not laboring beings, the absence of toil therefore becoming a sine qua non for human flourishing (Schippen 24–25).[3] As Josef Pieper shows, the Ancient Greek word for leisure, σχολή—from which the Latin *scola*, the Portuguese *escola*, the French *école*, the English *school*, and the German *Schule* derive—points toward the centrality of a work-free environment for the development of learning, reflexive thought, and philosophy, the ultimate goals of human existence (25–26). Being exempt from labor was therefore not a synonym of a passive existence. Rather, one could "do leisure" (*scholen agein*) in Ancient Greek, and the centrality of the concept was such that the language only expressed industriousness negatively as "not-leisure" (*a-scholé*), a formulation that was also used, *mutatis mutandis*, in the Latin *negotium*, the negation of leisure (Pieper 26).

The view of work as something eminently negative lies at the root of the word in many Romance languages. The Portuguese "trabalho"—as well as the Spanish *trabajo* or the French *travail*—derives from the Latin *tripalium*, the name for a torture device used throughout the Roman Empire, in particular to punish those unable to pay taxes. To work, then, was to perform tasks associated with the poor and with slaves, tortuous activities unfit for the true citizens of Rome.

Within the Christian tradition, Jesus preached the superiority of the lilies of the field in his Sermon on the Mount, because they "toil not, neither do they spin" and nevertheless—or perhaps because of it—display a beauty that humans can never hope to achieve. A *vita contemplativa* (contemplative life) without labor and dedicated to worshipping God was considered to be the highest form of human existence throughout the

Christian Middle Ages and the ultimate goal of monasticism (Pieper 27; 33). Even though work was not necessarily condemned, leisure was viewed by theologians such as Thomas Aquinas as a way for us to transcend our human condition and come closer to divinity (Pieper 33).[4]

The Western stance toward work began to change rapidly with the advent of the Reformation and, later, of the Industrial Revolution. Contrary to the prevalent view of a cloistered life of prayer and contemplation as the supreme human calling, Luther rejected monasticism as being too cut off from the world, and regarded most occupations—with the notable exceptions of trade, banking, and other activities related to the nascent capitalism of his time—as dignified forms of divine worship in their own right. Calvin went even farther and considered the profits resulting from trade and finance as signs of God's favor, as long as they resulted from diligence and hard work (Veal 20–21). Such views on labor were at the root of the link established by Max Weber in his well-known *The Protestant Ethic and the Spirit of Capitalism* (1905) between Protestantism and the values associated with a capitalist economic and social organization.

The Industrial Revolution that transformed European manufacturing from the eighteenth century onward also contributed to a valorization of labor as a key component of people's lives. Former farmers and craftsmen who had often followed irregular, task-oriented schedules had to be turned into a disciplined workforce ready to toil regularly for many hours a day performing monotonous and often strenuous jobs.[5] As E. P. Thompson pointed out, capitalism had to inculcate the importance of industriousness, the need to abide by the time of the clock, and time-thrift in the minds of workers, an ideological shift achieved through legislation, religious sermons, schooling, pamphlets, and so on (79–85). It was this concerted onslaught on the values of leisure and idleness that prompted Robert Louis Stevenson to write his "Apology for Idlers" (1877), where he criticizes diligence and "extreme business" as a "symptom of deficient vitality" and praises the existence of the idle as a form of resistance against the ethos of the day and the surest path not only to wisdom but also to mastering the "Art of Living" (48; 47).[6]

A critique of the work ideology also drove the Marxist take on industrial capitalism. Marx did not disapprove of labor as such, which he regarded as the essence of humanity. It is in and through work that we became human, the product of our labor being merely an objective reflection of this process. Capitalism, however, alienated work by an excessive division of labor, as well as by proletarians' lack of control over the means of production and over the goods produced. This separation of the worker from the product of her toil culminated in social alienation that could only be overcome in a communist, classless society, where workers would be in control of the entire production process.

While orthodox Marxism embraced the thesis that work functioned as the defining element of human life, taking issue only with alienated forms of labor, some leftist thinkers questioned the centrality of toil and linked it to capitalist exploitation. One of the most cogent critiques of a society of labor came from Marx's son-in-law Paul Lafargue in his "The Right to be Lazy." According to Lafargue, work had become a "dogma" and a "religion" that "contaminated" the proletariat (13; 16). Even though arduous toil was touted as a means to curb the vices of the poor, it was work itself that became a vice, leading to "pain, misery and corruption" (14; 17; 24). Abiding by the dictates of "Christian ethics, economic ethics and free-thought ethics," proletarians overworked themselves to a point where industrial crises of overproduction became inevitable and convulsed the entire social organism (24; 29). The result was that workers grew increasingly impoverished while capitalists were forced to overconsume and constantly look for new markets to sell their products.

Lafargue's solution to the problem involved two distinct measures that resonate with many debates on work and leisure today. He believed that, on the one hand, it is necessary to raise wages and to diminish working hours in order to force capitalists to improve factory machines that should, in the future, perform most of the hard labor (47).[7] On the other hand, the proletariat must renounce their "blind, perverse and murderous passion for work," "return to its natural instincts," and "proclaim the Rights of Laziness, a thousand times more noble and more sacred than the anaemic Rights of Man concocted by the metaphysical lawyers of the bourgeois revolutions" (29; 31). Lafargue ended his text with an exhortation to laziness that, in contrast to work, is regarded as the true human essence: "O Laziness, have pity on our long misery! O Laziness, mother of the arts and noble virtues, be thou the balm of human anguish!" (57).

Following in the footsteps of Lafargue, many later authors have condemned the work ideology that dominates capitalist society and praised leisure, idleness, and play as the hallmarks of humanity. Joffre Dumazedier, for instance, was confident that, in the second half of the twentieth century, industrialized countries were entering a stage of social development during which leisure would play an increasingly important role, and Josef Pieper goes as far as regarding leisure to be the foundation of all culture. Johan Huizinga proposes that "civilization arises and unfolds in and as play," which he identifies as the basis of law, literature, art, and philosophy (ix). In fact, in the 1960s and '70s, the leisure society thesis, according to which we would be in the process of transitioning away from a society of work, gained ground in sociological circles, as the mechanization of production and the reduction of the work week contributed to an increase in free time for most employees in industrialized nations. However, the dream of a society of leisure did not come to pass. The restructuring of world economy from the 1980s onward under the banner of neoliberalism, deregulation of job markets, and the outsourcing of work, thanks to a rapid process of economic globalization, resulted in growing labor instability in the West, an increase in part-time and fixed-term labor contracts, and a general erosion of workers' rights such as occupational welfare and paid vacations (Rojek 21). As Juliet Schor points out, the average American worked longer in the 1990s than in the 1950s, with labor time steadily increasing since the 1960s (1–6).

Still, some authors have predicted a drastic overhaul of work fueled by the digital age. In his *The End of Work*, Jeremy Rifkin argues that, while the previous mechanization of production replaced the physical power of human labor, new information and communication technologies are substituting for the human mind itself (3). He foresees that automated machinery and sophisticated computers can potentially perform up to 75 percent of the tasks now carried out by the labor force in industrial nations (5). "The idea of a society not based on work is so utterly alien to any notion we have about how to organize large numbers of people into a social whole," writes Rifkin, "that we are faced with the prospect of having to rethink the very basis of the social contract" (12). Since human societies and human beings have been, for as long as we can remember, determined by the ways they engage in productive activities, the absence of mass formal employment will be, for Rifkin, the "seminal issue of the coming age" (235–36). He suggests, somewhat idealistically, a turn to volunteering and community service—the so-called third sector—as a means to solve the problem of mass unemployment and to offer people a meaningful occupation freed from the pressures of the marketplace.[8]

Resonating with Rifkin's predictions of the end of labor as we know it, Ulrich Beck has also identified stable work as one of the casualties of the "neo-liberal free market utopia" that marked the passage from the first to the second Modernity, a time during which smart technologies are ousting people from paid employment. Significantly for the purposes of this chapter, Beck believes that insecurity and risk have been the steady companions of work in the global South, a tendency that is now spreading to (North-) Western societies: "The social structure in the heartlands of the West is thus coming to resemble the patchwork quilt of the South, characterized by diversity, unclarity and insecurity in people's work and life" (12–13). He describes this trend as the "Brazilianization of the West," Brazil being, in his view, a country where those who have regular waged jobs are a minority. For Beck, this is tantamount to a reversal, whereby supposedly premodern nations with their informal labor practices "reflect back the future of the so-called 'late-modern' countries of the Western core" (210).

The shift implied in Beck's Brazilianization thesis not only undoes a neat understanding of the world in terms of core and periphery but, more importantly, also signifies a broader upending of the commonplace linear view of historical progress as moving from less to more developed societies, from more informal to more stable lifestyles. But is the Brazilianization of the West a simple regression from more to less affluence and social well-being? Although Beck regards the end of the work society and the emergence of a society of risk as inevitable, the consequences of this development are yet to be fully fleshed out. The new regime certainly condemns workers to insecurity but this flexibility can potentially "be converted into a blossoming of social creativity" (164). The unbinding of old class, gender, and other hierarchies that structured the first wave of Modernity opens the possibility for a "concrete utopia of a political civil society" and may spell out "anew the original idea of politics and democracy" (164). In other words, the Brazilianization of the West does not necessarily mean a world of jobless people leading aimless, destitute lives. Rather, it can be regarded as an opportunity for the creation of a more open, "multi-activity society in which housework, family work, club work and voluntary work are prized alongside paid work" (280). For Beck, as for Rifkin, the end of rigid work models will mean more civil labor, political engagement, and a stronger civil society that will pave the way to pluralistic national and transnational communities grounded upon political freedom. Far from being seen as outdated models to be overcome by the triumphant march of progress, the social arrangements of the global South, and of Brazil in particular, point toward a more pliable social structure to be developed in the rest of the world.

Beck recognizes that his Brazilianization of the West thesis runs the risk of reproducing stereotypes and of renewing "through negative inversion, the romantic image that Westerners tend to have of Brazil" (211). But even though his broad-strokes portrayal of Brazilian social and economic features does often smack of Eurocentrism,[9] the association of the country to informality, flexibility, and, above all, to a ductile approach to organized, formal work and its rules has strong roots in the Brazilian cultural tradition that we will explore in this chapter.

From the texts of early European colonizers, who represented South American lands as an earthly paradise of plenty where the need for work was obviated by the abundance of nature, to the writings of twentieth-century authors, who formulated their conception of Brazilian identity around the figure of the idle *malandro*, Brazil has consistently been regarded as a utopian land of leisure, the laid-back mindset of its inhabitants contrasting sharply with the industrious spirit of both Europe and the United States. Brazilian thinkers such as Oswald de Andrade, Antônio Cândido, or Roberto da Matta believed that these features contributed to making the country less rigid in its societal structures, more open to play and artistic pursuits, and, ultimately, more hospitable to social experimentation. In the rest of this chapter, we will revisit some of the utopias of leisure that have taken shape throughout the history of Brazil and consider how these are indebted to and distinguish themselves from the European visions of a work-free Golden Age and Garden of Eden, on the one hand, and respond to the increasing pressure of the Industrial Age to impose a capitalist work ideology throughout the world, on the other. In embracing leisure, idleness, and even laziness, Brazilians intellectuals saw themselves at the forefront of a social revolution and construed the carefree, laid-back lifestyle of their society as an archetype for a future world civilization.

But before we delve into the different contours of Brazil's utopias of worklessness, it is worth noting that free time, leisure, idleness, and laziness, though often employed interchangeably in this chapter, cannot be conflated as synonymous. Free time is a loose notion that refers to the moments when one is not engaged in working or in other occupations necessary for subsistence. The concept of leisure as we use it today, in turn, is a product of industrial capitalism and arose in tandem with the growing relevance of formal, mass employment that followed the time of the clock. Leisure studies focus primarily on hobbies and other activities performed outside of work time, as a way to develop skills and interests that are denied outlet at work.[10] Nichole Schippen put forth the notion of discretionary time as an alternative to both free time and leisure. Discretionary time, she argues, "helps highlight the relevance of individuals having control over their time for developing and exercising autonomy, or more specifically 'temporal autonomy,'" and thus moves beyond the logic of production and consumption that limits the other two terms (18–19). Still, discretionary time refers primarily to a situational juncture: one can have or not have such time, a condition that does not determine a person's essence.

Free time, leisure, and, I would add, discretionary time "remain negatively imprisoned in the value imperialism of work" and, therefore, cannot function as linchpins for a critique of the work society (Beck 22). Labor has been regarded, with a few exceptions, as the measure of a human being's worth at least since the Industrial Revolution, and "only those things which are proven and recognized to be work count as valuable" (Beck 22). As Beck pointedly states, "[a]ny vision worthy of the name must therefore cast off this spell of work, and begin by breaking the taboo on any antithesis to the work society" (27). This is Lafargue's end goal when he pits the ideology of work against the "right to be lazy." Contrary to free time and leisure, idleness and, especially, laziness stand for a complete negation of work, instead of constituting its necessary supplements. They are ontological conditions, rather than transient states. The negative connotations of both terms speak to the power that the ideology of work wields in Modernity. What is at stake in the praise of a workless life by Brazilians is precisely the ontological dimension that elevates idleness and laziness to an existential condition and an identity trait. Taking up a stereotypical image of Brazil cultivated by foreigners and often deployed to denigrate the country, Brazilian intellectuals highlight its utopian, redemptive features and present it as a state of grace that others can only hope to emulate.

Leisure and Labor in Paradise

As we have seen in the previous two chapters, the first Europeans to arrive in the New World were persuaded that they had reached an earthly paradise, where nature was bountiful and the local inhabitants amiable. Sérgio Buarque de Holanda analyzes in detail the influence of Edenic motives on the early colonization of South America in his *Vision of Paradise*

(*Visão do Paraíso*, 1959). For Holanda, the Medieval belief in the concrete existence of paradise, situated at a recondite earthly location—a paradise travelers incessantly looked for and cartographers placed in different geographic areas on the outskirts of the known world—materialized in South American territory. The lush environment and the warm climate of the new continent, different from the often-arid European landscapes, contributed to cementing the conviction of early explorers that they had reached the Garden of Eden (x–xi).

In the case of Brazil, the paradisiac elements of the land already feature prominently in Pêro Vaz de Caminha's Letter to the Portuguese King discussed in chapter 3. Caminha mentions some staple traits of paradise, such as the abundance of natural resources, which made the labor of agriculture unnecessary. "The brook," writes Caminha, "has plenty of very good water. Along it are many palms, not too high, where one can find very good hearts of palm. We plucked and ate many of them" ("[A] ribeira, a qual é de muita água e muito boa. Ao longo dela há muitas palmas, não muito altas, em que há muito bons palmitos. Colhemos e comemos deles muitos"). Farther on, he comments: "[G]iven that the trees are plenty and large and of many shapes, I do not doubt that there are many birds throughout the land!" ("[S]egundo os arvoredos são muitos e grandes, e de infindas maneiras, não duvido que por esse sertão haja muitas aves!"). His overall conclusion is that the land has a very good climate ("bons ares"), is beautiful ("formosa") and gracious ("graciosa"). The inhabitants of such a blessed environment have no need to exert themselves in order to procure sustenance: "They [the indigenous population the Portuguese encountered] do not till the soil nor do they raise cattle. There are no bulls, cows, goats, sheep, chicken, nor any other animal used to the life of men" ("Eles não lavram, nem criam. Não há aqui boi, nem vaca, nem cabra, nem ovelha, nem galinha, nem qualquer outra alimária, que costumada seja ao viver dos homens"). Instead, they eat yam "and the seeds and fruit of the land and the trees" ("e dessa semente e frutos, que a terra e as árvores de si lançam"). Caminha realizes the advantages of such food, as "their [the Native Brazilians'] bodies are as clean, plump and beautiful as can be" ("os corpos seus são tão limpos, tão gordos e tão formosos, que não pode mais ser") and favorably compares the Brazilian to the Portuguese diet, in one of the several moments of cultural relativism that made the letter famous: "And with this [nourishment] they are stronger and stouter than us, despite the wheat and vegetables we eat" ("E com isto andam tais e tão rijos e tão nédios, que o não somos nós tanto, com quanto trigo e legumes comemos").

Given that they do not have to engage in farming and cattle raising, Native Brazilians spend a lot of their time "dancing and relaxing" ("dançando e folgando"). Caminha notes at several points in the letter how they rested, had fun, and, on a given day, how, "while they were there, they danced and swirled always with our own men … in a manner that shows that they are much more our friends than we are theirs" ("enquanto ali andaram, dançaram e bailaram sempre com os nossos … em maneira que são muito mais nossos amigos que nós seus"). As in the Garden of Eden, where Eve and Adam could easily pluck their food from every tree, and in the Greco-Roman legends of the Golden Age, when labor was unnecessary and humans could devote themselves to idleness, Caminha paints a portrait of Native Brazilians as inhabiting a paradise of plenty and leading a carefree existence. This auspicious environment made them more lighthearted and trusting than the Europeans who had to work hard for a living. In spite of his cultural bias, which makes him, at points, depict the indigenous population with childish features, Caminha cannot help but let his admiration for their leisurely way of life, which diverges so drastically from the European mindset, come through in his Letter.

The representation of Native Brazilians as idlers became a mainstay in descriptions of the country's indigenous population both by settlers and by other European intellectuals. Published eight decades after Caminha drafted his Letter, Montaigne's "Of Cannibals," part of his *Essays*, repeated many of the tropes already mentioned in the Portuguese's text. Montaigne's goal was to refute the accusation leveled against Brazilian Indians of being savage and barbaric because they resorted to ritualistic cannibalism. Not only did he relativize these charges, arguing that we tend to deem inhuman those practices that differ from our own, but he also mounted a spirited defense of Native Brazilians, who, in his opinion, still retained the virtue of simplicity that had been lost in Europe.[11] Quoting Seneca, he calls them "men fresh from the gods," whose customs derive directly from nature. He praises their "very pleasant and temperate" country and notes that people are rarely sick over there and do not suffer from the physical ailments that afflict the Europeans.[12]

More importantly for the argument of this chapter, Montaigne directly links the Native Brazilian way of life to that of the Classical Golden Age: "[W]hat we now see in those nations, does not only surpass all the pictures with which the poets have adorned the golden age, and all their inventions in feigning a happy state of man, but, moreover, the fancy and even the wish and desire of philosophy itself." He goes on to remark that indigenous society is kept with "little artifice," as they have "no manner of traffic [trade], no knowledge of letters, no science of numbers...; no...riches or poverty...no properties, *no employments, but those of leisure... no agriculture*, no metal, no use of corn or wine" [my emphasis] and adds, a little farther down the text, that their "whole day is spent in dancing." Native Brazilians, like the fortunate inhabitants of the mythical Golden Age, led a life of leisure and dance, agriculture and other forms of toil being unnecessary for their simple and natural existence.

The leisure that, according to Europeans, characterized indigenous Brazilian culture, was not unanimously praised as a positive feature. While early authors such as Caminha and Montaigne viewed the idleness of indigenous peoples as a sign of superiority vis-à-vis their Old Word counterparts, fated to incessant toil in order to meet basic needs, others came to regard these leisurely ways as evidence of sloth, one of the seven deadly sins. As the need for slave labor intensified with the establishment of large plantations in Brazil, most notably of sugar cane, settlers forcefully removed Indians from their villages to work in the fields. Concurrently, efforts to evangelize South America meant that religious orders strove to persuade the country's indigenous inhabitants to adopt European customs. The famous dispute between Jesuit Priest Antônio Vieira and the colonizers of Maranhão about the fate of the enslaved indigenous population, which we discussed in chapter 1, revealed two visions of Native Brazilians that shared a common root. While the Maranhão landowners wanted to employ them as slaves, Vieira believed they should live in villages organized by the Jesuits and work in exchange for a salary. Beyond the obvious power struggle between secular and religious authorities, the conflict uncovers a shared understanding of the need to bring the "idle Indians" into the fold of colonizer society with its nascent capitalist work ideology.

The conception of Brazilian Indians as living in a prelapsarian state outside historical time, which contributed to their association with the Golden Age and the Garden of Eden, gradually gave way to the idea that they stood in the way of progress and civilization. Unaccustomed to large-scale, sedentary agriculture, Indians made for a poor workforce (Brookshaw 2) and were soon replaced by Africans as the main source of slave labor. Still, the notion that indigenous villages, which lay outside the sphere of Portuguese political power, were places of darkness, associated with pagan practices and a lazy, devilish way of life, spread after the first decades of colonization. As David Brookshaw points out, Eden no longer lay in nature, now regarded as perilous and satanic, and salvation required the move to European towns and to religious missions that would evangelize the native population (20).

The Jesuits in particular created a network of missions spread throughout the area that is now Paraguay, Northeastern Argentina, and Brazil, where Indians were brought to live and learn the ways of Catholicism. Their time was divided between agricultural work, together with other activities necessary to meet the everyday needs of the community, and religious teachings and prayer (Brookshaw 20). There is no consensus about the effects of Jesuit missions on native populations. On the one hand, they prevented mass enslavement and extermination at the hands of settlers but, on the other hand, they profoundly disrupted Indian cultures by imposing upon them a foreign belief and a harsh labor regime. The Society of Jesus, which was becoming a parallel power rivaling that of the monarchy, was removed from the Portuguese Empire by the king's prime minister in 1757 and finally expelled from the country in 1773 (Brookshaw 22). But the legacy of the Jesuit missions remained in the cultural memory of Brazil as a symbol of a rural Arcadia. This nostalgic appreciation of native existence no longer centers on a wild and bountiful environment that allowed for a toil-free life but on an agrarian utopia, where nature is tamed and ordered by virtue of indigenous labor (Brookshaw 21).

Throughout the history of Brazil, the perceived indigenous idleness was subject to widely divergent interpretations. Early explorers saw in it proof that the New World was either akin or amounted to the real location of the Biblical paradise, a place where humans did not have to work as all needs were provided for by a bounteous nature. This spatial identification of the country with paradise was complemented by the notion that the leisurely ways of the Indians stood for a turn back in time, to a Golden Age when humanity was free from labor and could dedicate itself exclusively to pleasurable pursuits. But the utopia of native leisure soon began to be condemned as laziness with the advancement of colonization and the evangelization of the land. Jesuit missions provided a new model for Indian life, predicated on agricultural work and religious worship. The dichotomy leisure/labor, then, has not only reflected changing attitudes toward the Brazilian native population but also Brazilian intellectuals' and other Europeans' projections of utopian social arrangements onto the New World.

Brazilian Romanticism, which recovered the Indian as one of the pillars of national identity, harked back nostalgically to the missions as an Arcadia that could provide a blueprint for a utopian Brazilian rural society. But the vision of the Indian as a fiercely independent noble savage, free from the constraints of work and living in tune with wilderness, remained as an even more powerful trope in Brazilian letters. As the Modernist movement rose to prominence in the country's cultural milieu, the scales decisively tipped in favor of an idealized image of the

idling Indian, who challenged the work ethics of the developing industrial society burgeoning in the nation's large metropolises.

A New World of Rest: *Ócio* vs *Negócio*

The first words the audience hears from the indigenous protagonist
Macunaíma (Grande Otelo) in Joaquim Pedro de Andrade's homonymous 1969 film are "Oh! what laziness!" ("Ai! que preguiça!").
The exclamation is a *leitmotif* both of the movie and of Mário de
Andrade's 1928 novel, upon which the film is based. Macunaíma, characterized by the narrator in the first few words of Andrade's text as the
"hero of our people" ("herói de nossa gente"), is a consummate idler,
who takes pleasure in watching others work while he whiles his time
away resting in a hammock.[13] As mentioned in chapter 2, Andrade was
a member of the irreverent Modernist movement that came together in
the 1920s in the city of São Paulo and strove to renew Brazilian culture
and society by freeing it from undue foreign influences. The hailing of the
lazy Macunaíma as the hero of all Brazilians has a clear satirical intent.
Andrade is following a strategy also adopted by his friend Oswald de
Andrade in his renowned "Anthropophagous Manifesto" ("Manifesto
Antropófago," 1928), namely, that of taking up negative stereotypes about
Brazil and presenting them in a new light. The idleness often attributed
to the country's indigenous population by national and foreign intellectuals and condemned as an impediment to economic and social progress
is here regarded as a positive trait. Macunaíma is considered the "hero of
our people" not simply because he stands for the distillation of a national
feature, common to all Brazilians. Rather, his heroic status stems from
his example as a model of idleness, a trait that Brazilians should be proud
of, embrace, and consciously cultivate.

But Andrade's positing of Macunaíma as a hero has even farther-
reaching consequences. The novel's lazy protagonist belies the bourgeois
morality of São Paulo's upper and middle classes, which endeavored to
bring European and North American-style capitalism, with its attendant

values of time-thrift and industriousness, to Brazil's large cities. For Andrade, then, Macunaíma stands for his country's difference vis-à-vis other, richer, and more industrialized nations. Far from advocating the bridging of the gap between Brazil and its more developed counterparts in the North, Andrade suggests through his idle hero that this rift should be deepened. Such a stance goes beyond the Modernist refusal to emulate foreign tendencies. It points in the direction of an alternative conception of Modernity, at the forefront of which we find the leisurely life of native Brazilian Indians.

Oswald de Andrade will lend philosophical and historical credence to Mário de Andrade's literary vision of idleness as Brazil's contribution to a more just and egalitarian future world. When we discussed his take on matriarchy and utopia in chapter 2, we hinted at the fact that, for Oswald de Andrade, civilization is moving toward a renewed, classless, and communitarian society. He pits the leisure allowed "in the easy fields of the matriarchal jungle" against the patriarchal business ethos prevalent in his day ("ócio da selva," "Marcha," 164; "na seara fácil da selva matriarcal," "Matriarcado," 209). For him, the fact that the Portuguese word for business, *negócio* (from the Latin *neg-otium*), is formed by the negation of leisure or idleness, *ócio* (from the Latin *otium*), signals that the business-as-usual work mentality of the capitalist world is at odds both with the primeval *ócio* of Brazilian indigenous communities and with the new *ócio* of a future utopian world.[14]

According to Andrade, history unfolds in the move from the first to the second coming of *ócio*. "For me," he writes, "there is only one leisure and the whole of humanity is marching toward it" ("Para mim o ócio é um só e para ele caminha toda a humanidade," "Marcha," 193). But the move toward the age of *ócio* is mediated by a dark period of work that coincided with the development of capitalism and exploitation—the time of *negócio*. Such an understanding of Western history explains why the utopias of the Renaissance, triggered by the encounter of Europeans with the idle "natural man" (*"homem natural,"* "Achado," 210) of South America, systematically advocated for hard work. "It is a prophetic paradox," writes Andrade, "that the discovery of the leisurely man of the

American jungle brought to light and to action the great intents of social organization and of work" ("É um paradox profético esse de ter a descoberta do homem ocioso da selva Americana trazido à luz e à ação grandes propósitos de organização social e de trabalho," "Marcha," 160). Labor plays a key role in the communitarian utopian states imagined by More or Campanella because work was necessary at their particular stage of sociopolitical and economic development. It is as if the two utopian writers understood that "only through technical conquests and through human labor would a later Re-conquest of the leisure for which man was born be possible" ("somente através das conquistas da técnica e do trabalho humano, fosse possível, mais tarde, a Reconquista do ócio para que o homem nasceu," "Marcha," 160). In order to achieve "that life on the hammock that is, after all, the general human preoccupation" ("essa vida de rede que afinal é a geral preocupação humana"), humanity had to live through a "long and sweaty path of social inequality, elevated to a dogma during the Reformation" ("longo e suarento caminho da desigualdade social, elevado a dogma pela Reforma," "Marcha," 194). It is, therefore, dialectically through *negócio*, key for technological development, that human beings will be able finally to enter a time of *ócio*.

Andrade argues that Brazil played and will continue to play a pivotal role in the advent of the new age of *ócio*. The nation was "the prophecy and the utopian horizon of leisure" ("a profecia e o horizonte utópico do ócio," "Marcha," 193), sowing the egalitarian ideals of idleness of which Native Brazilians were living proof in the hearts and minds of the citizens of the Old World. The very history of the country is regarded as a faceoff between the forces of leisure and those of industriousness. For instance, Andrade interprets the victory of the faction loyal to Portugal in the "utopian war" waged against the invading Dutch forces in Brazil (in the late sixteenth and early seventeenth centuries) as a triumph of "a playful and amiable understanding of life that contrasted with a utilitarian and business-oriented concept" ("guerra utópica"; "uma compreensão lúdica e amável da vida, em face dum conceito utilitário e comerciante," "Marcha," 182; 184). The very miscegenation that took place in the country, where the idle indigenous mixed with immigrants of European and African stock, is regarded as a sign of the nation's superiority: "[W]e Brazilians, champions of miscegenation both of race and of culture ... are a concretized utopia in the face of the mercenary and mechanic utilitarianism of the north" ("[N]ós brasileiros, campeões da miscigenação tanto da raça como da cultura ... somos a utopia realizada, bem ou mal, em face do utilitarismo mercenário e mecânico do Norte," "Marcha," 153). Brazil's resistance to becoming a society of work indicates its place at the forefront of a march toward the imminent world civilization of *ócio*.

How will the new utopian age of leisure come about? And what will it look like? In his answer to these questions, Andrade replays some of the reasoning already adduced by nineteenth-century socialists and anarchists, including Paul Lafargue. Remaining true to dialectics, he believes that "the world of work, thanks to technology and human progress, passes its social burden on to the machine and tries to fulfill on earth the leisure promised by religions in heaven" ("o mundo do trabalho, graças à técnica e ao progresso humano, passa os encargos sociais para a máquina e procura realizar na terra o ócio prometido pelas religiões no céu," "Filosofia Messiânica," 127). It is, therefore, through much suffering and hard toil that humankind conquered the right to leisure, achieved by virtue of technological progress that frees human beings from strenuous tasks and affords them the freedom to dedicate themselves to more rewarding activities such as artistic pursuits, as we will discuss below. Andrade anticipates here the conviction that a coming society of leisure made possible by the mechanization of the means of production is about to materialize, an idea that, as we have seen, gained in popularity in social scientific circles in the 1970s and was later revived by authors such as Rifkin and Beck in the aftermath of the digital revolution. "It is the sharing of leisure to which every man born of a woman has the right," Andrade writes, "[a]nd the common ideal will henceforth be that of retirement, which is the metaphysics of leisure" ("É a partilha do ócio a que todo homem nascido de mulher tem direito. E o ideal comum passa a ser a aposentadoria, que é a metafísica do ócio," "Filosofia Messiânica," 83). The toil-free human life in an age of *ócio* will be tantamount to the Messianic dream of heaven achieved on earth and democratically available to all.

Andrade never spells out the specific place Brazil will occupy in the future era of leisure. Given that it carried the torch of *ócio* throughout the grim era of business, it is probable that the country will be one of the nations at the forefront of the social revolution that will soon transform the world. Also, if humankind is about to "leave its condition of slavery and cross again the threshold of the Age of Leisure," ("[o homem] deixa a sua condição de escravo e penetra de novo no limiar da Idade do Ócio," "Filosofia Messiânica," 83), the Brazilian past of slavery should make the coming time of idleness all the more meaningful. In fact, Andrade's hailing of the Indian as the symbol of a Golden Age of idleness, to which humans are about to return thanks to technology, tends to bracket African slaves from Brazil's past and leave them out of the country's racial identity. Such a blatant sidelining of a large segment of the population has deep roots in the nation's intellectual history. As we mentioned above, it had already begun in colonial times, when African slaves were deemed more fit for work than Indians, and continued with Romanticism, which conceived the mix of indigenous peoples and European colonizers as the foundation for modern Brazilian society, leaving Africans outside the picture. Andrade's utopian age of leisure could potentially redress this wrong by promising *ócio* to all, including those who have traditionally been marginalized both in terms of actual labor conditions and with regard to the country's self-image.[15] Be this as it may, Andrade was persuaded that Brazil was perfectly positioned to lead the rest of the world by example, away from *negócio* and into a time of *ócio*. In the following section, we will see how the Brazilian traits of cordiality and social flexibility render the country particularly apt for ushering in a more egalitarian, leisurely society.

Between Order and Disorder:
From the Cordial Man to the *Malandro* Slacker

In a short text published in 1950 and titled "An Anthropophagic Aspect of Brazilian Culture: The Cordial Man" ("Um Aspecto Antropofágico da

Cultura Brasileira: O Homem Cordial"), Oswald de Andrade identifies alterity, or "the feeling of the other" ("o sentimento do outro," 141), as one of the key features of the leisurely Indian. For Andrade, the empathy of the "cordial man" toward other members of the group is not only characteristic of the indigenous population but has also become a prominent trait of Brazilian culture as a whole. He sets the cordial person against the individualistic worldview of societies predicated on egoism and private property—the values of *negócio*—where the ties that bind the members of the community have all but disappeared. As we enter the new age of leisure, he foresees a return to the values of cordiality that have been forgotten in industrialized nations ("Homem Cordial," 143–44).

Andrade draws the idea of the "cordial man" as the epitome of Brazilianness from Sérgio Buarque de Holanda's 1936 study *Roots of Brazil* (*Raízes do Brasil*). In this book, Holanda analyzes the development of the country from colonial times onward, signaling the ways in which key historical circumstances have contributed to shaping its collective character and culture. When he discusses the traits of Iberian societies that would later be transposed onto South America, he underscores the "invincible repulsion that all morality grounded upon the cult of work has always inspired in them" ("invencível repulsa que sempre lhes inspirou toda moral fundada no culto ao trabalho," 38). He goes on to add that "amongst Hispanic people, the modern religion of work and the value of utilitarian activity was never naturalized" ("jamais se tenha naturalizado entre gente hispânica a moderna religião do trabalho e o apreço à atividade utilitária," 38). For the Portuguese, a "dignified idleness" always seemed to be much more of a mark of excellence than the "senseless fight for our daily bread," and the "morality of work" was always an "exotic fruit" ("digna ociosidade"; "a luta insana pelo pão de cada dia"; "moral do trabalho... fruto exótico," 38; 39). It follows that the colonization of Brazil was primarily the result of an adventurous impulse, and not of steady hard work, which explains why talent and intelligence are valued more highly than strenuous effort and labor in the nation (44–45; 82–83). What Holanda is hinting at is that, beyond the lazy indigenous population, the Portuguese, one of the other matrixes of Brazilian racial and cultural identity, were likewise prone to idleness.[16]

The Portuguese dislike of work went hand in hand with their aversion to economic virtues. They praised wealth and material goods but, at the same time, also favored prodigality and lavish behavior. Formal economic relations based upon legally binding contracts were less relevant than personal ties of friendship (133–37). For Holanda, they had a "certain, one would say congenital, incapacity for making any form of impersonal and mechanical organization prevail over relations of an organic and communal character, like the ones based upon kinship, ties of neighborhood and friendship" ("certa incapacidade, que se diria congênita, de fazer prevalecer qualquer forma de ordenação impessoal e mecânica sobre as relações de carácter orgânico e communal, como o são as que se fundam no parentesco, na vizinhança e na amizade," 137). Holanda believes the Portuguese tendency toward idleness and their reluctance to abide by general rules that go beyond informal social ties established among family and friends formed the basis for the Brazilian "cordial man."

While intellectuals such as Ribeiro Couto approvingly identified cordiality as the main Brazilian contribution to world civilization, Holanda is more ambiguous in his discussion of the "cordial man" (146). For him, the origins of cordiality go back to a strong patriarchal family that prevents the development of independent individuals and of a well-structured civil society. He rejects the usual understanding of the term as politeness and good manners and sees it as an "organization of defense against society," a "disguise that allows each person to preserve intact their sensibility and emotions" ("organização de defesa ante a sociedade"; "um disfarce que permitirá a cada qual preservar intata sua sensibilidade e suas emoções," 147). Cordiality is therefore an outward manifestation of the inability to abide by social norms. It creates the illusion that a community is composed exclusively of friends and acquaintances, which would make societal regulations redundant. Given that all forms of sociality are based upon sentiment, at the national level confusion reigns between the private and the public spheres, even among those who hold public office (144–49). Furthermore, solidarity and social unity depend upon feeling and not upon a sense of common purpose or interest (39).

Holanda concludes about cordiality: "The private life of Brazilians is neither cohesive nor disciplined enough to envelop and dominate their personality, integrating it as a conscious piece of the social whole" ("A vida íntima do brasileiro nem é bastante coesa, nem bastante disciplinada, para envolver e dominar toda a sua personalidade, intergrando-a, como peça consciente, no conjunto social," 151). The predisposition toward idleness and the inability to behave with impartiality in business dealings can be explained by this lack of social discipline. Still, cordiality is not devoid of positive aspects. Holanda ends his chapter on the subject by pointing out that the cordial man is "free … to abandon himself to the complete repertoire of ideas, gestures and forms that he may find along his path, often assimilating them without major difficulties" ("livre … para se abandonar a todo o repertório de idéias, gestos e formas que encontre em seu caminho, assimilando-os freqüentemente sem maiores dificul-dades," 151). He does not elaborate any further upon the advantages of the cordial man's adaptability to different customs and environments, leaving it up to the reader to speculate about the implications of such qualities in a colonial and postcolonial setting. Antônio Cândido will take up Holanda's reflections to foreground precisely this element of the Brazilian collective psyche in his discussion of the country's identity traits and highlight its advantages in an open world society.

Cândido's best known foray into the intricacies of the Brazilian national character can be found in his essay "Dialectics of *Malandragem*" ("Dialética da Malandragem"), first published in 1970. The word *malan-dragem*—which I will use in the Portuguese original throughout this chapter—can be translated into English in a variety of ways, includ-ing "trickery," "cunning," or "idleness," and the *malandro*, the one who practices or engages in *malandragem*, is the English "trickster," "crook," "scoundrel," "idler," "slacker," or "layabout," depending on the con-text. The polysemy of the two words already reveals their centrality in Brazilian culture: they agglutinate several related notions while preserving the vagueness that is part and parcel of the concept. Cândido's approach to the topic was to choose the novel *Memoirs of a Militia Sergeant* (*Memórias de um Sargento de Milícias*, 1952–53) by Manuel Antônio de Almeida as the point of departure for his analysis of the term, the narrative's protagonist representing, in his view, "the first great *malandro* who enters the Brazilian tradition of the novel" ("o primeiro grande malandro que entra na tradição novelística brasileira," 25).

For Cândido, the roots of the literary *malandro* go back to the picaresque heroes of Iberian fiction. However, the Brazilian character distinguishes itself from its predecessors in several important ways. First, while the picaresque hero lets go of scruples out of necessity, being a *malando* is an ontological condition: one is born *malandro*, rather than turned into one by the circumstances (22). Second, the main character of the picaresque novel often works as a servant for the rich and powerful, while the *malandro* tends to be idle and survive through a variety of ploys and maneuvers that involve avoiding labor at all costs (22). Cândido teases out the implications of these divergences between the two literary figures: unlike the picaresque hero, the *malandro* is a typically Brazilian creation. He sees the lazy Macunaíma, the protagonist of Mário de Andrade's narrative discussed in the previous section, as an inheritor of the *malandro* tradition that began with Almeida's novel and can be found in many literary works, as well as, more broadly, as a central feature of Brazilian culture and society (25–26).[17]

The *malandro* inhabits a world that wavers between order and disorder. According to Cândido, the upper classes in Brazil live in an orderly environment where everyone abides by the rule of law, whereas the lower classes correspond to the sphere of disorder. The *malandro* oscillates between these two poles in a constant, broken dialectical movement without sublation. The circulation between order and disorder results in an absence of moral judgment that renders meaningless the conventional distinctions between good and evil, creating "a universe that appears to be free from the weight of mistakes and of sin," in other words, "a universe without culpability and even without repression" ("um universo que parece liberto do peso do erro e do pecado"; "[u]m universo sem culpabilidade e mesmo sem repressão," 47). "We glimpse," writes Cândido, "a land without definitive or irremediable evils, ruled by a charming moral neutrality" ("uma terra sem males definitivos ou irremediáveis, regida por uma encantadora neutralidade moral," 53).

Cândido correlates the moral indeterminacy of the *malandro* to his equivocal relationship toward work. While those who form part of orderly society have stable, well-paid jobs, the ones belonging to the domain of disorder are either criminals who make their living by engaging in illegal activities or, at the time when Almeida wrote his novel, slaves forced to toil for others. It is as if Cândido is unwittingly espousing the strict labor ethics of Protestantism that equated moral uprightness with organized work. "In the parasitic and indolent society of [poor] free men in Brazil at the time," people lived off "the brutality of slave labor" ("Na sociedade parasitária e indolente, que era a dos homens-livres do Brasil de então"; "brutalidade do trabalho escravo," 53–54), and the *malandros* occupied an in-between position "idling hither and thither, harvesting the remains of parasitism, of scams, of donations, of luck or of petty theft" ("flauteavam ao Deus dará, colhendo as sobras do parasitismo, dos expedientes, das munificências, da sorte ou do roubo miúdo," 44–45). In other words, the *malandro* does not have a steady job but neither is he a slave nor does he engage in full-fledged criminal enterprises. He survives in a "universe without guilt," where *"one does not work, but one also does not experience need,* everything can be remedied" ("universo sem culpa"; *"não se trabalha, não se passa necessidade, tudo se remedeia,"* 53; my emphasis). The idling *malandro* envisioned by Cândido is thus reminiscent of the lazy, carefree indigenous population described by early colonizers and explorers, of the archetypical Indian portrayed by Modernist writers as a symbol of *ócio,* as well as of the work-averse "cordial man." He lives in a state (of precarious) grace where regular social norms have been suspended or, rather, he occupies a limbo in which these rules do not apply and playfully exploits the loopholes inherent in the dialectics of order and disorder.

The relaxed, leisurely lifestyle of the *malandro,* which represents the quintessentially Brazilian way of being-in-the-world, generated a society where regulations are lax, and so can be easily bent to accommodate different customs and traditions. "Not wishing to create a homogeneous group and, consequently, not needing to defend it rigidly, Brazilian society opened itself more broadly to the penetration of dominated or foreign communities. And it gained in flexibility what it lost in integrity and coherence" ("Não querendo construir um grupo homogêneo e, em consequência, não precisando defendê-lo asperamente, a sociedade brasileira se abriu com maior larqueza à penetração dos grupos dominados ou estranhos. E ganhou em flexibilidade o que perdeu em inteireza e coerência," 51).[18] Cândido contrasts Brazil to the United States, where, in his view, the strict rule of law dehumanizes the relations between people who belong to different communities and easily alienates those considered to be pariahs, as illustrated in Nathaniel Hawthorne's masterpiece *The Scarlet Letter* (1850) (50).

In contrast to the rigidity of American morality, Brazilians have a flexible, often irreverent approach to authority and the law, which allows them to joke about and subvert society's strictest rules. For Cândido, this attitude "blunts sharp corners and gives way to all sorts of accommodations (or negations) that sometimes make us look inferior before a vision that is stupidly nourished from puritan values, like the one of capitalist societies; but it will facilitate our insertion into an open world to come" ("amaina as quinas e dá lugar a toda sorte de acomodações [ou negações], que por vezes nos fazem parecer inferiores ante uma visão estupidamente nutrida de valores puritanos, como a das sociedades capitalistas; mas que facilitará a nossa insersão num mundo eventualmente aberto," 53). As did Holanda before him, Cândido emphasizes Brazilians' ability to adjust to and to incorporate different habits into the country's *modus vivendi*, in contrast to the austere, puritan values of capitalist societies that exclude alternative viewpoints.[19]

In his comments on the notion of the *malandro*, Roberto Schwarz speculates about the contours of the "open world" mentioned in the quote above, which Cândido does not further elaborate upon. Schwarz suggests that the expression might refer to a coming postbourgeois, socialist society and buttresses his interpretation by referring to the fact that "Dialectics of *Malandragem*" was most likely written in the late 1960s, during the so-called "lead years" ("anos de chumbo"), or the most repressive period of the Brazilian Military Dictatorship (1964–1985) (Schwarz 150; 152). "[T]he claim of the dialectics of *malandragem* against the spirit of capitalism," writes Schwarz, "is perhaps a response to the brutal modernization that was underway" during the dictatorship, whose goal was to bring industrial capitalism to Brazil, no matter the social, environmental, or other costs ("[A] reivindicação da dialética da malandragem contra o espírito do capitalism talvez seja uma resposta à brutal modernização que estava em curso," 154).

The modes of conviviality of the poor where *malandragem* originated would, consequently, stand for an alternative view of Brazilian society, meant as a form of resistance against the unilateral vision of the country's destiny that the dictatorship was trying to impose.[20] If Cândido's "open world" was indeed an allusion to a future socialism, such a society would differ significantly from the ones of historical socialist countries such as the USSR, which depended upon the dignity of work for their conception of postproletarian classless nations. Cândido's utopian, postbourgeois world would, rather, approximate Oswald de Andrade's universe of *ócio*, a community of tolerance and leisure, the foundations of which would extend back to the sociability of the *malandro* slacker. In the next section, we will turn to a possible instantiation of the permissive, idle world without guilt of Cândido's *malandro* in our discussion of Carnival.

Idling in a State of Exception: Carnival

The suspension of orderly society culminates in Brazil in the celebration of Carnival. During this period, we witness an inversion of regular habits and forms of behavior that put into question political, economic, gender, and other norms of the day: the pauper behaves as a prince, the poor act like the rich, women dress as men, and so on. Much has been written about the subversive potential of such inversions, as well as about their ultimately reactionary function.[21] For if Carnival's abolition of customary hierarchies offers a foretaste of a universe where each person can freely fashion her- or himself as they please, the end of the festivities means a return to established mores. The Carnivalesque world-upside-down is revealed as nothing more than a means for those at the bottom of the social ladder to come to terms with their oppression, knowing that, in a year's time, they will again have a chance to experience, even if in the make-believe fleeting situation of Carnival parades and balls, how it feels to belong to the club of the rich and powerful. According to this view, then, the function of Carnival is to bolster the status quo by staging a mock revolution that will ultimately serve to forestall real social change.

We will skirt, for now, the hotly debated issue of the emancipatory and/or conservative social function of Carnival and focus instead on its relationship to work and idleness. Like all other "national rituals," ("rituais nacionais," 36), as anthropologist Roberto da Matta calls them in his landmark study *Carnivals, Malandros and Heroes* (*Carnavais, Malandros e Heróis*, 1979), Carnival always implies an "abandonment or 'forgetting' of work" ("um abandono ou 'esquecimento' do trabalho," 36), "demanding a kind of special, empty time, that is to say, without work, a holiday" ("exigindo um tipo de tempo especial, vazio, isto é, sem trabalho, um feriado," 41). Contrary to festivities such as military parades or religious processions, however, Carnival is not only celebrated on days officially exempt from work but, more importantly for our argument, it is also the celebration *of worklessness*.

For Matta, the idle *malandro* is a symbol of the Carnavalesque spirit. "[T]o create a 'Carnival' basically means to try and fulfill the role of a *malandro*," someone "fatally excluded from the job market, that is to say, someone defined by us as totally averse to work" ("criar um 'carnaval' significa basicamente procurar desempenhar o papel de malandro"; "fatalmente excluído do mercado de trabalho, aliás definido por nós como totalmente avesso ao trabalho," 204). The *malandro* relativizes all "laws, regulations, codes and moralities that stifle the individual without noble birth in the yoke of work" ("leis, regulamentos, códigos e moralidades que sufocam o indivíduo sem berço no jugo do trabalho," 214) and adopts a "life of idleness" ("vida de 'sombra e água fresca,'" 206). His rejection of the work ideology complements the Carnivalesque subversion of ordinary circumstances and is an intrinsic part of the social anomie created by Carnival.

For Matta, as for Cândido before him, the *malandro* occupies the interstitial spaces of society, the grey areas where "it is difficult to say what is right and wrong, fair and unfair" ("é difícil dizer onde está o certo e o errado, o justo e o injusto," 214). He "does not completely renounce order but also does not belong to complete marginality. His choice... is the intermediary sphere, that zone of inconsistencies [...]" ("não renuncia completamente à ordem, mas também não fica na plena marginalidade. Sua escolha... é da esfera intermediária, aquela zona das inconsistências [...]," 234–35). Matta places the *malandro* in between two other Brazilian heroes: the *caxias*, a stickler for order who stands for legality and authority and who is linked to the festivities surrounding military parades; and the *renunciador*, a Messianic figure who lives on the margins of the established society he wishes to overhaul in order to institute a Millenarian kingdom and who is associated to religious processions (203). Of these three archetypal characters, only the *malandro* displays an innate aversion to work that characterizes not just his particular loose ethical stance but also the very unraveling of morality that takes place during Carnival.[22]

Matta identifies two salient characteristics of Carnivalesque *malandragem* that chime in with our discussion of idleness. First, the main activity of the Carnival's *malandro* is *play*, in Portuguese *brincar*, a verb whose etymology goes back to the Latin word *vinculum*, that is to say, "bond," "link," or "tie." In Brazil, one "plays" Carnival, which points toward "getting together, suspending the borders that individualize and compartmentalize groups, categories and people" ("unir-se, suspender as fronteiras que individualizam e compartimentalizam grupos, categorias e pessoas," 49), in tune with the term *brincar*'s original meaning. *Fantasies* (*fantasias*)—a word that in Portuguese stands both for "dream" or "reverie," and for "costume," both for an imagined scenario and for its materialization—fulfill a key function in *playing* Carnival, in that they "create a social field of encounter, of mediation and of social polysemy" ("um campo social de encontro, de mediação e de polissemia social," 49). Carnivalesque *fantasies* produce a cosmopolitan, open society that contrasts with the rigid hierarchy of Brazilian social structure (49). Matta concludes that "the world of Carnival is the world of conjunction, of license, of *joking*; that is to say, the world of metaphor" ("o mundo do Carnaval é o mundo da conjunção, da licença e do *joking*; vale dizer, o mundo da metáfora," 49). Play, fantasy, and metaphor take us to the domain of the imagination, where things are never quite what they seem and we give free rein to our inventiveness. In the workless sphere of Carnival, unrestrained by the fetters of often mind-numbing labor, the playful *malandro* experiments both with new social constellations and with an artistic approach to life, according to which the world is dramatized in song and dance (112–13). As toil recedes intro the background, the boundaries between life and art loosen, until the one merges with the other. We shall return to this point in the conclusion to this chapter, in our discussion of playfulness as an intrinsic part of leisure.

A second significant feature of Carnival for our consideration of idleness is that the Carnivalesque *malandro* dwells fully in the present, unlike the *caxias*, who is bound to rules inherited from the past, and the *renunciador*, who has his eyes exclusively on a Millenarian future (233–34). "Only the *malandro*," writes Matta, "lives off the present, uses the present and, thus, connects the past to the future" ("É somente o malandro . . . que vive do presente, usa do presente e, assim, liga o passado com o futuro," 233). Carnival's focus on the present moment is indebted to its moratorium on norms and its reversal of ordinary frameworks that engender a quasi-enchanted world of freedom and fantasy. Carnival brackets regular life outside it and thereby allows for play and the enactment of alternative identities and social structures.

By halting the cogs' predetermined movement in the machinery of time and opening a free realm of experimentation, Carnival institutes a state of exception, a space-time of anomie, where the usual rules and laws do not apply. Theorists of the state of exception, from jurist Carl Schmitt to philosopher Giorgio Agamben, have defined it both as a suspension of legality and as the foundation for any system of law: the anomic place outside the law from which a sovereign power institutes a legal system.[23] For Agamben, the grounding of the law in the state of exception and of sovereignty in anomie comes to light in periodic feasts such as Carnival "that are characterized by unbridled license and the suspension and over-turning of normal legal and social hierarchies" (*State*, 71). The periods of "legal anarchy" reveal "in a parodic form the anomie within the law, the state of emergency as the anomic drive contained in the very heart of the *nomos*" (*State*, 72). Carnivalesque celebrations dramatize the "irreducible ambiguity of juridical systems," that is to say, the fact that they depend upon an anomic state of exception as the basis for legality (*State*, 73).

Agamben's theorization of Carnival as a parodic re-presentation of the paradoxes inherent in modern legal systems holds only up to a point, though. For, if the state of exception is the groundless, anomic point of departure for a sovereign power's institution of the law, its Carnivalesque parody lacks any such sovereign moment. The beginning of Carnival is lost in the anonymous mass of the people participating in the celebrations and it does not produce a unified leader who would point toward the reinstitution of the status quo once the festivities have come to a close. In other words, Carnivalesque play is anarchy without any sovereign *arché*; it is an end in itself that completely eschews the logic of the *nomos* and is, as a result, fully divorced from regular sociopolitical power. Or, if we want, it is a state of exception where each participant is sovereign, creating her own rules of behavior within a generalized social anomie.

Perhaps it would be fruitful to consider Carnival under the double lens of an anarchic state of exception without sovereignty, as well as of inoperativeness, a notion Agamben develops in his more recent work. Inoperativeness stands for a pause that interrupts and brings to a halt the regular days of work. In the Jewish tradition, it culminates in the Sabbath, and its modern Christian version would be the day of rest on Sunday (*Kingdom*, 239). Agamben traces the history of the concept from Aristotle's claim that man was born workless, *argon* (*a+ergon*; literally, "without work" in Ancient Greek), through the Fathers of the Church's dream of an eternal Sabbath, the notion with which Augustine ends his *City of God*, to philosophical takes on repose, such as Spinoza's idea that inoperativeness is the greatest freedom and joy of human beings, because it allows them to contemplate their own potentiality for acting (Agamben, *Kingdom*, 239–42; 250–51). For Agamben, inoperativeness is not a synonym of inertia or inactivity. Rather, it connotes perfection, the final condition of human beings once they have reached, in theological terms, a state of blessedness after the Final Judgment. He regards the feast as one possible example of inoperativeness: it is eating performed not to nourish the body but out of sheer pleasure. The excess of the feast makes food unproductive and turns it into a celebration of its uselessness (*Seminar*).

Even though he does not discuss Carnival in the context of inoperativeness, one could extend Agamben's arguments to encompass Carnivalesque festivities. For one, Carnival makes the whole of society inoperative, not only because it is a time without work but, more importantly, because its festivities take place in the domain of fantasy, imagination, and make-believe, and are performed—indeed, are themselves a performance—with the sole aim of enjoyment, beyond the productive rationale of means and ends. The inoperativeness of Carnivalesque celebrations is, hence, another name for *ócio*, the animated rest or workless activity that is the opposite of *negócio*. Secondly, Agamben considers play and art as two secular instantiations of inoperativeness, when humans put their bodies and minds to unproductive uses (*Seminar*). Carnival's playfulness, then, is a sign of its inoperativeness, as are the artistic manifestations of Carnivalesque play, such as song and dance.

It is in Carnival's inoperativeness, in its "creative and free" universe of useless activity, more than in the reversal of established hierarchies, that lies its true subversive potential ("criativo e livre," Matta 204). The celebrations allow us to imagine a utopian sphere of inoperative play that is considered "madness" under the parameters of the work ideology ("loucura," Matta 68). As Matta points out, Carnival mirrors our society;

however, this reproduction is neither direct nor automatic but, rather, dialectic. The festivities show that another world is possible, that "society can change," and that the idle, lighthearted, inoperative life of the *malandro* might one day be available for all ("sociedade pode mudar," Matta 68). And that is why, when faced with Carnivalesque *malandragem*, we are "filled with hope" ("encher-se de esperança," Matta 68).

A Leisurely Sexual Haven

From the idle Indians to the *malandro* slacker, from the coming time of *ócio* to the playful Carnival, leisure has always been linked to a loosening of sexual boundaries, if not to outright promiscuity. Caminha mentioned in his Letter to the King that none of the Indians, men or women, could be bothered to cover their genitals, something that must have greatly impressed the Portuguese, as he refers to this custom several times throughout the text. The lack of modesty and the sexual availability of indigenous women, in particular, would become a staple of European stereotypes about Native Americans for most of the colonial period. Centuries later, Cândido also mentions permissive sexuality as a trait of the *malandro* behavior. In the social sphere of *malandragem* "there were twenty love affairs for each marriage and a thousand one-night-stands for each love affair" ("vinte mancebias a cada casamento e mil uniões fortuitas a cada mancebia," 44). The lazy *malandro* Macunaíma in Mário de Andrade's novel, a parodic precursor of a future time of *ócio*, is notorious for his lasciviousness, constantly preying on unsuspecting women, including the wives of his brothers. And debauchery has become tied to the imaginary of Carnival, not only because of widespread cross-dressing but also due to the erotic potential of scantily clad revelers dancing the night away in the streets. Whence the link between leisure and sexuality? What does idleness have to do with sexual liberation?

Freudian psychoanalysis and variations on its original theory have dwelled at length upon the correlation between sexuality, work, and civilization. For Freud, the human body as a whole is originally sexualized in all its activities and relationships. However, this eroticized body, entirely delivered to the sexual instinct, resists any form of labor. In the words of Herbert Marcuse, who has dealt with the implications of Freudian theory for social organization, the fully sexualized body is "unproductive in the deepest sense: unproductive for the alienated productivity that is the motor of cultural progress" (*Five Lectures*, 11). Freud insists that the sexual instinct had to be repressed and channeled into nonsexual pursuits such as work through a process of sublimation in order for humans to prevail over harsh surroundings. The violent repression of the sexual instinct, then, finds its justification in the difficult conditions humanity had to face in the process of its development: "Freud sees in the repression of the instincts [especially the sexual instinct] a cultural and a natural necessity: scarcity, the struggle for existence, and the anarchical character of the instinct place limits on freedom which cannot be trespassed" (*Five Lectures*, 23). As Marcuse points out, "[b]ecause men are too weak and the human environment too poor and cruel, the denial and suppression of instincts became from the beginning fundamental conditions of all the unpleasurable work, the denials and renunciations that ... make the progress of civilization at all possible" (Marcuse, *Five*, 33). In a nutshell, instinctual freedom had to be curtailed in order for progress to take place and for culture to flourish.

Civilization requires directing the original, polymorphous sexual instinct into genital sexuality that aims at the reproduction of family structures and into productive labor: "In limiting Eros to the partial function of sexuality ... the individual becomes, *in his very nature*, the subject-object of socially useful labor" (Marcuse, *Five Lectures*, 11).[24] The process of civilization, therefore, runs counter to human pleasure in the fulfillment of our instincts and to the freedom to do so, which are subordinated to social goals (Marcuse, *Five Lectures*, 34–35).[25] For Freud, this is a "traumatic wound, a disease that culture has inflicted on man" and that causes "growing anxiety and 'discontent with civilization'" (Marcuse, *Five Lectures*, 23–24). But, even though Freud recognizes the downside of sexual repression, he does not envision a solution to this quandary, except for a therapeutic reduction of blockages that impede the drives in the case of severe neurosis. Instinctual repression and domination are, for him, "the internal logic of the development of civilization" (Marcuse, *Five Lectures*, 11). He believes that de-repression and de-sublimation would mean a regression to a disorganized world of instantaneous gratification of the instincts: "Instinctual liberation ... would explode civilization itself, since the latter is sustained only through renunciation and work (labor)—in other words, through the repressive utilization of instinctual energy. Freed from these constraints, man would exist without work and without order; he would fall back into nature, which would destroy culture" (Marcuse, *Eros*, 175).

Going back to the Brazilian case, Freud would regard the leisurely indigenous as an example of nonsublimated instinctual existence. He would probably concur with reactionary detractors of the Indians, who saw in their aversion to work a sign of uncivilized customs, but would, at the same time, regard their freedom from repression as a more pleasurable way of life than that of civilized humanity. Processed through the Freudian apparatus of interpretation, both the lazy debauchery of the *malandro* and the idle eroticism of Carnival would be nothing more than regressions from civilization to barbarism, soon to be overcome by the reinstatement of orderly society, of sexual boundaries, family values, and the ideology of work.[26] The *malandro* and the period of Carnivalesque festivities would stand as nothing more than nostalgic reminders of a time of generalized, free eroticism, when the human body was not regarded as an instrument for labor but, rather, as the locus for the free fulfillment of instincts. According to this reading, *malandragem* and Carnival celebrations would be just interregna—pockets of resistance or, in the context of generalized repression, interludes to blow off steam—in the inexorable progress toward increasing heights of civilization.

While Marcuse agrees with Freud's verdict on the need to limit instinctual freedom "to the extent that it makes possible the ascent from a human animal to a human being, from nature to civilization," he asks: "does it remain rational when civilization has developed completely?"

(*Five Lectures*, 12). In answering this question, he follows two possible lines of inquiry. First, he suggests that, even though repression may have been necessary in order to overcome scarcity, humankind has reached a level of development where it has become superfluous. Marcuse's argumentation here is reminiscent of Oswald de Andrade's take on the opposition between the world of *negócio* and the coming time of *ócio*. The former was needed at earlier stages of human evolution, but the moment has arrived for it to give way to a more leisurely life. Similarly, Marcuse contends that "the repressive modification of the instincts ... has its quite definite limit. This becomes apparent after instinctual repression and progress have fulfilled their historical function and mastered the condition of human impotence and the scarcity of goods, and when a free society for all has become a real possibility" (*Five Lectures*, 39).[27] Once labor has been largely mechanized, and humans no longer have to engage in a daily struggle for existence, society reaches a tipping point, where "[t]he achievements of repressive progress herald the abolition of the repressive principle of progress itself" (Marcuse, *Five Lectures*, 39). "It would no longer be the case," writes Marcuse, "that time spent in alienated labor occupied the major portion of life and the free time left to the individual for the gratification of his own needs was a mere remainder. Instead, alienated labor time would not only be reduced to a minimum but would disappear and life would consist of free time" (*Five Lectures*, 39).[28] With the need for labor obviated, all instincts, including the sexual instinct, could be freed from the dams of repression channeling them into work and given their full expression in a society of leisure.

What would such a nonrepressive society look like? Marcuse portrays this utopian social order in the following way: "No longer used as a fulltime instrument of labor, the body would be resexualized. ... [It] would become ... a thing to be enjoyed—an instrument of pleasure. This change ... would lead to a disintegration of the institutions in which the private interpersonal relations have been organized, particularly the monogamic and patriarchal family" (*Eros*, 201). Marcuse is well aware of the fact that, by advocating for a free Eros in the context of a libidinous civilization, where the entire human body would again be sexualized, he would invite the accusation of wishing to create "a society of sex maniacs—that is, . . . no society" (*Eros*, 201). He defends his position by pointing out that the liberation of sexual instincts would allow for the recovery of energy used for alienated labor "and its release for the fulfillment of the autonomously developing needs of individuals" (*Five Lectures*, 4). Instead of a relapse into barbarism, this move would "not destroy the 'spiritualized' manifestations of human energy but rather take them as projects for and possibilities of happy satisfaction" (*Five Lectures*, 4–5). In more concrete terms, the release of eroticism from the clutches of repression would not entail a complete de-sublimation but the ability to direct one's instinctual energy into more pleasurable, fulfilling pursuits than repetitive work, such as cultural and artistic creation. The result would be a higher form of civilization, in which all would have the leisure and the freedom to dedicate themselves to the activities that afford them the greatest enjoyment.[29] The future world of *ócio* postulated by Oswald de Andrade coincides with such a community, where idleness would not betoken a negative condition but the possibility for free experimentation, as the difference between sexual and intellectual pleasure would all but disappear.

Marcuse also proposes a slightly different answer to the question of the relation between repression and civilization. Not only does he argue, as we have seen, that repression becomes unnecessary after humanity has surpassed a certain threshold of progress, but he also speculates on the possibility that, contrary to the Freudian theory of instinctual repression, civilizational development can thrive without the repression of sexual instincts. He points out that "[t]he traumatic transformation of the organism into an instrument of alienated labor is *not* the psychic condition of civilization as such but only of civilization as domination," which would open the possibility for thinking about another kind of civilization that would not depend upon instinctual domination (*Five Lectures*, 20). This idle, unrepressed, eroticized society would not arise *only after* a certain technological level had been reached but, rather, it would be the condition of possibility for any free civilization. For Marcuse, then, the leisurely life of Native Brazilians would qualify as an example of a social arrangement, in which work and leisure are not determined by repression and domination.[30] Indian communities would be the instantiations of an unrepressed civilization, where sexual pleasure is not divorced from but integral to everyday activities.

A corollary to this line of thought, according to Marcuse, is that, perhaps, all forms of civilization are grounded upon liberated sexual instincts. What if "[t]he *work* that has contributed so essentially to the development of man from animal is *originally libidinous*"? What if "[m]an begins working because he finds pleasure in work, not only after work, pleasure in the play of his faculties and the fulfillment of his life needs, not as a means of life but as life itself"? (*Five Lectures*, 20). If this is the case, Marcuse concludes, "[c]ivilization arises from pleasure: we must hold fast to this thesis in all its provocativeness" (*Five Lectures*, 19). Such a thesis would have far-reaching implications for the relation between labor and sexuality, between work and worklessness.

Marcuse envisions a society in which the aesthetic-erotic dimension takes center stage, a "possible society in which work becomes play . . . in which even socially necessary labor can be organized in harmony with the liberated, genuine needs of men" (*Five Lectures*, 68). Human beings do not need to be compelled to work when labor is the "free play of human abilities," that is, when there is a "convergence of technology and art and the convergence of work and play" (*Five Lectures*, 68). This work would be free from the values of productiveness and performance, in the same way as "play is unproductive and useless precisely because it cancels the repressive and exploitative traits of labor and leisure; it 'just plays' with the reality" (Marcuse, *Eros*, 195). To put it differently, work would become, like play, an end in itself, the result of a pleasurable impulse. If labor is driven by the energy of sexual instincts and can, indeed, be pleasurable, then the distinction between civilizational work and *aesthe-sis*—the capacity for feeling through the senses, and the basis for artistic experience—collapses. In an eroticized, libidinal civilization, *to work* and the *work of art* become one and the same thing, an aestheticized mode of being that is, for Marcuse, the authentic goal of human life, "the only mode of existence worthy of man" (*Five Lectures*, 42).

The idle *malandro* libertine, who stands for a release from the strictures of moral codes and the work ethics implicit in them, represents a nondomineering approach to civilization. This figure can be interpreted as an incarnation of free sexual instincts in a workless, artistic society of leisure. Thinking in terms of a dialectics of *malandragem* that moves between order and disorder would no longer make sense, in that orderly and disorderly conduct, the world of labor and the world of play, become one and the same. The *malandro*, usually viewed as lazy in terms of the parameters established by a work ideology, heralds a time when these distinctions have already been erased. By the same token, the eroticized costumes, singing, and dancing typical of Carnival can be regarded as an outcome of liberated sexual instincts that have opened the path to artistic creativity, to a union between art and life.

Idleness and Art

The imbrication of worklessness, play, and art is a central element in Brazilian utopias of leisure. Oswald de Andrade, for instance, establishes a parallel between religion and art, based upon their common root in *ócio*. If the sacredness of religion can be traced back to leisurely activities that eschew the everyday routine designed to guarantee the necessary ingredients for living—the Portuguese word for "priesthood," *sacerdócio*, is a combination of the Latin terms *sacer* and *otium*, meaning "sacred leisure" [31]—artistic impulses, at their inception deeply embedded in religious practices, are also predicated upon idleness. In a secular world, art becomes emancipated from cult while keeping its link to leisure and, to a certain extent, its sacred character that Walter Benjamin famously called "aura." For Andrade, human beings' "innate laziness," is the "mother of fantasy, of invention," and the ultimate source of art ("preguiça inata";

"mãe da fantasia, da invenção," "Filosofia Messiânica," 83). The coming
society of leisure will therefore be a new "playful world" of creativity, in
which "over the Faber, the Viator and the Sapiens, Homo Ludens will
then prevail." ("mundo lúdico," "Filosofia Messiânica," 127; "sobre a [*sic*]
Faber, o Viator e o Sapiens, prevalecerá então o Homo Ludens," "Filosofia
Messiânica," 83). The "playful instinct" will dominate the new age of
ócio, when work dissolves into pleasurable, artistic activities and human
beings occupy themselves not with trite pursuits but with "sacred" artistic
endeavors ("instinto lúdico," "Filosofia Messiânica," 83).

Andrade inherits a long tradition of Western thought in his reflections on the coming creative age of *ócio*. Most notably Friedrich Schiller,
in his *Letters on the Aesthetic Education of Man* (1795), had already
identified in the aesthetic realm the ultimate goal of humanity. Even
though Schiller does not draw an explicit connection between leisure
and art, he accuses "necessity" and "utility" of being the idols of his age,
condemning human beings to a life of drudgery and suppressing their
sensibility (26; 36–37). He finds a solution to this grim state of affairs
in the "play impulse," which is another name for the aesthetic drive. For
him, the artistic sphere is where humans are free, since it is a "joyous realm
of play," independent of need and emancipated from moral judgments,
that focuses solely on what is enjoyable, in other words, the opposite of
mindless toil (137). Furthermore, art is not only a precondition for freedom but also a great equalizer, since aesthetic pleasure can be enjoyed
by all, and so "fulfills the ideal of equality" (140).

Writing almost a century after Schiller, Oscar Wilde reiterates the
German writer's praise of art over enforced labor in his essay *The Soul
of Man under Socialism* (1891). For Wilde, "[i]t is mentally and morally
injurious to man to do anything in which he does not find pleasure, and
many forms of labor are quite pleasureless activities." Touching upon a
point reiterated by thinkers from Lafargue to Andrade, Wilde believes
that "all monotonous, dull labor, all labor that deals with dreadful things,
and involves unpleasant conditions, must be done by machinery," while
the individual is only "to make what is beautiful." For Wilde, then,

humanity should be "amusing itself, or enjoying cultivated leisure—which, and not labor, is the aim of man—or making beautiful things, or reading beautiful things, or simply contemplating the world with admiration and delight." Aesthetics, not the ethics of work, is human beings' true calling.

From the twentieth century onward, the belief in a utopian time of leisure when humans can devote themselves to the arts or, differently put, when there is no distinction between work and play, labor and aesthetics, has become a staple of progressive thought. Marcuse's psychoanalytic approach, discussed above, is one possible avenue into the topic. Others have followed a more overtly political route. Jacques Rancière elaborates on what he calls the "distribution of the sensible," the aesthetic grounds upon which social and political decisions are based. Given that society depends upon our subjective and aesthetic—in the original sense of *aesthesis*, as sense—understanding of reality, any real political change implies an artistic transformation of the ways in which we experience the world. Serge Latouche, one of the foremost advocates of the de-growth movement, also highlights the positive political consequences of a less consumerist society, more attuned to art than to incessant labor. In a de-growth world, "the pleasure of leisure and the ethos of play should replace the obsession with work" (34), and human beings will be free to explore their artistic inclinations without the constant pressure to produce more goods.

How do Brazilian utopias of leisure fit into these various approaches to art? What can the emphasis on idleness and even laziness, so prevalent in the country's self-image, add to contemporary reflections on a future leisurely and artistic human civilization?

For the first chroniclers who described the customs of Native Brazilians, such as Caminha or Montaigne, as well as for later Brazilian thinkers like Andrade, Cândido, or Matta, the leisurely ways of the region's population were always tied to artistic sensibility. Indians were routinely depicted as engaging in song and dance, the same being true, centuries later, for the *malandro* and, in general, for Carnival revelers.

The drive toward play, *brincar*, is consistently portrayed as stronger than the urge to labor, which demarcates Brazil from other nations hostage to a work ideology stifling their creativity. If art is a great equalizer, as Schiller would have it, making humans free and independent from moral judgments, then salient tropes of Brazilian culture such as *malandragem* and Carnivalesque celebrations certainly stand for a freer society, in which economic and social hierarchies crumble in a relaxed, playful environment. For Brazilian intellectuals, the propensity toward playfulness is interpreted as a sign of the nation's difference, a positive marker of its joyful, artistic bent. A Brazilianization of the West, then, would entail not only a more informal approach to work and idleness but, most of all, placing the arts center stage, following the Brazilian lead into a utopian, leisurely world to come.

Epilogue

The Country of the Future

> Here the world's labyrinth and the heart's paradise become visible discretely; the world in the *focus imaginarius*, in the more hidden, intelligible part of our subjectivity, begins to appear as hope for the future.
>
> —Ernst Bloch, *The Spirit of Utopia*

IN THIS BOOK, we have revisited key facets of utopian thought as it developed throughout Brazilian history. We began by addressing the link between Messianism and utopia in the prophetic writings of Antônio Vieira. For the preacher, the evangelization of Brazil, made possible by the Portuguese arrival in the New World, was a clear sign of the impending advent of a Messianic age, when Christians, Jews, and Native Americans would come together as one people, united by Catholicism. This so-called Fifth Empire would be a utopian time of plenty: an earthly reign of perpetual peace, devoid of suffering and hardship. By emphasizing that the perfect Kingdom of Christ he anticipated was located on earth, Vieira entangled his theological musings with sociopolitical reflections. His conception of a better time to come was to remain a matrix for subsequent utopian thought. Later utopias, where an improved future community would develop not thanks to divine Providence but through human ingenuity, still harked back to a theological paradigm, to the image of Brazil as an earthly paradise or a Garden of Eden with

153

bountiful nature, whose native inhabitants led a leisurely life devoted to pleasurable pursuits.

Often regarded as a space separated from the historical development of the rest of the country, an infernal area hiding incalculable dangers but also a paradisiac region harboring prodigious wealth, the Amazon river basin was the perfect location to project utopian dreams. The fabled community of the Amazons, who, according to legend, inhabited a recondite area of the rainforest, embodied the divergent views on the Amazon prevalent in Brazil. Metonymically standing for American land, which was often feminized, the Amazons were depicted in early writings as ferocious warriors who instilled fear in the hearts of explorers and settlers. In later texts, the all-women tribe acquired utopian overtones. It was imagined as a matriarchy, where each person worked according to her abilities and was provided for according to her needs. Intellectuals such as Oswald de Andrade regard such a utopian community as a blueprint for a future world society that would replace global, patriarchal capitalism.

The utopian, paradisiac conception of the Brazilian natural environment, apparent in texts on the Amazon, is a mainstay of the country's letters. Brazilian writers such as Guimarães Rosa or Clarice Lispector paint a portrait of interspecies communities, in which humanity interacts with animals and plants in such a way that nonhumans become co-creators of literary texts, producing a kind of writing I call *zoophytographia*. This form of interspecies literature presupposes that animals and plants have their own modes of expression, which are articulated in human cultural productions. Zoophytographic literature therefore implies a collaborative interspecies utopia that portends a profound transformation both of literary language and of the very notions of human and nonhuman existences.

The conception of Brazilian land as a new Garden of Eden in the first decades of colonization was coterminous with the understanding of Native Brazilians as inheritors to Eve and Adam's leisurely life before the Fall. Later authors built upon this view of the country's indigenous population to describe their nation as a bastion of leisure, idleness, and even laziness. The idea that the typical Brazilian is a "cordial" person or a *malandro* who avoids labor at all costs has become engrained in national identity. Carnival festivities, during which work gives way to enjoyable activities, would therefore be the expression of a quintessentially Brazilian quality. Far from considering an idle way of life as a negative trait, Brazilian intellectuals regard it as a form of resistance against the mindless pursuit of financial gain typical of industrialized, European, and North American nations. The leisurely Brazilian mode of being in the world is deemed a beacon of hope for a new global order, in which the boundaries separating work and play, industry and art, would progressively fade and each person could devote herself to pleasurable or artistic tasks in a utopia free from the drudgery of unwanted labor.

This book's journey through Brazilian utopian thought, which we have just recapped, brings into focus two crucial elements of utopianism in the country. The various iterations of utopia foregrounded in this study share a view of Brazil as a sociopolitical alternative to the ruling global order. In other words, the current state of affairs is seen as beyond repair and, rather than its gradual improvement, only a complete overhaul of the present situation—a veritable *revolution*—would allow for utopian aspirations to come true. For Antônio Vieira, the constant wars and prejudice against Jews and Native Brazilians that proliferated in his age should give way to equality and perpetual peace in the earthly Kingdom of Christ. And both the communitarian tribe of the Amazons and the utopia of a work-free era stand in sharp contrast to our individualistic, work-intensive societies. Brazil is seen as a country with one foot already firmly planted in an imminent utopian age that others can only dream of. Being a country of the future, it is often at odds with the present, not conforming to the models of political organization, economic development, and social, as well as interspecies, relations accepted in other regions of the world. This disjunction between Brazil and other nations is transposed, in turn, onto an internal split. In all the texts discussed in this book, the promise of utopia lies in the more marginalized members of society—community-oriented women, leisurely Indians, poor *malandros*, and so on—whereas the elite and, to a certain extent, the middle classes, try to emulate the industrial-capitalist way of life prevalent in other countries. The take-home lesson, then, is that, instead of struggling to imitate foreign ideals and constantly falling short of these extraneous standards, Brazil should turn to examples available within its borders. It is not surprising, these writings implicitly tell us, that those most derided under the current circumstances are the kernel of the utopian time to come.

The different strands of Brazilian utopianism discussed in this study also partake of another decisive feature, namely, the centrality of the environment to a utopian future. The mythical Amazons are praised for living in tune with their surroundings, and the leisurely life of Native Brazilians is made possible by the region's plentiful nature. Such connection to the environment translates into many Brazilian writers' close ties to plants and animals, making zoophytographic literature possible. The prominence of nature in the nation's utopian thought signals that the improved, future time heralded by Brazil will necessarily entail an end to environmental destruction and a rethinking of our relations to nonhumans.

Positing Brazil as a country of the future, as the utopias analyzed in this study do, hubristically ascribes to the nation the pivotal role of leading the world in its quest for a more egalitarian and just society. Nevertheless, the projection of utopia onto a concrete space—Portugal and its South American colonies, in the case of Antônio Vieira, the Amazon river basin, or, in later texts, the entire territory of Brazil—highlights a certain incongruousness between that area's reality and the utopian expectations placed upon it. A specific region, limited by its geophysical characteristics and historical circumstances, Brazil will inevitably fail to embody fully all utopian aspirations. The nation's intellectuals have responded to this cognitive dissonance in opposing but ultimately complementary ways.

On the one hand, the significance of utopia for Brazilian national identity contributed to the *ufanista* ("proud"), self-congratulatory attitude of nationalists. Disregarding their country's problems, this group believes theirs is the greatest nation on earth, surpassing even the wildest utopian expectations. Afonso Celso's book *Why I Am Proud of My Country* (*Porque me Ufano do meu País*), published in 1900 to celebrate four centuries since the arrival of the Portuguese in the region, exemplifies this approach. Following in the footsteps of early colonizers, Celso praises the immensity of Brazilian territory, its natural beauty and riches, its mild climate, as well as its glorious history, brave people, and indomitable national character.

This *ufanista* mindset has resurfaced at vital moments in Brazilian cultural and political history. For instance, one of the factions that emerged during Modernism espoused a radically nationalistic, *ufanista* agenda. Intellectuals such as Menotti del Picchia, Cassiano Ricardo, and Plínio Salgado formed the Verde-Amarelo group (Green-Yellow group, using the colors of the Brazilian flag) that advocated the superiority of Brazilian values and conservative policies. Later transformed into the Anta School—the "anta," or tapir, was a mythical animal in the Native Brazilian tupi culture—this segment of Modernism was associated with far-Right political movements such as Integralism, some key tenets of which, in turn, fed into the nationalism of Getúlio Vargas's totalitarian New State government (Estado Novo, 1937–1945). The military dictatorship that ruled Brazil between 1964 and 1985 again went back to *ufanista* tropes, waxing lyrical about the glory of the nation and, concomitantly, of its rulers, in an effort to secure the support of the population for its policies.

While allegiance to the core tenets of one's land is not necessarily something negative, *ufanismo* often entails a racist posture, as its ultranationalism and exaltation of Brazilianness goes hand in hand with the debasement of other nations or even of certain groups, such as Afro-Brazilians, within the country. One can outline a direct trajectory from the view of Brazil as a place where utopia has already been realized to the *ufanista* belief in the region's flawlessness, outside influences being considered an adulteration of national purity. At the limit, this laudatory perception of the region covers over its social, economic, and ecological problems to make it coincide with its utopian ideal, or, to put it differently, the nation in the present is conceived as having caught up with its futural, utopian version. Even progressive thinkers sometimes fall prey to such perfunctory attitudes. An example is writer and singer Jorge Mautner, according to whom "[e]ither the world becomes Brazilianized, or it will be Nazified," a statement meant to present the country as a beacon of racial and sexual tolerance that clearly does not correspond to the concrete situation in the nation ("[o]u o mundo se brasilifica ou vira nazista," quoted in Dunn 173). Such a stance stifles all criticism and precludes progressive cultural and political action, given that the status quo is seen as the best possible state of affairs.

The influence of utopia in Brazilian thought can produce, on the other hand, an overly critical, fatalistic appraisal of the nation, according to which it permanently falls short of utopian expectations. This constant fault-finding can be observed, at a mundane level, in the tendency to invoke the "exterior"—the outside, often meaning North European and North American nations—as a point of reference in a comparison between national and international standards, in which the former usually do not live up to the latter. The root of such self-debasement lies in an interpretation of Brazil as being plagued by a fundamental deficiency that different intellectual movements have struggled to pinpoint. For the Northeastern group of "regionalist" writers such as Graciliano Ramos, Rachel de Queiroz, and the early Jorge Amado, this flaw was the profound economic inequality that created a small class of wealthy landowners and a mass of landless, destitute peasants. Members of New Cinema (Cinema Novo) movement subscribed to this vision, adding endemic corruption as another major source of the country's ills. In his renowned film *Entranced Earth* (*Terra em Transe*, 1967), for example, New Cinema director Glauber Rocha depicts the dystopian, Latin American republic of El Dorado, ravished by political infighting, corruption, and the traffic of influences, as a fictional representation of Brazil. Others have identified slavery's legacy of profound racism as the nation's most significant obstacle in fulfilling its utopian dreams.

These intellectuals are more than justified in drawing attention to their nation's shortcomings as a first step in trying to address them. Still, the enormity of the task facing those who strive to tackle these issues sometimes results in a pessimistic stance, whereby one gives up hope of ever solving them. Such hopeless may play into the hands of a reactionary worldview, bent on showing that there is no alternative to the way things are at present. Accurate as critiques of Brazil's problems certainly are, its socioeconomic, political, and ecological predicaments hardly affect the nation alone. They neither warrant a permanent feeling of inadequacy vis-à-vis its utopian potential, nor do they condemn it to lag behind a better version of itself as a country of the future. The critical impulse was, after all, part of utopia from the outset, one of the main goals of Thomas More in writing his famous book having been precisely to denounce the social dilemmas of his native England. More than anything, the Brazilian self-consciousness of inadequacy, when juxtaposed to utopian models, reveals that dystopia always inheres in utopia as its attending and unavoidable reversal. Dystopia is embedded in the very fabric of utopianism, and the gap between a society and its better version, which can trigger criticism and a sense of frustration, is the very engine that instigates a community to improve.

Our study of utopian thought in Brazil reveals that utopia determined the country's history from its inception and that it is, and will most likely remain, a central element of its collective identity. Utopian ideals, be they Messianic, socialist-communitarian, ecological or economic, are an immanent component of the nation's lived experience, part and parcel of its DNA. The very nature of utopia, though, is to open up a rift between what is and what could be, the real and its exponential betterment. Brazilian intellectuals often respond to this tension intrinsic to utopianism by hovering between the two extremes of *ufanismo* and excessive criticism, the chauvinistic confidence of already embodying a future utopia and the feeling of doom for remaining tied to the inequities of the past. By giving in to an exacerbated version of either of these tendencies, Brazil risks never fully embracing the present and its utopian potential.

This book hopes to demonstrate that Brazilian utopias determine the nation's current circumstances, denouncing prefabricated views of what it is to be Brazilian and instigating the country to move out of its comfort zone and live up to its promise. *Ufanismo* and defeatist, fatalistic criticism are facile responses to utopianism that ultimately fail to meet its challenge in that, in one way or the other, they subscribe to the current state of affairs as the only available and conceivable option. Rejecting these two paths, Brazil will remain a country of the future insofar as it continues to be open to the immanent, utopian possibilities that are woven into the fabric of its historical and sociopolitical becoming. The Brazilian utopias of perpetual peace, communitarianism, interspecies collaboration, and a leisurely, artistic way of life we have contemplated in these pages are a reminder that utopia is operative in the present and that a utopian time to come begins today.

Notes

Introduction

Sections from this Introduction were previously published as the Introduction to the Special Dossier on Brazilian Eco-Criticism of the *Journal of Lusophone Studies* 2.2 (2017). I thank the editors of the journal for their permission to reprint here a revised version of these sections.

1. The Latin "u" of "utopia" is usually considered to be a rendition of the Greek "ou" but it could also be interpreted as deriving from "eu," thus creating an ambiguous term that can mean both "no place" and "good place."

2. The premise implicit in early dreams of a better society to be built in the Americas was that the continent was virtually empty. The native inhabitants of the region were either disregarded or it was assumed that they would adopt European customs and ideals.

3. For an overview of utopianism in Latin America, see Beauchesne and Santos 6–11.

4. This and all other quotes in a foreign language throughout the book are rendered into English in my translation, followed by the original in brackets, unless the text is listed in the bibliography in its English translation. The page numbers refer to the edition of the work listed in the bibliography.

5. See Norman Cohn's *The Pursuit of the Millennium* for a detailed analysis of Millenarian movements in Europe from the Middle Ages onward.

6. For an in-depth discussion of intrahistorical, immanent utopia, see the Introduction to my co-edited book *Existential Utopia*, as well

as the chapter I co-wrote with Michael Marder, "Existential Utopia: Of the World, the Possible, the Finite."

7. The Canudos War has inspired a number of literary and cinematic works in Brazil and beyond, including, for instance, Glauber Rocha's film *Black God, White Devil* (*Deus e o Diabo na Terra do Sol*, 1964) and Mario Vargas Llosa's novel *The War of the End of the World* (*La Guerra del fin del mundo*, 1981).

8. I chose not to focus on Canudos in this study not only because it was an actual historical occurrence but also because the event and its cultural ramifications have already been analyzed in depth in numerous scholarly works, including, among many others, Robert Levine's *Vale of Tears: Revisiting the Canudos Massacre in Northwestern Brazil 1893–97*, Simone Garcia's *Canudos: História e Literatura*, and Adriana Johnson's *Sentencing Canudos: Subalternity in the Backlands of Brazil*.

Chapter 1. The Theologico-Political Utopia of Father Antônio Vieira

A shorter, earlier version of this chapter was published as a chapter in the book *Utopia in Portugal, Brazil and Lusophone African Countries*, edited by Francisco Bethencourt (Berne: Peter Lang, 2015) under the title "António Vieira's Utopian Kingdom of Christ on Earth." Sections of the same chapter have also been published in Portuguese in *Romance Quarterly*, under the title "Estado de Graça: A Utopia Teológico-Política do Padre António Vieira" (61:1, 2014: 65–78) and in the *Revista do Centro de Estudos Portugueses da UFMG*, under the title "A Experiência Transatlântica do Padre António Vieira e o Quinto Império" (49, 2013: 171–84). I thank the editors of these publications for their permission to reprint here a revised version of these previously published sections.

1. For an in-depth analysis of Vieira's position on Indian labor, see António José Saraiva's "O Padre António Vieira e a Liberdade dos Índios" in *História e Utopia*, 11–52. Saraiva also addresses Vieira's controversial position on African slavery in the same book, 55–72.

2. The target audience of Vieira's prophetic writings changed over time. The text "Hopes of Portugal" ("Esperanças de Portugal") was primarily addressed to Queen Luísa de Gusmão, the widow of King John IV; the *History of the Future* was written mainly for a Portuguese audience and the *Key of the Prophets* had a more universal scope and aimed at reaching all Christians, which is why it was written in Latin and not in Portuguese (Buescu 16). Beyond these works, Vieira also developed his Messianic vision in the *Representation before the Tribunal of the Holy Office* and in the *Apology of Things Prophesied* (*Apologia das Coisas Profetizadas*), which were meant for the members of the Inquisitorial Tribunal as a defense of some of the author's positions considered to be blasphemous.

3. In the *Apology*, Vieira also mentions the universality of the Fifth Empire: "Because the Empire of Christ will be properly, rigorously, entirely and absolutely universal and all scriptures mention this proper, entire and absolute universality" ("Porque o Império de Cristo há de ser própria, rigorosa, inteira, e absolutamente universal, e desta própria, inteira, e absoluta universalidade falam todas as escrituras," 94).

4. Aníbal Pinto de Castro points out that Vieira's Messianic thought permeated also his nonprophetic writings such as the sermons, the goal of which was to "shape the mind and the soul of their addressee so that he would consciously work to build the Kingdom of Christ on Earth" ("modelar a mente e a alma do seu destinatário, de modo a fazer dele um construtor consciente do Reino de Cristo na Terra," Castro 100).

5. Vieira understands the difficulties in upholding such thesis and therefore dedicates a large section of Book II of the *History of the Future* to the analysis of quotes from the Scriptures and from canonical authors that he interprets in such a way as to corroborate his opinion.

6. Vieira develops a similar argument in the *History of the Future*: "To Tertullian's argument based upon the eternity of the Fifth Empire, we have already replied that its continuation in Heaven will be truly eternal in all acceptations and meanings and of this word" ("Ao argumento de Tertuliano que se fundava na eternidade do Quinto Império, já temos dito que a continuação dele no Céu há-de ser verda-

deiramente eterna em toda a propriedade e largueza da significação desta palavra," II, 50).

7. Vieira states, also in the *History of the Future*: "[T]his is why the writings of the Church Fathers frequently point out the difference between His Kingdom [of Christ] and the kingdoms of the World; they do not deny to Christ as King, as we were saying, the dominium and temporal empire over all of it [the World], but ennoble that Empire because of [Christ's] disdain for pomp and vain splendor, which the kings of Earth equate to greatness and majesty" ("[P]or isso é tão frequente nos escritos dos Padres a diferença do seu Reino [de Cristo] aos reinos do Mundo, não negando a Cristo Rei, como dizíamos, o domínio e Império ainda temporal sobre todo ele, mas engrandecendo esse mesmo Império pelo desprezo da pompa e aparato vão em que põem os reis da Terra sua grandeza e majestade," II, 66).

8. In the *History of the Future*, Vieira mentions Christ's negative exercise of His freedom, when he decided not to exert His dominium over the world: "[E]ven though Christ's temporal dominium did not have those acts and positive actions that characterize the kings and princes of earth, it nevertheless had a most excellent action and a continuous exercise, never before seen in the World, which we can call negative, namely, that fact that Christ never wanted to use His dominium. And to have the power to use one's dominium and not wanting to do it (which is a heroic act of humanity and modesty that necessarily presupposes the same dominium) is not to have this dominium in an idle way but rather to exercise it very gloriously. In this sense, therefore, (which is neither vulgar nor violent) we can say that Christ did not lack the temporal dominium that we attribute to Him, but that the usage He made of this dominium was the privation of this usage, i.e., not wanting to use it" ("[A]inda que o domínio temporal de Cristo não teve aqueles actos ou exercício positivo que costuma ter nos reis e príncipes da terra, teve porém um acto excelentíssimo e um exercício contínuo, nunca visto até então no Mundo, a que podemos chamar negativo, que foi o não querer Cristo usar do mesmo domínio. E ter o domínio para poder e não querer usar dele (que é um

acto heróico de humanidade e modéstia, o qual necessariamente supõe
o mesmo domínio) não é tê-lo ocioso, se não mui gloriosamente exer-
citado, de maneira que neste sentido (que nem é vulgar nem violento)
podemos dizer que não careceu Cristo do uso do domínio temporal que
nele consideramos, e que o uso que teve daquele domínio foi a privação
do mesmo uso, ou não querer usar dele," II, 109).

9. We find the same idea in the *History of the Future*: "Christ did not
have only one crown but two: one as the Supreme Priest, which belonged
to the spiritual Empire; and another as Supreme King, which belonged
to the temporal one" ("Cristo não teve uma só coroa, senão duas: uma
como Supremo Sacerdote, que pertencia ao Império espiritual; e outra
como Supremo Rei, que pertencia ao temporal," II, 62).

10. The first coming of Christ inaugurated His dominium over the
earth, since, through the hypostatic union, the Son became the heir
to the Father's empire. This dominium is different from the effective
possession of the earth that began with the Christianization of the
world and will only be complete with the advent of the Fifth Empire
(*Representação* II, 53).

11. Vieira continues in the same passage: "[B]ecause Christ was a true
and complete man, it was very convenient that he had not only a spiritual
Empire, that refers to the souls, but also a temporal one, that is proper to
the bodies" ("[P]or Cristo ser verdadeiro e inteiro homem, composto não
só de espírito, se não de carne, foi muito conveniente que não só tivesse
o Império espiritual que pertence às almas, se não também o temporal
que é próprio dos corpos," *História* II, 104).

12. Vieira adds in the *Representation*: "[B]ecause one cannot accept,
without damage to Christ's Providence, that this Providence would be
less attentive to the temporal part of His perfect Empire than it has
been to its spiritual part, considering the proportion and need of each
according to their kind" "([P]ois se não pode bem entender, sem agravo
da Providência de Cristo, que seja ela menos atenta sobre a parte temporal do seu perfeito Império do que o tem sido na parte espiritual dele,
conforme a proporção e necessidade de cada um em seu género," II, 235).

13. In Vieira's words: "And just like the same two planets, with admirable harmony, uniformity and concord, go through their path and movement and share the virtue of their influence over all the bodies subjected and inferior to it [*sic*], out of which the conservation of the whole world depends, so those two Supreme Monarchs, in perpetual union, peace and conformity, will each exert the virtue and efficiency of their powers over the world and its parts (i.e., over all men, equally subject to both monarchies), and their jurisdictions will not clash, their orders will not be entangled and their effects will not be disrupted, but, rather, they will help and favor each other so that, with the same gentleness and efficiency, they will reach and completely accomplish the goals of that most perfect of states" ("E assi como os mesmos dous planetas, com admirável concerto, uniformidade e concórdia, fazem seu curso e movimento e repartem a virtude de suas influências sobre todos os corpos que lhe [*sic*] ficam sujeitos e inferiores, de que depende a conservação de todo o mundo, assi aqueles dous Supremos Monarcas, em perpétua união, paz e conformidade, influirá cada um a virtude e eficácia de seus poderes sobre o mesmo mundo e sobre as mesmas partes dele (que serão todos os homens, sujeitos igualmente a ambas as monarquias) sem que as jurisdições se encontrem, nem as ordens se confundam, nem os efeitos se perturbem, mas antes se ajudem e favoreçam reciprocamente, para que, com igual suavidade e eficácia, se consigam e se logrem inteira e consumadamente os fins daquele perfeitíssimo estado," *Representação* II, 224).

14. Vieira acknowledges that, according to some commentators, the secular emperor would be French, but he states that the majority of nations believes this Emperor to be a "Prince of Spain," an expression that refers to a monarch from the Iberian Peninsula (*Representação* II, 442).

15. The letter "Hopes of Portugal" was intended for Queen Luísa de Gusmão, the widow of King John IV, as the Bishop of Japan was the confessor to the Queen. In the *Representation* Vieira indicates that the Fifth Empire would begin around 1666 (II, 440), that is, ten years after the death of King John IV, whom the author identified as the secular monarch

of the coming Kingdom of Christ. Toward the end of the *Representation*, the preacher apologizes before the members of the Inquisitorial Tribunal for his possible mistake in identifying a Portuguese king as the secular emperor of the Fifth Empire: "The only human aspect of the matter, the rest of it being sacred and divine, was that I said the main instrument for the conquest and temporal dominium was or would be a Portuguese Prince. But if in this issue I was mistaken (like many others) because of the love and devotion I dedicate to my Homeland, *causas habet error honestas*" ("Só tinha de humano o dito assunto, sendo todo sagrado e divino, dizer-se que o instrumento principal dele para a conquista e dominação temporal é ou havia de ser Príncipe Português. Mas, se nesta aplicação me enganou (como a muitos outros) o amor e piedade da Pátria, *causas habet error honestas*," II, 469).

16. The imbrication of Portugal's universalist calling with a colonizing and a missionary project remained alive in Lusophone thought and coalesced in the concept of Lusotropicalism developed by Brazilian sociologist Gilberto Freyre (1900–1987). According to Freyre, Portuguese rule over its colonies was not as harsh as other forms of colonization due to the Portuguese predisposition to adapt to other cultures and to interact with other races, an idea that was to be harshly criticized by scholars and activists both in Brazil and in Portugal.

17. For more information about this topic in Vieira's writings, see Margarida Vieira Mendes, *A Oratória Barroca de Vieira* 523–27.

18. In the *Apology*, Vieira also writes: "This Kingdom of Christ is nothing other than the faith and the Church of Christ, dilated, spread, known, received, obeyed and executed all over the world: and the means through which the said faith and Church will extend, dilate, became known, be obeyed and executed in the world is the preaching of the Gospel, as stated by all the Doctors and the texts from the Scriptures" ("Este Reino de Cristo nenhuma outra coisa é senão a fé, e a Igreja do mesmo Cristo dilatada, estendida, conhecida, recebida, e obedecida e executada em todo o mundo: e o meio por onde a dita fé e Igreja se há de estender, dilatar, conhecer, e obedecer, e executar no mundo é a pregação

do Evangelho, como conformemente dizem todos os Doutores e textos da Escritura," 223–24).

19. Vieira mentions four kinds of infidelity: Hereticism, that is, those who are Christian but deviate from Church doctrine; Judaism; Gentiles, who never knew God; and Pagans, who are for him the followers of Islam. In the *Representation*, Vieira shows, based on the Scriptures, how all of these will cease to exist in the Kingdom of Christ (II, 152–70). However, in the case of the Heretics and the Muslims, the preacher mentions only that, according to the Sacred Texts, they will disappear in the Messianic age. As to the Jews and the Gentiles, with whom he had closer contact, Vieira goes more in-depth into the process of their conversion to Christianity.

20. As Vieira puts it in *Key of the Prophets*: "We therefore conclude that the barbarians raised in the jungles, who have not heard the Gospel and have not by other means been purified from their innate ignorance of God, are immune from any mortal guilt, as well as from any immortal punishment, that is, one that would last eternally, and are not guilty in any other way" ("Donde se conclui que os bárbaros criados nas selvas, os quais não ouviram o Evangelho ou por outra fonte não foram purificados da ignorância inata de Deus, assim como estão imunes de toda a culpa mortal, assim também estão isentos de toda a pena immortal, isto é, que há-de durar eternamente, e não são culpados por qualquer outro motivo" (*Chave dos Profetas*, 89).

21. For a detailed analysis of the influence Menasseh Ben Israel's thought exerted on Vieira, see António José Saraiva's "António Vieira, Menasseh Ben Israel e o Quinto Império" in *História e Utopia*, 75–106.

22. The Jews were expelled from Portugal by King Manuel I in 1496.

23. Vieira reiterated in the *Apology* that all the different kingdoms will keep their sovereignty: "Not because the other Kingdoms, Republics and Empires would not have the same superiority as before over the lands and the people of their jurisdiction, but because that superiority will have a new subjection that it did not use to have <namely the recognition of the> Universal Monarchy" ("Não porque os outros Reinos, Repúblicas

e Impérios não hajam de ter a mesma superioridade que dantes sobre as terras e pessoas de sua jurisdição, mas porque essa superioridade há de ter um nova [*sic*] sujeição que dantes não tinha <que é o reconhecimento da> Monarquia Universal," 285–86).

24. For a discussion of the bodily functions of the blessed, including nutrition and sexuality, as they were portrayed by the Church, see Giorgio Agamben, *The Open*, 17–19.

Chapter 2. Amazons in the Amazon

A section of this text, titled "Utopian Amazons: A Communitarian Matriarchy in the Jungle," was published in the *Revista da UFMG* 24 (2017): 98-115. I thank the editors of the journal for giving me permission to reprint here a revised version of this article.

1. For Aristotle, natural bodies are a combination of matter and form (II, 2). Traditionally viewed as passive, women have been associated to the material substratum of life throughout the history of Western thought, whereas men tend to be regarded as its formative element.

2. The figure of Iracema in Brazilian popular culture plays a role similar to that of Pocahontas in the United States. The two women stand both for the feminized American land and for its native peoples. Their romantic relationships with male European colonizers frame the conquest of American territory in terms of a love affair, thus eliding its more violent features, hidden under sentimental trappings.

3. Afro-Brazilians were conspicuously absent from Alencar's *Iracema* and from considerations of nationality during Romanticism. The African contribution to Brazil only came to be fully recognized from the mid-twentieth century onward.

4. Jorge Bodanzky and Orlando Senna's 1975 film *Iracema, an Amazonian Love Affair* (*Iracema, uma Transa Amazônica*) goes back to the protagonist of Alencar's novel to depict the destruction wrought by unbridled exploitation of Amazonian resources. For an in-depth

discussion of the movie, see my book chapter "Laws of the Jungle: The Politics of Contestation in Cinema about the Amazon," 137–40.

5. In Alencar's novel, Iracema stood for a wild version of nature before she met Martim. She was then "tamed" by her love for the Portuguese soldier and became an instantiation of the motherly, benevolent, sacrificial nature.

6. See my article "*Phytofables*: Tales of the Amazon," 120–23, for a detailed analysis of the Amazon's dichotomous depiction as either a green hell or an earthly paradise.

7. In Ancient Greek mythology, the Amazons were an all-women society of powerful warriors. They had sexual encounters with men to produce offspring but kept only their daughters, killing or abandoning the sons. One of the etymological explanations for the term "Amazon" is that it combines the privative *a* with *mazos*, or breast, to mean "without breast." This goes back to the idea that the Amazons severed their right breast in order to better use their bows and spears, a notion that pointed to the elision of their feminine side and adoption of male traits in order to become better fighters.

8. Holanda describes the transformation of the Amazon myth from the idea that the tribe lived on an island to the belief that they inhabited the American continent (28–38). The Amazon River basin, conceived as a space separated from the rest of South America for its remoteness, climate, and geography, and, thus, almost like an island, is a fitting abode for the legendary women. It is worth recalling, furthermore, that many utopias, including Thomas More's, were located on islands. The utopian portrayal of the Amazons in texts from the first half of the twentieth century therefore follows in a long line of insular utopias.

9. This 1637–39 expedition was the first trip to cross the Amazon from the Atlantic Ocean to Quito and back, and the first time the river was navigated countercurrent for all its length.

10. The conflict between Brazil and Bolivia over the Acre region was the background for Amazonian writer Márcio Souza's 1976 satirical novel *Galvez, Emperor of Acre* (*Galvez, Imperador do Acre*).

11. Euclides da Cunha's Amazon writings were collected in *Contrastes e Confrontos*, from 1907, and in *À Margem da História*, first published in 1909. All of Cunha's Amazonian texts were later published in *Um Paraíso Perdido*, from 1976.

12. Cunha lists several failed attempts to bring Western-style civilization to the Amazon in the past in order to show the area's resistance to progress—mainly due to the specificities of its natural environment and population—and, therefore, the need to invest in robust development projects in the region (123–26).

13. For a detailed analysis of the rhetoric of progress in the Amazon, see my article "*Phytofables*: Tales of the Amazon," 123–26.

14. The vast majority of migrants to the Amazon River basin were young males. It is therefore not surprising that the land was routinely depicted as a female lover to be won over by her male suitors. Female characters are usually underdeveloped in rubber boom literature and the scarcity of women in the region is often identified in these narratives as a reason for crime.

15. Pedro Maligo already noted that the Amazon is frequently depicted as a space apart from the rest of the Brazilian territory (55–56, 70, 153). Conservationist thought is, paradoxically, based upon the same image of the Amazon as a land separated from the rest of the country, an area that is in need of protection so that it would be left untouched. The oft-patronizing discourse of conservationism underlines the idea that the center of decision making about the Amazon is located elsewhere, in the large cities of Southern Brazil (Maligo 155).

16. See my book chapter "Laws of the Jungle: The Politics of Contestation in Cinema about the Amazon," for an analysis of the Amazon as a space onto which aspirations of social and political emancipation are projected.

17. Cruls later toured the region and wrote down his impressions in his 1930 book *The Amazon I Saw* (*A Amazônia que eu Vi*).

18. The narrator expounds the theory that the Amazons descended from women who had fled the Spanish when the latter conquered the Inca Empire. According to the German doctor, the women had either

rebelled against their husbands because they had been defeated by Francisco Pizarro or they were vestal virgins from the Temple of the Sun, who had escaped the rage of the *conquistadores* by leaving the Andes and moving to the Amazon River basin (114–15).

19. The Amazons had sexual encounters with males from a neighboring tribe once a year but they kept only the female offspring resulting from this union. All male children were sent to live with their fathers.

20. Cruls goes back to edenic discourses in his description of pre-Columbian America through the eyes of Atahualpa: "This was a blessed continent that God graced with every favor, giving it all the climates, a soil that is rich and fertile, boundless treasures, very high mountains, the largest rivers and immense lakes. It was not without a reason that Columbus, when he arrived in the New World, believed he had found paradise, and thought that the Orinoco was one of the four large rivers that . . . came out of Eden to irrigate the recently formed world" ("Isto era um continente abençoado e com o qual Deus se desmediu em prodigalidades, dando-lhe todos os climas, um solo rico e feraz, tesouros inesgotáveis, altíssimas montanhas, os maiores rios, lagos imensos. Não foi sem razão que Colombo, ao chegar ao Novo Mundo, supôs ter descoberto o Paraíso e julgou o Orinoco um dos quatro grandes rios que . . . saíam do Éden para banhar a terra recentemente formada," 166–67).

21. The German doctor explains that the Amazons were traditionally considered to be belligerent because they had to fight with local tribes for their territory when they descended from the Andes into the Amazon River basin (116). Since then, they have lived in peace with their neighbors.

22. The Amazons channel their energy into communitarian activities. When they come from work, their organized manner of walking reminds the narrator of an army, but this is a peaceful formation returning from agricultural and similar tasks, not from battle: "Judging by the way they all marched, in a distinguished manner, at the same distance from one another and without speaking, they looked like small platoons which observed the strictest of disciplines. . . . Those are the *ccossanac*, the virgins returning from work" (À maneira por que todas marchavam, em postura

garbosa, equidistantes e sem falar, tinha-se a impressão de pequenos pelotões nos quais se observasse a mais rigorosa disciplina.... Aquelas são as *ccossanac*, as virgens que voltam do trabalho," 99).

23. The German doctor needed human subjects to perform his experiments and decided to move to a remote region, where tribes often sacrificed their prisoners of war, in order to use these prisoners in his scientific pursuits. He also used twins, since local tribes usually killed one of the twins at birth, children with physical disabilities, who were also killed at birth, and the male offspring of the Amazons (220–23). Even though the professor tries to persuade the narrator that his experiments are ethically sound, the latter is never fully convinced.

24. Rosina recounts that her husband also experimented on healthy subjects, including a Syrian merchant who arrived at the city of the Amazons by mistake. After the experiments, the Syrian lost the ability to speak Portuguese and the use of one of his arms. Furthermore, the German doctor tried to persuade his wife to give birth to a being that would be half-human, half-monkey, an experiment he later performed on one of the Amazons (249–51).

25. The connection between Cruls and the protagonist of his novel comes through in the travel book *A Amazônia que eu Vi*, where he writes: "What if on a turn of the river we were imprisoned by one of those tribes who protected the *Land of the Amazons* and I was taken once again to Professor Hartmann?" ("E se a uma curva do rio fôssemos aprisionados por uma daquellas tribos que guardavam o *País das Amazonas* e de novo eu me visse levado à presença do Professor Hartmann?" 214).

26. The similarities between this fictional plot and the real-life story of the Canudos community, recounted by Euclides da Cunha in *The Backlands*, are striking: as in Canudos, a group of downtrodden peasants fight against the Brazilian army and look for a promised land of plenty.

27. The word *Icamiaba* derives from a Tupi language expression that means "broken breast," an allusion to the legend of the Ancient Greek Amazons, who supposedly mutilated their right breast. More likely, Icamiaba refers to the name of the region that the Amazons supposedly inhabited, as already hinted at by Acuña in the seventeenth century. Cruls

mentions this etymology in *The Mysterious Amazon*: "One of the areas where one finds more green stones is in the mountain of Itacamiaba, and that is why the Amazons are also called Itacamiabas" ("Uma das zonas em que se encontram mais pedras verdes é a serra Itacamiaba, por isso se chamaram às Amazonas também Itacamiabas," 111). The "green stones" were gifts that the Amazons purportedly bestowed upon their lovers when they visited them once a year. "Itacamiaba" was then shortened to "Icamiaba."

28. The narrator writes, in one of the novel's tirades against foreigners: "The Brazilian is irreplaceable. Still, every day, ships unload in national harbors packs of foreigners. They bring no money" ("O brasileiro é insubstituível. No entanto, todos os dias os navios despejam nos portos nacionais matilhas de forasteiros. Não trazem vintém," 94).

29. Early Brazilian Modernism can roughly be divided into two distinct groups: a left-wing Modernism that tempered nationalism with an openness to foreign artistic trends, to which Mário de Andrade and Oswald de Andrade belonged; and a more radically nationalistic, "proud" ("ufanista") Modernism associated with right-wing political movements such as Integralism, which included intellectuals like Menotti del Picchia and Cassiano Ricardo.

30. The title of the text is usually translated into English as "Cannibalist Manifesto." I prefer "Anthropophagous Manifesto," in light of Andrade's distinction between anthropophagy and cannibalism: "[Anthropophagy] is opposed, in its harmonious and communal sense, to cannibalism, which is anthropophagy motivated by gluttony and also by hunger, known through the chronicles of cities under siege and of lost travelers" ("[A Antropofagia] contrapõe-se em seu sentido harmônico e comunial, ao canibalismo que vem a ser a antropofagia por gula e também a antropofagia por fome, conhecida através da crônica das cidades sitiadas e dos viajantes perdidos," "Filosofia Messiânica," 77).

31. Andrade highlights the link between patriarchy and capitalist exploitation: "Patriarchy, whose biggest achievement was the discovery of the hydrogen bomb and whose identity card is capitalism, from its most obscure and embryonic forms to the glory of Wall Street" ("o Patriarcado,

cuja maior façanha é a descoberta da bomba de hidrogênio e que tem como sua carta de identificação o capitalismo, desde as suas formas mais obscuras e larvadas até à glória de Wall Street," "Marcha," 189).

Chapter 3. Zoophytographia

Parts of this chapter were published in the *Journal of Lusophone Studies* 2.2 (2017) under the title "Interspecies Literature: Clarice Lispector's Zoophytographia". I thank the editors of the journal for granting me permission to reprint here a revised version of this section of the text.

1. The description of Iracema, when she is first introduced in the novel, suffices to show her imbrication with Brazilian nature: "Iracema, the virgin with honey lips, whose hair was darker than the wing of the *graúna* bird, and longer than her palm-tree shape. The honeycomb of the *jati* bee was not as sweet as her smile; nor was the vanilla fragrance stronger in the woods than in her perfumed breath. She was faster than the wild doe" ("Iracema, a virgem dos lábios de mel, que tinha os cabelos mais negros que a asa da graúna, e mais longos que seu talhe de palmeira. O favo da jati não era doce como seu sorriso; nem a baunilha recendia no bosque como seu hálito perfumado. Mais rápida que a corça selvagem," 16).

2. This identification of Brazil with the rainforest is problematic, as we saw in chapter 2. Even though, with urbanization, the tropical forest becomes increasingly removed from the everyday lives of most Brazilians, it continues to undergird the country's self-perception (McNee 15).

3. For a more detailed analysis of posthumanism in Machado de Assis, see Maria Esther Maciel, *Literatura e Animalidade*, 74–82.

4. A *crónica* is a short journalist text, usually triggered by a current or recent event. It is a versatile text that can be descriptive, narrative, or essayistic.

5. For an in-depth, theoretical discussion of the notion of "phytographia" and of plant inscription in literary texts, see my article "*Phytographia*: Literature as Plant Writing."

6. See my co-edited volume *The Language of Plants: Science, Philosophy, Literature* for recent scientific studies on the language of plants, as well as philosophical reflections on plant language and literary criticism on this subject.

7. In Castro's words: "Where the latter [multiculturalist ontologies] are founded on the mutually implied unity of nature and multiplicity of cultures ... the Amerindian conception presumes a spiritual unity and a corporeal diversity" ("Exchanging Perspectives," 466).

8. Animals were originally human and they still retain traces of this condition: "While our [Western] folk anthropology holds that humans have an original animal nature that must be coped with by culture—having been wholly animals, we remain animals 'at bottom'—Amerindian thought holds that, having been human, animals must still be human, albeit in an unapparent way" ("Exchanging Perspectives," 465).

9. As Castro puts it: "To say that humanity is the original common condition of humans and nonhumans alike is tantamount to saying that the soul or spirit—the subjective aspect of being—is the universal, unconditioned given (since the souls of all nonhumans are humanlike), while objective bodily nature takes on an a posteriori, particular, and conditioned quality. In this connection, it is also worth noticing that the notion of matter as a universal substrate seems wholly absent from Amazonian cosmologies" ("Exchanging Perspectives," 466).

10. For Amerindians, every entity that has a point of view is a subject: "Amerindian perspectival ontology proceeds as though the point of view creates the subject: whatever is activated or 'agented' by the point of view will be a subject" ("Exchanging Perspectives," 467).

11. As Castro points out: "The essential difference between this 'perspectivism' and our own 'multiculturalism' is that this variation of point of view does not only affect our 'way of seeing' a world that would otherwise be objectively exterior to the point of view and larger than any possible point of view; it is an ontologically and epistemologically infinite world. In the first place, the perspectivist 'world' is a world exhaustively composed of points of view: all beings and things in the world are

potential subjects, hence the entities that 'we see' are always seeing beings" ("Interview"). Castro adds that perspectivism may, at first glance, appear to be just another name for relativism, but he highlights the differences between the two stances: "[A]ll beings perceive ('represent') the world in the same way. What varies is the world that they see. Animals impose the same categories and values on reality as humans do—their worlds, like ours, revolve around hunting and fishing, cooking and fermented drinks, cross-cousins and war, initiation rituals, shamans, chiefs, spirits, and so forth. Being people in their own sphere, nonhumans see things just as people do. But the things that they see are different" ("Exchanging Perspectives," 472).

12. Uexküll famously gave the example of the tick and its *Umwelt*, or environment, wholly different from that of humans (44ff).

13. For Maria Esther Maciel, the community of humans and bulls acquires utopian undertones since "humans and non-humans forge relationships of friendship, complicity, conflicts" ("convivem em relação de amizade, cumplicidade, conflitos," *Literatura*, 67).

14. Hélène Cixous found that Clarice Lispector's novel *Água Viva* was a perfect example of *écriture féminine*, namely, "a writing, based on an encounter with another—be it a body, a piece of writing, a social dilemma, a moment of passion—that leads to an undoing of the hierarchies and oppositions that determine the limits of most conscious life" (Conley vii).

15. Lispector, together with Rosa, were singled out as the two Brazilian writers belonging to the boom of Latin American literature in the 1960s (Peixoto xviii).

16. Lispector's Hebrew name would disappear once the family moved to Brazil, only to reappear in her tombstone (Moser 33). In his biography of Lispector, Benjamin Moser writes: "People who met her frequently compared her to an animal, often a feline: elegant, unknowable, potentially violent. 'She was perfectly dressed, long and beautiful, like one of those Egyptian cats,' one friend remembered. 'Her Slavic face impressed me, strong and beautiful, with something of a feline animal,' the poet Ferreira Gullar remembered.... 'Other people think I seem like a tiger,

like a panther,' Clarice told an interviewer. He replied, 'Because of your eyes—but that's not it. It's because you have a cat's inner composure, that feline way of always being on the lookout'" (55–56).

17. Lispector reflects in the same text that humans are fated to be carnivores, and gloomily concludes that it is still better to eat animals than our fellow human beings: "When I think about the voracious happiness with which we eat chicken with grey sauce, I become aware of our barbarism. I, who would be unable to kill a chicken, because I like them so much while alive, moving their ugly neck and looking for worms. Should we not eat them and their blood? Never. We are cannibals and should not forget about it. We should respect our violence. And, who knows, if we were not to eat chicken with grey sauce, we would eat people with their blood" ("Quando penso na alegria voraz com que comemos galinha ao molho pardo, dou-me conta de nossa truculência. Eu, que seria incapaz de matar uma galinha, tanto gosto delas vivas mexendo o pescoço feio e procurando minhocas. Deveríamos não comê-la e ao seu sangue? Nunca. Nós somos canibais, é preciso não esquecer. É respeitar a violência que temos. E, quem sabe, não comêssemos a galinha ao molho pardo, comeríamos gente com seu sangue," *Aprendendo*).

18. Lispector published a first version of this story, "The Crime" ("O Crime"), in a Rio de Janeiro newspaper on August 25, 1945. She later expanded and renamed the text to include it in the collection *Family Ties*.

19. The author writes about "A Hen:" "I also saw that I had written a short story, and that the fondness I always had of animals was there" ("Vi também que escrevera um conto, e que ali estava o gosto que sempre tivera por bichos," *Não Esquecer*). She adds later in the same text: "I believe that this short story ['The Smallest Woman in the World'] also comes from my love of animals; it seems like I feel animals as one of the things that are still very close to God, a material that did not invent itself, something still warm from its birth" ("Creio que também este conto ['A Menor Mulher do Mundo'] vem de meu amor por bichos; parece-me que sinto os bichos como uma das coisas ainda muito próximas de Deus, material que não inventou a si mesmo, coisa ainda quente do próprio nascimento," *Não Esquecer*).

20. At first, the professor believed that his relationship with the dog was based upon a give and take: "'While I made you in my image, you made me in yours'.... 'We understood each other only too well'" ("'Enquanto eu te fazia à minha imagem, tu me fazias à tua'.... .'Nós nos compreendíamos demais...'" *Laços*). Later in the narrative, the man recognizes that the dog is merely humoring him when he abides by his rules, retaining its animal nature untouched: "'How you smelled the streets!'... 'This was your childish side. Or was it your true fulfilment of being a dog? and the rest was just you playing at being mine? Because you were irreducible'" ("'E como cheiravas as ruas!'... 'Este era o teu lado infantil. Ou era o teu verdadeiro cumprimento de ser cão? e o resto apenas brincadeira de ser meu? Porque eras irredutível,'" *Laços*). The dog only pretends to have been domesticated, all the while remaining true to its wild, animal self.

21. Some of Lispector's autobiographical short stories also feature the trope of becoming animal. In "The Disasters of Sophia" ("Os Desastres de Sofia"), for instance, the narrator states: "She felt inside her a perfect animal, full of inconsequences, of selfishness, of vitality" ("Sentia dentro de si um animal perfeito, cheio de inconsequências, de egoísmo e vitalidade," *Contos*, 17).

22. Lispector writes about becoming a plant in several other narratives. In *An Apprenticeship*, the protagonist, Lóri, often imagines herself as a fruit: "Sometimes she compared herself to fruit, and disregarding her external appearance, she ate herself internally, full of the live juice that she was"; "She never imagined that the world and herself would once reach that point of ripe wheat" ("Às vezes comparava-se às frutas, e desprezando sua aparência externa, ela se comia internamente, cheia de sumo vivo que era"; "Nunca imaginara que uma vez o mundo e ela chegassem a esse ponto de trigo maduro," 101; 116). The short story "Remains from Carnival" ("Restos do Carnaval") ends with the following statement from the first-person female narrator: "And I, then, an eight-year-old little woman, considered for the rest of the evening that finally someone had recognized me: yes, I was a rose" ("E eu então, mulherzinha de 8 anos, considerei pelo resto

da noite que enfim alguém me havia reconhecido: eu era, sim, uma rosa," *Contos*, 107).

23. Michael Marder developed the idea of our relationship to plants as an encounter, a meeting halfway, neither humanizing them nor rendering humans totally vegetal, in his "Introduction" to *Plant-Thinking*, especially 10–13.

24. Another facet of Lispector's work that approximates it to the philosophy of Levinas is the sense of being responsible for nonhumans. For Levinas, the I is absolutely responsible for the Other, a responsibility that is independent from the Other's deeds. Lispector transforms this absolute responsibility into an urge to take care of nonhuman others and of the world as a whole. The protagonist of *Água Viva* writes: "I am tired. My tiredness is very much because I am an extremely busy person: I take care of the world.... Especially in the Botanical Garden, I get exhausted. I have to take care with my gaze of thousands of plants, trees and, above all, of the giant water lily" ("Estou cansada. Meu cansaço vem muito porque sou pessoa extremamente ocupada: tomo conta do mundo.... No Jardim Botânico, então, fico exaurida. Tenho que tomar conta com o olhar de milhares de plantas e árvores e sobretudo da vitória-régia," 49). A little farther in the same text the first-person female narrator adds: "You will ask me why I take care of the world. It is because I was born with this duty. / When I was a child I took care of a line of ants." ("Você há de me perguntar por que tomo conta do mundo. É que nasci incumbida. Tomei em criança conta de uma fileira de formigas," 50).

25. For an in-depth analysis of Levinasian philosophy and its relation to animals see Matthew Calarco's *The Question of the Animal from Heidegger to Derrida*, 55–77.

26. For a Levinasian reading of Lispector's *The Passion*, see Joseph Ballan's "Divine Anonymities." Ballan argues that Levinas's work opens the door to an undecidability between absolute materiality and concreteness, on the one hand, and absolute distance and anonymity, on the other hand (540). For Ballan, this is exacerbated in the writings of Lispector. While Levinas never abandons an aspiration toward transcendence,

though, Lispector tends to side with creatureliness and materiality, finding divinity in immanence (552–54).

27. I translate the feminine pronoun *ela*, referring to the cockroach, as "it." The word *cockroach* is feminine in Portuguese and therefore *ela* would be the pronoun usually used to refer to the animal. However, critics such as Benjamin Moser have argued that *ela* is employed because Lispector identifies the cockroach as female. G.H. points in this direction when she writes: "I only thought of it [the cockroach] as female, since that which is crushed by the waist is female" ("Eu só a [à barata] pensara como fêmea, pois o que é esmagado pela cintura é fêmea," 73). In general, *The Passion* could be read as an attempt to condemn both anthropocentrism and phallocentrism, as Hilary Owen points out: "The displacement of the *phallogocentric* universe in *A Paixão* is at the same time the displacement of the *anthropocentric* universe" (176). A. M. Wheeler also establishes a link between animal imagery and gender roles in an essay on the collection of short stories *Family Ties*.

28. G.H. describes the appearance of the cockroach in detail: "It was a face without contours. The antennas came out like moustaches from the sides of the mouth. The brown mouth was well delineated. The thin and long moustaches moved lowly and dryly.... The cockroach has no nose. I looked at it, with its mouth and its eyes: it looked like a mulatto woman about to die" ("Era uma cara sem contorno. As antenas saíam em bigodes dos lados da boca. A boca marrom era bem delineada. Os finos e longos bigodes mexiam-se lentos e secos.... A barata não tem nariz. Olhei-a, com aquela sua boca e seus olhos: parecia uma mulata à morte," 44).

29. G.H. writes that her feeling of disgust when facing cockroaches stems from the fact that the insects are very old, in evolutionary terms: "What I always found repugnant in cockroaches was that they were obsolete and, nevertheless, actual. To know that they were already on Earth, and the same as today, even before the first dinosaurs appeared; to know that the first human to appear had already found them proliferated and crawling alive; to know that they had witnessed the formation of the large oil and coal reservoirs of the world, and that they were there during the

great move forward and then the great retreat of the glaciers—the passive resistance" ("O que sempre me repugnara em baratas é que elas eram obsoletas e no entanto atuais. Saber que elas já estavam na Terra, e iguais a hoje, antes mesmo que tivessem aparecido os primeiros dinossauros, saber que o primeiro homem surgido já as havia encontrado proliferadas e se arrastando vivas, saber que elas haviam testemunhado a formação das grandes jazidas de petróleo e carvão no mundo, e lá estavam durante o grande avanço e depois durante o grande recuo das geleiras—a resistência pacífica," 37).

30. In another passage later in the novel, G.H. adds: "We will be inhuman—as the highest conquest of man. To be is to be beyond the human" ("Seremos inumanos—como a mais alta conquista do homem. Ser é ser além do humano," 134).

31. Lispector's first novel, *Near to the Wild Heart*, is the text where her indebtedness to the philosophy of Spinoza is clearer (Moser 122–23) but his thought permeates all her writings.

32. G.H. describes primordial life as an inferno throughout the novel: "Because a world completely alive has the force of Hell"; "hell of live matter"; "the hell of raw life"; "[t]he orgy of hell is the apotheosis of the neutral" ("É que um mundo todo vivo tem a força de um Inferno"; "inferno de matéria viva"; "inferno de vida crua"; "[a] orgia do inferno é a apoteose do neutro," 17; 46–47; 47; 97).

33. In another passage, G.H. writes: "I would also have to abandon the beauty of salt and the beauty of tears. That also, for what I was seeing was still before the human" ("Também a beleza do sal e a beleza das lágrimas eu teria de abandonar. Também isso, pois o que eu estava vendo era ainda anterior ao humano," 66).

34. G.H. realizes that beauty can be misleading: "I will have to nostalgically say goodbye to beauty. Beauty was a gentle enticement, it was the way in which I, weak and respectful, adorned the thing to be able to tolerate its nucleus" ("Terei que dar com saudade adeus à beleza. Beleza me era um engodo suave, era o modo como eu, fraca e respeitosa, enfeitava a coisa para poder tolerar-lhe o núcleo," 123).

35. G.H. recognizes that, similar to the way in which she tried to kill the cockroach, the animal would have killed her if it had a chance, not out of malevolence but simply because that is how life works: "If it [the cockroach] had not been imprisoned and if it were bigger than me, it would kill me with a neutral and busy pleasure. In the same way as the violent neutral of its life allowed that I would kill it, because I am not imprisoned and because I am bigger than it. That was the kind of tranquil, neutral ferociousness of the desert where we were" ("Se ela não estivesse presa e se fosse maior que eu, com neutro prazer ocupado ela me mataria. Assim como o violento neutro de sua vida admitia que eu, por não estar presa e por ser maior que ela, que eu a matasse. Essa era a espécie de tranqüila ferocidade neutra do deserto onde estávamos," 67). Cruelty is absent from the most basic level of existence, where only the drive for life prevails.

36. According to Hilary Owen, Lispector's *The Passion* draws on Western mysticism but inverts its main tenets. While Western mystics seek to unite with transcendence, Eastern mysticism remains in the nothing, the latter being the path advocated in the novel (166).

37. Even though G.H. emphasizes the radical alterity of the animal other, siding with Levinas, she still believes, *contra* Levinasian thought, that, at a very basic level, both humans and animals share the fact of being alive. The Levinasian transcendence of the other is therefore moderated, in the case of Lispector, by Spinozan immanence.

38. As the protagonist of *Água Viva* put it: "That beatitude is not in itself laic or religious" ("Essa beatitude não é em si leiga ou religiosa," 72).

39. G.H. also describes the state of grace as a condition beyond language farther on in the novel: "We will be live matter manifesting itself directly, without knowing the word, going beyond thought that is always grotesque" ("Seremos a matéria viva se manifestando diretamente, desconhecendo palavra, ultrapassando o pensar que é sempre grotesco," 134).

40. For a more in-depth discussion of Walter Benjamin on language see my essay "*Phytographia*: Literature as Plant Writing," 210–13.

41. As Benjamin put it: "All nature, insofar as it communicates itself, communicates itself in language, and so finally in man. Hence, he is the lord of nature and can give names to things" (65).

42. The novel also begins with the same set of dashes, suggesting that the whole narrative transpires in the middle of a process, the ongoing becoming of life.

Chapter 4. Idling in the Tropics

1. For a more detailed analysis of the Platonic stance on work, see Anthony 15–16.

2. Daedalus was a legendary sculptor whose statues were so lifelike they had to be chained to prevent them from running away.

3. See Schippen 22–37 for an in-depth analysis of Aristotle's concept of leisure.

4. Pieper discusses the Medieval concept of *acedia*, often translated as "idleness," as the opposite of *vita contemplativa*. He points out that, rather than connoting leisure, *acedia* was considered to be a kind of restlessness or even despair, that is to say, the inability to be truly at leisure. In the code of life of the Middle Ages, idleness was therefore associated to *acedia* because it meant "the restlessness of work-for-work's-sake" (Pieper 47). While leisure and the *vita contemplativa* were valued positively, idleness was linked to restlessness and considered a sin: "Idleness in the old sense, then, has so little in common with leisure, that it is the very inner disposition to non-leisure, that it is really 'lack of leisure.' There can only be leisure, when man is at one with himself, when he is in accord with his own being. *Acedia*, therefore, is 'disagreement with oneself.' Idleness and lack of leisure belong with each other; leisure is opposed to *both*" (Pieper 50). As the ideology of work developed in tandem with the Industrial Revolution, leisure and idleness acquired more similar connotations, even though the latter term never lost its negative undertones.

5. As Veal points out, the concept of regular working hours was foreign to most laborers in premodern times and workers had to progressively

become accustomed to this new idea: "One feature of the non-industrial work culture which industrialists found frustrating was the tendency for employees to work until they had earned a certain amount of money, sufficient for their needs, and then to stop, perhaps disappearing from the workplace for extended periods.... The idea of wealth from hard work, particularly in the New World, transformed the hopes and aspirations of many ordinary people. It was no longer necessary to persuade the masses that work was a moral duty or for the glory of God, with its rewards in the hereafter; work now had its own, increasing, rewards here on earth" (24).

6. This is what Stevenson has to say about those who are too industrious: "As if a man's soul were not too small to begin with, they have dwarfed and narrowed theirs by a life of all work and no play; until here they are at forty, with a listless attention, a mind vacant of all material of amusement, and not one thought to rub against another, while they wait for the train" (49).

7. Lafargue, like many thinkers after him, places his trust in machines, which will perform the work that is tying human beings to the chains of hard toil: "Our machines, with breath of fire, with limbs of unwearying steel, with fruitfulness, wonderful inexhaustible, accomplish by themselves with docility their sacred labor. And nevertheless the genius of the great philosophers of capitalism remains dominated by the prejudice of the wage system, worst of slaveries. They do not yet understand that the machine is the savior of humanity, the god who shall redeem man from the sordid arts and from working for hire, the god who shall give him leisure and liberty" (Lafargue 62).

8. Here is Rifkin's idealistic take on community work: "Community service is a revolutionary alternative to traditional forms of labor. Unlike slavery, serfdom, and wage labor, it is neither coerced nor reduced to a fiduciary relationship. Community service is a helping action, a reaching out to others. It is an act entered into willingly and often without expectation of material gain. In this sense, it is more akin to the ancient economics of gift giving. Community service stems from a deep understanding of the interconnectedness of all things and is motivated by a personal sense of indebtedness. It is, first and foremost, a social exchange,

although often with economic consequences to both the beneficiary and the benefactor. In this regard, community activity is substantially different from market activity, in which the exchange is always material and financial and where the social consequences are less important than the economic gains and losses" (242).

9. For instance, Beck rashly dismisses Brazilian politics by saying that "Brazilian political discourse often has little to do with reality; wishful thinking, belief in miracles and a longing for salvation can here be unproblematically dressed up and 'marketed' in 'modern' social and economic terminology" (176).

10. As Kenneth Roberts points out, "for many members of the workforce, leisure offers opportunities to compensate for the frustrations and monotony of work in modern industry.... [S]ome individuals use leisure to compensate by devoting spare time to hobbies and handicrafts which employ skills and talents denied outlet in employment. An alternative response to boring work..." (53).

11. Montaigne comments upon the advantages of South America's indigenous population, who live closer to nature than Europeans: "They [Native Brazilians] are savages at the same rate that we say fruits are wild, which nature produces of herself and by her own ordinary progress; whereas, in truth, we ought rather to call those wild whose natures we have changed by our artifice and diverted from the common order. In those, the genuine, most useful, and natural virtues and properties are vigorous and sprightly, which we have helped to degenerate in these, by accommodating them to the pleasure of our own corrupted palate."

12. Montaigne, like Caminha, praises the healthy state of Native Americans, which compares positively to the situation in Europe: "[A]s my witnesses inform me, 'tis rare to hear of a sick person, and they moreover assure me, that they never saw any of the natives, either paralytic, bleareyed, toothless, or crooked with age."

13. For a more detailed analysis of Macunaíma's contradictory character as the hero of all Brazilians, see my chapter, "Heróis sem Carácter. Particularismo e Identidade Nacional em *Macunaíma*."

14. Throughout this chapter, I mostly translate *ócio* as "leisure." In some cases, when the context points in this direction, I render it as "idleness" or "laziness." In general, though, I avoid the two latter terms given their negative connotations.

15. Arguably, Indians have been as marginalized as Africans in Brazil. Still, in the country's self-understanding, the native population came to represent, together with Europeans, the origin of Brazilian society from very early on, while Africans were only acknowledged as part of this original matrix in the twentieth century. Native Brazilians have therefore played a big part in the nation's intellectual history, even though this role has not been matched by their social reality.

16. This is what Holanda has to say about Native Brazilians, which coincides with the stereotypes about the indigenous population we discussed in the previous sections: "Even though they were extremely versatile, they could not grasp certain notions of order, constancy and exactitude that, for the European, are like a second nature and seem to be fundamental prerequisites for a social and civil existence" ("Versáteis ao extremo, eram-lhes inacessíveis certas noções de ordem, constância e exatidão, que no europeu formam como uma segunda natureza e parecem requisitos fundamentais da existência social e civil," *Raízes*, 48).

17. As Roberto Schwarz argues, "the dialectics of order and disorder is built initially as the experience and perspective of a social segment, in the context of a historically determined class antagonism. While in another moment it is the Brazilian *mode of being*, i.e., a cultural trait through which we compare ourselves to other countries and that can help us in favorable historical circumstances" ("a dialética de order e desordem é construída inicialmente enquanto experiência e perspectiva de um setor social, num quadro de antagonismo de classes historicamente determinado. Ao passo que noutro momento ela é o *modo de ser* brasileiro, isto é, um traço cultural através do qual nos comparamos a outros países e que em circunstâncias históricas favoráveis pode nos ajudar" (150).

18. Cândido also mentions the idea that Brazilian society is particularly flexible when he discusses the novel *Memoirs of a Militia Sergeant*: "In its most intimate structure and in its latent vision of things, this

book expresses the vast general accommodation that dissolves extremes, removes the meaning of law and order, manifests the reciprocal penetration of the most disparate groups, ideas, and attitudes, creating a kind of moral no-man's-land, where transgression is just a shade in the spectrum that comes from norms and moves to crime" ("Na sua estrutura mais íntima e na sua visão latente das coisas, este livro exprime a vasta acomodação geral que dissolve os extremos, tira o significado da lei e da ordem, manifesta a penetração recíproca dos grupos, das idéias, das atitudes mais díspares, criando uma espécie de terra-de-ninguém moral, onde a transgressão é apenas um matiz na gama que vem da norma e vai ao crime," 51).

19. For João Cezar Rocha, what defines the *malandro* is not only laziness but a kind of ontological indeterminacy, a "lack of character"—recall that the subtitle of Mário de Andrade's *Macunaíma* was "the hero without any character" ("o herói sem nenhum carácter")—or of fixed character traits. This indistinctness is at the root of the openness that Cândido identifies as key to understanding the *malandro*.

20. As Schwarz points out: "Antônio Cândido identifies the dialectics of order and disorder as a mode of being of the lower classes. Further on he generalizes it to the whole country.... The matrix for some of the best aspects of Brazilian society would thus be in the sociability developed by poor people, to which the future might present an opportunity" ("Antônio Cândido identifica a dialética da order e desordem como um modo de ser popular. Mais adiante ele a generaliza para o país.... Assim, a matriz de alguns dos melhores aspectos da sociedade brasileira estaria na sociabilidade desenvolvida pelos homens pobres, à qual o futuro talvez reserve uma oportunidade," 150–51).

21. For an in-depth discussion of Carnival, its inversion of established hierarchies and the subversive potential of such reversals see Mikhail Bakhtin's *Rabelais and His World*.

22. For Matta, the popular figure of Pedro Malasartes, is "the paradigm of the so-called *malandro*" ("o paradigma do chamado malandro," 204). Matta also regards Mário de Andrade's character Macunaíma as a *malandro* (211, 214).

23. Agamben defines the state of exception as follows: "that temporary suspension of the rule of law that is revealed instead to constitute the fundamental structure of the legal system itself" (*Means*, iii–iv).

24. Or, differently put: "Only the limitation of Eros makes possible the limitation of free, that is, pleasurable time to a minimum deducted from full-time labor" (*Five Lectures*, 10).

25. For Freud, then, both pleasure and freedom cannot be found in civilization: "According to him [Freud], happiness is as little a product of civilization as is freedom. Happiness and freedom are incompatible with civilization" (Marcuse, *Five Lectures*, 33).

26. It is telling that, for Freud, an "intensification of the feeling of guilt" is typical of civilization (Marcuse, *Five Lectures*, 17). The world of the *malandro*, by contrast, is usually described as being guilt-free.

27. Marcuse argues that "[t]he realm of freedom is envisioned as lying beyond the realm of necessity: freedom is not within but outside the 'struggle for existence.' Possession and procurement of the necessities of life are the prerequisite, rather than the content, of a free society. The realm of necessity, of labor, is one of unfreedom because the human existence in this realm is determined by objectives and functions that are not its own and that do not allow the free play of human faculties and desires" (*Eros*, 195).

28. In other words, "the degree of domination of nature and of social wealth attained makes it possible to reduce ungratifying labor to a minimum; quantity is transformed into quality, free time can become the content of life and work can become the free play of human capacities. In this way the repressive structure of the instincts would be explosively transformed: the instinctual energies that would no longer be caught up in ungratifying work would become free and, as Eros, would strive to universalize libidinous relationships and develop a libidinous civilization" (Marcuse, *Five Lectures*, 22).

29. As Marcuse puts is: "A reactivation would be possible of all those erotic forces and modes of behavior that were blocked off and desexualized under the repressive reality principle. I should like to emphasize sharply, because the greatest misunderstanding is possible on this point,

that sublimation would not cease but instead, as erotic energy, would surge up in new forces of cultural creation" (*Five Lectures*, 40).

30. Marcuse mentions that eroticized work relations are usually attributed by psychoanalysis to a "general maternal attitude as the dominant trend of a culture," and are therefore considered a "feature of primitive societies rather than as a possibility of mature civilization" (*Eros*, 216). It is therefore significant that Oswald de Andrade regards the future age of *ócio* as a new matriarchy, as we saw in chapter 2. What both Andrade and Marcuse are suggesting is that such reactivation of erotic forces does not need to be relegated to the past and that matriarchy is not necessarily associated to primitivism but can also be projected onto a future civilization: "But while the psychoanalytical and anthropological concepts of such an order [of eroticized work relations] have been oriented on the prehistorical and precivilized *past*, our discussion of the concept is oriented on the *future*, on the conditions of fully mature civilization" (Marcuse, *Eros*, 216).

31. For Andrade, then, religious sentiment at its most authentic consists in the "beatific contemplation of God—pure *Ócio*" ("contemplação beatífica de Deus—Ócio puro," "Marcha," 158). Religious devotion requires a time of idleness, which is considered a supreme gift and, in Christianity, a reward for the trials and tribulations of the blessed in the future kingdom of heaven.

Works Cited

Acuña, Cristóbal de. "New Discovery of the Great River of the Amazons." *Expeditions into the Valley of the Amazons. 1539, 1540, 1639.* Ed. and Trans. Clements R. Markham. London: Hakluyt Society, 1859. 47–142. Print.

Agamben, Giorgio. *Means without Ends.* Minneapolis and London: U of Minnesota P, 2000 (1st. Italian ed. 1996). Print.

———. *The Open: Man and Animal.* Stanford: Stanford UP, 2004. Print.

———. *Seminar at Saas Fee.* European Graduate School. Saas-Fee, Switzerland. August 6–11, 2007. Lecture.

———. *State of Exception.* Chicago and London: U of Chicago P, 2005. Print.

———. *The Kingdom and the Glory: For a Theological Genealogy of Economy and Government.* Stanford: Stanford UP, 2011. Print.

Alencar, José de. *Iracema. Lenda do Ceará.* São Paulo: Editora Ática, 2001. Print.

Andrade, Joaquim Pedro de, dir. *Macunaíma.* Brazil: 1969. DVD.

Andrade, Mário de. *Macunaíma, o Herói sem nenhum Carácter.* Belo Horizonte: Livraria Garnier, 2001 (1st. ed. 1928). Print.

Andrade, Oswald de. "Manifesto Antropófago." *Zona Curva. Mídia Livre em Política e Cultura*; accessed April 27, 2016. Web.

———. "A Crise da Filosofia Messiânica." *Obras Completas. Vol. 6: Do Pau-Brasil à Antropofagia e às Utopias.* Rio de Janeiro: Civilização Brasileira, 1978. 75–138. Print.

———. "A Marcha das Utopias." *Obras Completas. Vol. 6: Do Pau-Brasil à Antropofagia e às Utopias.* Rio de Janeiro: Civilização Brasileira, 1978. 145–200. Print.

———. "Ainda o Matriarcado." *Obras Completas. Vol. 6: Do Pau-Brasil à Antropofagia e às Utopias*. Rio de Janeiro: Civilização Brasileira, 1978. 205–209. Print.

———. "O Achado de Vespúcio." *Obras Completas. Vol. 6: Do Pau-Brasil à Antropofagia e às Utopias*. Rio de Janeiro: Civilização Brasileira, 1978. 210–15. Print.

———. "Um Aspecto Antropofágico da Cultura Brasileira: O Homem Cordial." *Obras Completas. Vol. 6: Do Pau-Brasil à Antropofagia e às Utopias*. Rio de Janeiro: Civilização Brasileira, 1978. 139–44. Print.

———. "Variações sobre o Matriarcado." *Obras Completas. Vol. 6: Do Pau-Brasil à Antropofagia e às Utopias*. Rio de Janeiro: Civilização Brasileira, 1978. 201–204. Print.

Anthony, P. D. *The Ideology of Work*. London: Tavistock, 1977. Print.

Aristotle. *Physics*. Vol. I. Cambridge and London: Harvard UP, 2005. Print.

———. *The Politics*. London and New York: Heinemann and G. P. Putnam's Sons, 1932. Print.

Assis, Machado de. *Machado de Assis: Obra Completa*. Ministério da Educação do Governo Brasileiro. http://machado.mec.gov.br/obra-completa-mainmenu-123; accessed October 7, 2016. Web.

Bakhtin, Mikhail. "Discourse in the Novel." *The Dialogical Imagination: Four Essays*. Ed. Michael Holquist. Austin: U of Texas P, 2002. 259–422. Print.

———. *Rabelais and His World*. Trans. Hélène Iswalsky. Bloomington: Indiana UP, 1984. Print.

Ballan, Joseph. "Divine Anonymities: On Transascendence and Transdescendence in the Works of Levinas, Celan, and Lispector." *Religion and the Arts* 12 (2008): 540–58. Print.

Bastos, Abguar. *Terra de Icamiaba: Romance da Amazônia*. Rio de Janeiro: Andersen Editores, 1934. Print.

Beauchesne, Kim, and Alessandra Santos. "Introduction: The Theory and Practice of the Utopian Impulse in Latin America." *The*

Utopian Impulse in Latin America. Ed. Kim Beauchesne and Alessandra Santos. New York: Palgrave MacMillan, 2011. 1–26. Print.

Beck, Ulrich. *The Brave New World of Work.* Cambridge: Polity Press, 2000. Print.

Benjamin, Walter. "On Language as Such and on the Language of Man." *Selected Writings. Vol. 1, 1913–1926.* Ed. Marcus Bullok and Michael W. Jennings. Cambridge and London: The Belknap Press of Harvard UP, 1997. 62–74. Print.

———. "The Work of Art in the Age of Mechanical Reproduction." *Illuminations.* Trans. Harry Zohn. New York: Schocken Books, 2007. 217–51. Print.

Bloch, Ernst. *The Spirit of Utopia.* Stanford: Stanford UP, 2000. Print.

Bodanzky, Jorge, and Orlando Senna. dirs. *Iracema, an Amazonian Love Affair.* Brazil: VideoFilmes, 2006. DVD.

Bopp, Raul. *Cobra Norato.* Rio de Janeiro: José Olympio, 2001. Print.

Brookshaw, David. *Paradise Betrayed: Brazilian Literature of the Indian.* Amsterdam: CEDLA, 1988. Print.

Buescu, Maria Leonor Carvalhão. "Introdução." *História do Futuro.* Lisbon: Imprensa Nacional Casa da Moeda. 9–26. Print.

Calarco, Matthew. *The Question of the Animal from Heidegger to Derrida.* New York: Columbia UP, 2008. Print.

Caminha, Pêro Vaz de. *A Carta de Pêro Vaz de Caminha.* Jornal *Público.* https://www.publico.pt/culturaipsilon/noticia/a-carta-de-pe-ro-vaz-de-caminha-1627013; accessed April 27, 2016. Web.

Cândido, Antônio. "Dialética da Malandragem." *O Discurso e a Cidade.* São Paulo: Livraria Duas Cidades, 1993. 19–54. Print.

Carvajal, Gaspar de. *The Discovery of the Amazon according to the Account of Friar Gaspar de Carvajal and Other Documents.* Ed. in Spanish José Toribio Medina, Trans. and Ed. in English Bertram Lee. New York: AMS Press, 1970. Print.

Castro, Aníbal Pinto de. *O Essencial sobre o Padre António Vieira.* Lisbon: Imprensa Nacional Casa da Moeda, 2008. Print.

Castro, Eduardo Viveiros de. "Cosmological Deixis and Amerindian Perspectivism." *Royal Anthropological Institute of Great Britain and Ireland* 4:3 (1998): 469–88. Print.

———. "Exchanging Perspectives: The Transformation of Objects into Subjects in Amerindian Ontologies." *Common Knowledge* 10:3 (2004): 463–84. Print.

———. "Interview with Eduardo Viveiros de Castro: Some Reflections on the Notion of Species in History and Anthropology." *E-Misférica* 10:1 (2013). Web.

Celso, Afonso. *Porque me Ufano do meu País.* eBooksBrasil, 2002. Web.

Claeys, Gregory. *Searching for Utopia: The History of an Idea.* London: Thames and Hudson, 2011. Print.

Cohn, Norman. *The Pursuit of the Millenium.* New York: Oxford UP, 1970. Print.

Condamine, Charles de la. *Relation abrégée d'un voyage fait dans l'intérieur de l'Amérique Méridionale.* Mastricht: Jean-Edme Dufour and Philippe Roux, 1778. Print.

Conley, Verena Andermatt. "Introduction." *Reading with Clarice Lispector.* Ed. and Trans. Verena Andermatt Conley. Minneapolis: U of Minnesota P, 1990. vi–vxiii. Print.

Cruls, Gastão. *A Amazônia Misteriosa.* Rio de Janeiro: Livraria Castilho, 1926. Print.

———. *A Amazônia que Eu Vi.* São Paulo: Companhia Editora Nacional, 1945. Print.

Cunha, Euclides da. *Um Paraíso Perdido. Ensaios Amazônicos.* Brasília: Senado Federal, 2000. Print.

Deleuze, Gilles, and Félix Guattari. *A Thousand Plateaus: Capitalism and Schizophrenia.* Trans. Brian Massumi. Minneapolis and London: U of Minnesota P, 2005. Print.

Descola, Philipe. *Beyond Nature and Culture.* Chicago and London: The U of Chicago P, 2013. Print.

Dias, Gonçalves. *Primeiros Cantos.* Acervo Digital. http://objdigital. bn.br/Acervo_Digital/livros_eletronicos/primeiroscantos.pdf; accessed October 7, 2016. Web.

Dodman, Maria João. "Portuguese Environmental Perceptions of Brazil in the Sixteenth Century." *Portuguese Literature and the Environment*. Ed. Patrícia Vieira and Victor Mendes. Forthcoming. Print.

Dumazedier, Joffre. *Toward a Society of Leisure*. New York and London: The Free Press and Collier-MacMillan, 1967. Print.

Dunn, Christopher. "Jorge Mautner and Countercultural Utopia in Brazil." *The Utopian Impulse in Latin America*. Ed. Kim Beauchesne and Alessandra Santos. New York: Palgrave MacMillan, 2011. 173–85. Print.

Engels, Frederik. *The Origin of the Family, Private Property, and the State*. Chippendale: Resistance Books, 2004. Print.

Flannery, Kent, and Joyce Marcus. *The Creation of Inequality: How Our Prehistoric Ancestors Set the Stage for Monarchy, Slavery, and Empire*. Cambridge and London: Harvard UP, 2012. Print.

Gandavo. Pêro de Magalhães. *História da Província de Santa Cruz a que Vulgarmente Chamamos Brasil*. Secretaria da Educação do Governo do Paraná. http://www.educadores.diaadia.pr.gov.br/arquivos/File/2010/literatura/obras_completas_literatura_brasileira_e_portuguesa/PEROMGANDAVO/SANTACRUZ/SANTACRUZ.PDF; accessed October 7, 2016. Web.

Garcia, Simone. *Canudos: História e Literatura*. Curitiba: HD Livros Editora, 2002. Print.

Geoghegan, Vincent. *Utopianism and Marxism*. Oxford et al.: Peter Lang, 2008. Print.

Gray, John. *Black Mass: Apocalyptic Religion and the Death of Utopia*. New York: Farrar, Straus, and Giroux, 2007. Print.

Hesiod. *Theogony. Works and Days. Testimonia*. Ed. and Trans. Glenn W. Most. Cambridge and London: Harvard UP, 2006. Print.

Holanda, Sérgio Buarque de. *Visão do Paraíso. Os Motivos Edênicos no Descobrimento e Colonização do Brasil*. São Paulo: Brasilense e Publifolha, 2000. Print.

———. *Raízes do Brasil*. São Paulo: Companhia das Letras, 2003 (1st ed. 1936). Print.

Huizinga, J. *Homo Ludens*: *A Study of the Play Element in Culture*. London, Boston, and Henley: Routledge and Kegan Paul, 1949. Print.

Jameson, Fredric. *Archaeologies of the Future*: *The Desire Called Utopia and Other Science Fictions*. London and New York: Verso, 2005. Print.

Johnson, Adriana. *Sentencing Canudos*: *Subalternity in the Backlands of Brazil*. Pittsburgh: U of Pittsburgh P, 2010. Print.

Kant, Immanuel. "Perpetual Peace: A Philosophical Sketch." *Kant*: *Political Writings*. Ed. Hans Reiss. Cambridge: Cambridge University Press, 2008. 93–130. Print.

Lafargue, Paul, *The Right to Be Lazy and Other Studies*. Chicago: Charles H. Kerr, 1907. Print.

Latouche, Serge. *Farewell to Growth*. Trans. David Macey. Cambridge, UK, and Malden, MA: Polity Press, 2009. Print.

Levinas, Emmanuel. "Transcendence and Intelligibility." *Basic Philosophical Writings*. Ed. Adriaan Peperzak, Simon Critchley, and Robert Bernasconi. Bloomington and Indianapolis: Indiana UP, 1996. 149–59. Print.

———. *Totality and Infinity*: *An Essay on Exteriority*. Trans. Alphonso Linguis. The Hague, Boston, and London: Martinus Nijhoff, 1979. Print.

Levine, Robert. *Vale of Tears*: *Revisiting the Canudos Massacre in Northwestern Brazil 1893–97*. Berkeley: U of California P, 1992. Print.

Lispector, Clarice. *A Hora da Estrela*. Rio de Janeiro: Rocco Digital. 2013. E-book.

———. *A Paixão segundo G. H.* Lisboa: Relógio D'Água, 2013. Print.

———. *Água Viva*. Lisboa: Relógio D'Água, 2012. Print.

———. *Aprendendo a Viver*. Rio de Janeiro: Rocco Digital. 2013. E-book.

———. *Contos*. Lisboa: Relógio D'Água, 2006. Print.

———. *Laços de Família*. Rio de Janeiro: Rocco Digital. 2013. E-book.

———. *Para não Esquecer*. Rio de Janeiro: Rocco Digital. 2015. E-book.

———. *Perto do Coração Selvagem*. Lisboa: Relógio D'Água, 2000. Print.

———. *Uma Aprendizagem ou o Livro dos Prazeres*. Lisboa: Relógio D'Água Editores, 2013. Print.

Maciel, Maria Esther. *Literatura e Animalidade*. Rio de Janeiro: Civilização Brasileira, 2016. Print.

Maligo, Pedro. *Land of Metaphorical Desires: The Representation of Amazonia in Brazilian Literature*. New York et al.: Peter Lang, 1998. Print.

Marcuse, Herbert. *Five Lectures: Psychoanalysis, Politics, and Utopia*. Trans. Jeremy Shapiro and Shierry Weber. London: Allen Lane, Penguin, 1970. Print.

———. *Eros and Civilization: A Philosophical Inquiry into Freud*. Boston: Beacon Press, 1966. Print.

Marder, Michael. *Plant-Thinking: A Philosophy of Vegetal Life*. New York: Columbia UP, 2013. Print.

Matta, Roberto da. *Carnavais, Malandros e Heróis: Para uma Sociologia do Dilema Brasileiro*. Rio de Janeiro: Zahar Editores, 1978. Print.

McNee, Malcolm K. *The Environmental Imaginary in Brazilian Poetry and Art*. New York: Palgrave McMillan, 2014. Print.

Mendes, Margarida Vieira. *A Oratória Barroca de Vieira*. Lisbon: Caminho, 2003. Print.

Merchant, Carolyn. *The Death of Nature: Women, Ecology, and the Scientific Revolution*. New York: HarperOne, 1990. Print.

Montaigne, Michel de. "Apology for Raimond Sebond." *Essays of Michel de Montaigne*. Trans. Charles Cotton. Project Gutenberg, accessed October 13, 2016. Web.

———. "Of Cannibals." *Essays of Michel de Montaigne*. Trans. Charles Cotton. Project Gutenberg, accessed April 27, 2016. Web.

More, Thomas. *Utopia*. Cambridge: Cambridge UP, 1993. Print.

Moser, Benjamin. *Why This World: A Biography of Clarice Lispector.* Oxford: Oxford UP, 2009. Print.

Nascimento. Evando. *Clarice Lispector: Uma Literatura Pensante.* Rio de Janeiro: Civilização Brasileira, 2012. Print.

Nery, Barão de Santa-Anna. *O País das Amazonas.* Belo Horizonte and São Paulo: Editora Itatiaia and Editora da Universidade de São Paulo, 1979. Print.

Ovid, *Metamorphoses.* Trans. Charles Martin. New York: Norton, 2004. Print.

Owen, Hilary. "Clarice Lispector beyond Cixous. Ecofeminism and Zen in *A Paixão segundo G.H.*" *Gender, Ethnicity, and Class in Modern Portuguese-Speaking Culture.* Ed. Hilary Owen. Lewiston: Edwin Mellen; 1996. 161–84. Print.

Peixoto, Marta. *Passionate Fictions: Gender, Narrative, and Violence in Clarice Lispector.* London and Minneapolis: U of Minnesota P, 1994. Print.

Pieper, Josef. *Leisure: The Basis of Culture.* South Bend: St. Augustine's Press, 1998. Print.

Plato. *The Republic of Plato.* Trans. Allan Bloom. New York: Basic Books, 1991. Print.

———. *The Laws.* Cambridge and London: Harvard UP and Heinemann, 1914. Print.

Raleigh, Sir Walter. *The Discovery of Guiana.* 2006. Project Gutenberg. http://www.gutenberg.org/files/2272/2272-h/2272-h.htm; accessed December 12, 2015. Web.

Ramos, Graciliano. *Vidas Secas.* Rio de Janeiro: Editora Record, 2002. Print.

Rancière, Jacques. *The Politics of Aesthetics.* London: Bloomsbury, 2011. Print.

Rangel, Alberto. *Inferno Verde. Scenas e Scenários do Amazonas.* Genova: S.A.I. Clichés Celluloide Bacigalupi, 1908. Print.

Rifkin, Jeremy. *The End of Work: The Decline of the Global Labor Force and the Dawn of the Post-Market Era*. New York: G. P. Putnam's Sons, 1995. Print.

Roberts, Kenneth. *Leisure*. London and New York: Longman, 1981. Print.

Rocha, Glauber. dir. *Deus e o Diabo na Terra do Sol*. Rio de Janeiro: Copacabana Films, 1964. DVD.

Rocha, João Cezar. "Do Malandro ao Antropófago: Por uma Epistemologia da Ausência." *Mester* 24:1 (Spring 1995): 173–84. Print.

Rojek, Chris. *The Labor of Leisure: The Culture of Free Time*. Los Angeles: Sage, 2010. Print.

Rosa, João Guimarães. *Estas Histórias*. Rio de Janeiro: Nova Fronteira, 2001. Print.

———. *Sagarana*. Rio de Janeiro: Nova Fronteira. 2012. E-book.

Rousseau, Jean-Jacques. "Discourse on the Origins and Foundations of Inequality among Mankind," *The Social Contract and the First and Second Discourses*. Ed. Susan Dunn. New Haven and London: Yale UP, 2002. 69–148. Print.

Sahlins, Marshall. *Stone Age Economics*. Chicago and New York: Aldine Atherton, 1972. Print.

Saraiva, António José. *História e Utopia: Estudos sobre Vieira*. Lisbon: ICALP, 1992. Print.

Schiller, Friedrich. *On the Aesthetic Education of Man*. Trans. Reginal Snell. Mineola: Dover, 2004. Print.

Schippen, Nichole Marie. *Decolonizing Time: Work, Leisure, and Freedom*. New York: Palgrave MacMillan, 2014. Print.

Schor, Juliet. *The Overworked American: The Unexpected Decline of Leisure*. New York: Basic Books, 1992. Print.

Schwarz, Roberto. "Pressupostos, Salvo Engano, de 'Dialética da Malandragem.'" *Que Horas São? Ensaios*. São Paulo: Companhia das Letras, 1987. 129–55. Print.

Slater, Candace. *Entangled Edens: Visions of the Amazon*. Berkeley, Los Angeles, and London: U of California P, 2002. Print.

Souza, Márcio. *Galvez, Imperador do Acre*. São Paulo: Marco Zero, sd. Print.

Spinoza, Benedict de. *Ethics*. London: Penguin Books, 1996. Print.

Stevenson, Robert Louis. "An Apology for Idlers." *Essays of Robert Louis Stevenson*. Free Classic Books. 41–63, accessed April 27, 2016. Web.

Thompson, E. P. "Time, Work-Discipline, and Industrial Capitalism." *Past and Present* 38 (1967): 56–97. Print.

Uexküll, Jakob von. *A Foray into the Worlds of Animals and Humans with a Theory of Meaning*. Minneapolis and London: U of Minnesota P, 2010. Print.

Vargas Llosa, Mario, *La guerra del fin del mundo*. Barcelona: Seix Barral, 1987. Print.

Vasconcelos, Simão de. *Notícias Curiosas e Necessárias das Cousas do Brasil*. Lisboa: Comissão Nacional para as Comemorações dos Descobrimentos Portugueses, 2001. Print.

Veal, A. J. "A Brief History of Work and its Relationship to Leisure." *Work and Leisure*. Ed. John T. Haworth and A. J. Veal. London and New York: Routledge, 2004. 15–33. Print.

Vieira, Padre Antônio. *História do Futuro*. vols. I e II. Ed. Antônio Sérgio e Hernâni Cidade. Lisbon: Sá da Costa Editora, 1953 e 2008. Print.

———. *Apologia das Coisas Profetizadas*. Ed. Adma Fadul Muhana. Lisbon: Cotovia, 1994. Print.

———. *Cartas*. Vols. I–III. Ed. J. Lúcio de Azevedo. Lisbon: Imprensa Nacional Casa da Moeda, 1997. Print.

———. *Chave dos Profetas*. vol. III. Lisbon: Biblioteca Nacional, 2001. Print.

———. *Representação Perante o Tribunal do Santo Ofício*. vols. I e II. Lisbon: Imprensa Nacional Casa da Moeda, 2008. Print.

Vieira, Patrícia. "Heróis sem Carácter. Particularismo e Identidade Nacional em *Macunaíma*." *Colonial/Postcolonial Junction*: *Writing as Memory in Literature*. Ed. Inocência Mata. Lisbon: Colibri, 2012. 59–77. Print.

———. "Laws of the Jungle: The Politics of Contestation in Cinema about the Amazon." *The Green Thread*: *Dialogues with the Vegetal World*. Ed. Patrícia Vieira, Monica Gagliano and John Ryan. New York: Lexington Press, 2015. 129–45. Print.

———. "*Phytographia*: Literature as Plant Writing." *Environmental Philosophy* 12:2 (Fall 2015): 205–20. Print.

———. "*Phytofables*: Tales of the Amazon." *Journal of Lusophone Studies* 1:2 (2016): 116–34. Print.

———, and Michael Marder. "Existential Utopia: Of the World, the Possible, the Finite." *Existential Utopia*: *New Perspectives on Utopian Thought*. London and New York: Continuum, 2012. 35–49. Print.

———. "Introduction. Utopia: A Political Ontology." *Existential Utopia*: *New Perspectives on Utopian Thought*. London and New York: Continuum, 2012. ix–xv. Print.

Virgil, *The Poems of Virgil*. Trans. James Rhoades. Chicago, London and Toronto: Encyclopaedia Britannica and William Benton, 1952. Print.

Weber, Marx. *The Protestant Ethic and the Spirit of Capitalism*. New York: Oxford UP, 2011. Print.

Wheeler, A. M. "Animal Imagery as Reflection of Gender Roles in Clarice Lispector's *Family Ties*." *Critique* (Spring 1987): 125–34. Print.

Whitehead, Neil. "South America/Amazonia: The Forest of Marvels." *The Cambridge Companion to Travel Writing*. Ed. Peter Hulme and Tim Youngs. Cambridge: Cambridge UP, 2002. 122–38. Print.

Wilde, Oscar. *The Soul of Man under Socialism*. Project Gutenberg. accessed March 31, 2016. Web.

Williams, Claire. "*The Passion according to G.H.* by Clarice Lispector."
    The Cambridge Companion to the Latin American Novel. Ed.
    Efraín Kristal. Cambridge: Cambridge UP, 2005, 245–57.
    Print.

Zweig, Stefan. *Brasilien: Ein Land der Zukunft.* Feedbooks. https://
    archive.org/details/StefanZweigBrasilienLandDerZukunftFe
    edbooks; accessed November 4, 2016. Web.

Index